Building Community Capacity for Tourism Development

Building Community Capacity for Tourism Development

Edited by

Gianna Moscardo

School of Business
James Cook University
Townsville
Australia

CABI is a trading name of CAB International

CABI Head Office
Nosworthy Way
Wallingford
Oxfordshire OX10 8DE
UK

Tel: +44 (0)1491 832111
Fax: +44 (0)1491 833508
E-mail: cabi@cabi.org
Web site: www.cabi.org

CABI North American Office
875 Massachusetts Avenue
7th Floor
Cambridge, Massachusetts 02139
USA

Tel: +1 617 395 4056
Fax: +1 617 354 6875
E-mail: cabi-nao@cabi.org

A catalogue record for this book is available from the British Library, London, UK.

Library of Congress Cataloging-in-Publication Data

Building community capacity for tourism development / edited by Gianna Moscardo.
p. cm.
ISBN 978-1-84593-447-7 (alk. paper)
1. Tourism. 2. Community development. I. Moscardo, Gianna. II. Title.

G155.A1B83 2008
338.4'791--dc22

2008000821

ISBN: 978 1 84593 447 7

Typeset by SPi, Pondicherry, India.
Printed and bound in the UK by Biddles Ltd, King's Lynn.

Contents

Contributors

Anna Blackman, *School of Business, James Cook University, Townsville, QLD 4811, Australia. E-mail: anna.blackman@jcu.edu.au*

Carol S. Kline, *Hospitality and Tourism Administration, North Carolina Central University, 1801 Fayetteville Street, Durham, NC 27707, USA. E-mail: ckline7@nc.rr.com*

Haretsebe Manwa, *Department of Management, University of Botswana, Private Bag UB 00701, Gaborone, Botswana. E-mail: manwah@mopipi.ub.bw, hmanwa@yahoo.com.au*

Nancy Gard McGehee, *Hospitality and Tourism Management, Virginia Tech, 351 Wallace Hall, Blacksburg, VA 24061, USA. E-mail: nmcgehee@vt.edu*

Richard Monypenny, *School of Business, James Cook University, Townsville, QLD4811, Australia. E-mail: richard.monypenny@jcu.edu.au*

Gianna Moscardo, *School of Business, James Cook University, Townsville, QLD 4811, Australia. E-mail: gianna.moscardo@jcu.edu.au*

Philip L. Pearce, *School of Business, James Cook University, Townsville, QLD 4811, Australia. E-mail: philip.pearce@jcu.edu.au*

Pimrawee Rocharungsat, *Tourism Industry Development and Management Division, Faculty of Humanities and Social Sciences, Phetchaburi Rajabhat University, Phetchaburi, Thailand. E-mail: pimstudy@yahoo.com, pimstudy@gmail.com*

Joy Sammy, *School of Environmental Design and Rural Development, Ontario Agricultural College, University of Guelph, Guelph, Ontario, Canada, N1G 2W1. E-mail: jsammy@uoguelph.ca, joy.sammy@gmail.com*

Natalie Stoeckl, *School of Business, James Cook University, Townsville, QLD 4811, Australia. E-mail: natalie.stoeckl@jcu.edu.au*

Amanda Stronza, *Department of Recreation, Park and Tourism Sciences, Texas A&M University, College Station, TX 77843–2261, USA. E-mail: astronza@ag.tamu.edu*

Kaye Walker, *School of Business, James Cook University, Townsville, QLD 4811, Australia. E-mail: kaye.walker@jcu.edu.au, kwalker@austarnet.com.au*

Introduction

Gianna Moscardo

School of Business, James Cook University, Australia

How can we improve the process of tourism development and enhance its benefits for destinations in developing, rural and/or peripheral regions? This is the broad question that drives this book. All of the contributions in this book seek to improve our understanding of what happens when communities turn to, or are subjected to, tourism as a development strategy. All of these contributions seek to use that understanding to improve the process of tourism planning and development in ways that will lead to better outcomes for destination residents. Ideally, the focus of this book should be on what does and/or should happen in a community before any tourism development is initiated and several chapters provide advice and examples for communities where little or no tourism exists. But in reality many of the decisions about tourism development are prompted by either the increasing presence of tourists in a community and/or a growing awareness of impacts from existing tourism. Thus, much of the material presented in this book is based on studies of communities that have some, although often low, levels of tourism development.

Regardless of the level of existing development, a common thread through all the contributions to this book is that of the challenges faced by rural, remote and/or peripheral regions where development options are limited and where community capacity is often constrained. The book includes cases and examples from remote areas in Australia, including indigenous communities (Chapters 2 and 4), regional destinations in Asia (Chapter 5), emerging destinations in Africa (Chapters 6 and 9), remote areas of South America (Chapter 8), countries in the South Pacific (Chapter 4) and less-developed tourism destinations and sectors in the USA and Australia (Chapters 10 and 11). Although much of the evidence presented in this book is from peripheral and rural regions many of the lessons are likely to apply to any emerging destination or established destination where tourism development is seen as problematic in terms of its impacts on local resident communities.

In addition to a diversity of geographic regions there is also diversity among the authors. There are contributions from academic researchers focusing on literature reviews and systematic evaluations across a range of cases (e.g. Chapters 2, 3,

9 and 10). Additionally, there are contributions from academic practitioners with examples and evaluations of initiatives they have been involved with (e.g. Chapters 6, 7, 8 and 11) and chapters based more on experience from practice (e.g. Chapter 12). It is noteworthy that 11 of the 13 authors are women, which is unusual in academic literature in general, but also reflects the importance of diversity of perspectives in any exercise seeking to pursue sustainable development options.

This book is about destination communities, also referred to as host communities and/or destination residents. Despite the use of different labels all the chapters in this book can be seen as using a definition of a destination community that sees it as including 'all such persons and public and private bodies who are potentially affected, both positively and negatively, by the impacts of tourism development within the boundaries of the destination area' (Singh *et al.*, 2003, p. 9).

All of the chapters present a mixture of research and case studies that address various knowledge gaps and further develop aspects of building community capacity to better manage and benefit from tourism development. The contributions in this book are about compiling evidence and examples of how community capacity for tourism can be built and enhanced. In addition the chapters provide tools for actual practice, including suggested steps for building local capacity for development, models and frameworks and lessons from participants in real tourism development situations.

Chapter 1 establishes the need for a book such as this one with a critical review of the use of tourism as a tool for development. This review, of both the literature and of an extensive sample of case studies of tourism development from around the world, provides evidence that a major barrier to the effective use of tourism as a development strategy has been inadequate attention to building community capacity or readiness for development. This aspect of tourism development has been discussed by only a few tourism commentators (Bourke and Luloff, 1996; Reid *et al.*, 2004). Their conclusions have been consistent with those put forward in the literature on community readiness or capacity for development in other areas, such as health (Slater *et al.*, 2005) and agriculture (Bokor, 2001).

The broader literature on community readiness for participation in development highlights a number of key aspects of community capacity that must exist for new developments in any sector to be successful. These include existing development programmes and activities, community knowledge of these activities, leadership, knowledge about a particular development sector and resources or capital (Slater *et al.*, 2005). The themes of leadership, resources and community understanding of tourism have been identified as particularly important to tourism development (Bourke and Luloff, 1996; Reid *et al.*, 2004). The analysis of the case studies in Chapter 1 identifies all these themes and a set of knowledge gaps particular to tourism development that include a limited understanding of the processes that contribute to various tourism impacts, few studies into the effectiveness of different approaches to increasing community tourism knowledge and awareness and limited evidence supporting mechanisms for increasing community participation in tourism development. The subsequent chapters are arranged into three parts matching these three gaps: improving knowledge of tourism development and its impacts; improving community knowledge of tourism development; and improving community participation in tourism development.

Improving Knowledge of Tourism Development and Its Impacts

Tourism is often chosen or supported by governments and other development agencies for its potential positive impacts, and various policies and strategies are used to both encourage these positive impacts and to control or eliminate negative consequences. Such policies are based on assumptions about the processes that contribute to tourism impacts. The contributions in Part I provide a critical examination of what is known about these processes. Chapter 2 focuses on understanding processes related to economic impacts and describes some potential strategies for enhancing the financial benefits of tourism for communities. Chapter 3 provides a similar review and a framework for understanding and benefiting from tourism's sociocultural impacts. Chapter 4 takes a different perspective focusing on how tour operators can work with communities to improve resident awareness and understanding of tourism impacts. This chapter also offers some suggestions for incorporating such activities into sustainability indicators and accreditation schemes, thus making community awareness of tourism impacts a core element of sustainable development approaches.

Improving Community Knowledge of Tourism Development

A recurring theme throughout the book is the importance of community awareness and understanding of tourism and its potential consequences. Chapter 1 identifies a lack of experience with, and understanding of, tourism as the underlying contributor to a number of other barriers to sustainable tourism development. The most direct linkage is between limited understanding of tourism and constraints to community participation in tourism. This is the core theme of Part II and Chapter 5, which explores the concept of community-based tourism in a number of settings in Asia. Chapters 6 and 7 then expand on this theme, offering different insights into practical ways to work with destination residents.

Improving Community Participation in Tourism Development

While it can be argued that improving community knowledge of tourism is the central prerequisite for enhancing community participation in tourism development, this factor is best considered as a necessary but not sufficient condition for enhanced community capacity for tourism. Other factors have also been recognized as important and these include the use of effective partnerships to increase various forms of capital available for development (Chapter 8), the need in many regions to work with women as a particular group to improve standards of living (Chapter 9), the identification, development and support of entrepreneurs (Chapter 10) and the need to find ways to effectively develop tourism leaders (Chapter 11). The last chapter in Part III provides a very different perspective on community capacity for development providing a series of suggested action and steps derived from research and practice in the broader area of regional development.

Finally, Chapter 12 identifies and describes five important and recurring themes that exist across all the parts and chapters. These are:

- Community capacity for tourism development is about community capacity for development in general.
- There is a need to better understand the processes that result in tourism impacts.
- While community-based tourism and ecotourism have not on the whole been as effective or sustainable as promised, they still hold the greatest potential for many regions.
- The importance of tourism development knowledge generation and management.
- The critical role of social capital in community capacity and sustainable development.

References

Bokor, C. (2001) Community readiness for economic development: community readiness checklist. Ontario Ministry of Agriculture, Food and Rural Affairs Factsheet 01-035. Available at: http://www.gov.on.ca/OMAFRA/English/rural/facts/01-035.htm

Bourke, L. and Luloff, A.E. (1996) Rural tourism development: are communities in southwest rural Pennsylvania ready to participate? In: Harrison, L.C. and Husbands, W. (eds) *Practicing Responsible Tourism: International Case Studies in Tourism Planning, Policy and Development.* Wiley, New York, pp. 277–295.

Reid, D.G., Mair, H. and George, W. (2004) Community tourism planning: a self-assessment instrument. *Annals of Tourism Research* 31(3), 623–639.

Singh, S., Timothy, D.J. and Dowling, R.K. (2003) Tourism and destination communities. In: Singh, S., Timothy, D.J. and Dowling, R.K. (eds) *Tourism in Destination Communities.* CAB International, Wallingford, UK, pp. 3–18.

Slater, M.D., Edwards, R.W., Plested, B.A., Thurman, P.J., Kelly, K.J., Comello, M.L.G. and Keefe, T.J. (2005) Using community readiness key informant assessments in a randomized group prevention trial: impact of a participatory community-media intervention. *Journal of Community Health* 30(1), 39–54.

1 Community Capacity Building: an Emerging Challenge for Tourism Development

GIANNA MOSCARDO

School of Business, James Cook University, Australia

Tourism as a Tool for Development

> Tourism has become one of the world's most important sources of employment. It stimulates enormous investment in infrastructure, most of which also helps to improve the living conditions of local people. It provides governments with substantial tax revenues. Most new tourism jobs and business are created in developing countries, helping to equalize economic opportunities and keep rural residents from moving to overcrowded cities.
>
> (UNWTO, 2007)

Sentiments such as these have supported and encouraged governments and development agencies in many countries to use tourism as a key tool for development (Hall and Jenkins, 1998; Forstner, 2004). Tourism has been seen as a particularly useful option for developing countries, and in rural and/or peripheral regions all over the world. Substantial resources have been invested in tourism by communities, governments and aid and development agencies. In Europe, for example, the EU claims to have spent more than €7 billion in 5 years on tourism projects specifically aimed at creating alternative employment and revenue options for rural regions facing challenges in sustaining traditional agricultural practices (European Union, 2003). The Australian government spent AUS$31 million in 2 years on regional tourism development projects (AusIndustry, 2005), while in Africa, the World Bank alone has US$3 billion invested in tourism development projects (World Bank, 2006).

It is not only government and aid and development agencies that invest major resources in tourism. Residents also commit time, money, effort and hope in tourism believing it will bring a range of economic and social benefits to their communities. Ra Phea, for example, works at Angkor Wat and:

> is employed by a Cambodian company that sells entry tickets to the temple site, and the visitors there are essentially paying her salary. With her earnings, she has

> reduced her family's reliance on rice farming and been able to help pay for Japanese-language classes for her younger brother and sister. 'I want them to become tour guides because I am confident more tourists will visit here,' she said.
>
> (Munthit, 2006)

Despite these major investments for governments, agencies and residents, the benefits of tourism cannot always be easily demonstrated. In some places any benefits that can be described have been eroded by the negative impacts that can also accompany tourism. In many other situations, the benefits have been slow to emerge, modest at best and usually restricted to certain groups within the community (Moscardo, 2005a). Pearce *et al.* (1996), for example, reported that nearly 80% of residents surveyed in a rural region of Northern Australia felt that tourism had increased local job opportunities. Unfortunately, 90% reported a negative impact of tourism on their cost of living and 63% believed that tourism had damaged the local environment. Mbaiwa and Darkoh (2006) report a similar situation in their review of tourism in the Okavango delta in Botswana. They conclude that the benefits of tourism for local residents have been very limited, but the costs have included substantial environmental damage, cultural erosion and community conflict. The evidence suggests that the use of tourism as a development tool may not always be the best option and that more critical evaluations of tourism are needed.

Describing Negative Tourism Impacts

A review of 329 case studies of tourism development from 92 different countries identified a number of different negative impacts from tourism (see Moscardo, 2005b, for a description of the method used to find and review these case studies). Overall, negative impacts were reported in more than 80% of the 329 cases reviewed. Analysis of the descriptions of these impacts revealed five key clusters or themes – environmental degradation, conflict, cultural challenges, disruptions to daily life and disillusionment when tourism development fails to deliver the promised benefits.

Many different forms of negative environmental impact were identified in the case studies, including:

- destruction of ecosystems when tourism infrastructure is built;
- pollution and problems with waste disposal;
- depletion of natural resources in the local environment, including water and food stocks;
- changes in wildlife behaviour; and
- inappropriate architecture used for tourism facilities.

The second cluster of negative impacts of tourism was about conflict, with the most commonly discussed type of conflict being between community members. In virtually all the case studies there were groups within the destination community supporting, and groups opposing, various tourism development options with different vested interests vying for potential benefits. Breakdowns in trust and relationships were often reported as a result of these power struggles within the communities. Tourism also contributes to changes in patterns of employment and income in host communities, and this can result in another form of conflict – that between family members. Many cases reported changes to traditional age and gender roles within families resulting from tourism employment as contributing to interpersonal tension and stress. Another type of conflict described in the case studies was that between tourism and other activities. The development of resorts and lodges for tourism can limit local access to certain places and have a negative impact on their use of these places for both subsistence and recreation.

The third set of negative impacts identified were those related to cultural challenges. The need to change cultural practices for presentation and sale to tourism interests was a commonly cited problem. In this case the negative impacts reported by local residents related to changes to culture that were out of their control. Ironically, in other cases the major problem faced by local residents was the reverse – an inability to change culture. The use of certain images of local people and their culture to promote regions resulted in residents being trapped in certain lifestyles in order to meet tourist expectations. The patterns of employment associated with tourism also had negative impacts on destination cultures. In some cases the peak tourist season coincided with critical times for other traditional practices, especially in agriculture, creating a shortfall in the resources needed to sustain these other activities and a subsequent decline in traditional cultural practices.

Interruptions to daily life made up the fourth set of negative tourism impacts and these included:

- traffic congestion and general crowding;
- rises in the cost of living;
- the presence of strangers at traditional ceremonies and rituals; and
- changes to land use resulting in residents having to travel further to live, work and recreate.

The final theme in the descriptions of the negative tourism impacts was that of disillusionment and negative attitudes towards tourism resulting from the failure of the tourism development to live up to its promises. Less income and fewer jobs than expected were the most common complaints in this category. Even where the promised number of jobs was created by the tourism development, it was typical to report that many of these were taken up by newcomers moving into the community because the training required to allow locals to develop the necessary skills was never conducted or offered. In addition, many of these jobs were low level in terms of career potential and skills development, and usually part-time and seasonal. High levels of small business failure were also described in the case studies and these were attributed to either a lack of tourism skills and knowledge on the part of local business owners or inflated predictions for visitor numbers used to justify the tourism development.

Arguably some of the negative impacts discussed in the case studies could have been avoided or mitigated with planning and development controls. But a major challenge for managing tourism impacts is that we have a very limited understanding of these impacts. Much of the published research into tourism impacts has been focused on a limited range of situations with a strong focus on destinations with established and large-scale tourism sectors (Fagence, 2003). Further, there has been a narrow focus in the existing research on how impacts are related to resident–guest interactions (Apostolopoulos and Sonmez, 1999) or to resident characteristics (Pearce *et al.*, 1996). Pearce *et al.* (1996), for example, reviewed a large number of studies of resident perceptions of tourism impacts and reported a list of explanatory variables that had been considered in these studies. Of the 12 variables on this list, ten were characteristics of the residents. There has been very little research into the characteristics of the tourism development process that contribute to its impacts.

One consequence of this limited understanding of tourism development processes and how they contribute to impacts has been a tendency to falsely connect numbers of tourists to a destination with negative impacts on that destination, especially negative environmental impacts (Andersen, 1991; Southgate and Sharpley, 2002). Several authors have noted that this approach is overly simplistic and ignores the critical role of regulation and governance in managing tourism impacts (Andersen, 1991; Snow and Wheeler, 2000). This approach also ignores the substantial negative environmental impacts that can result from the presence of minimal numbers of uncontrolled tourists (Sulaiman, 1996; Andersen, 1991). In summary, our knowledge of the factors and processes that contribute to tourism impacts in a number of areas is very limited and requires much more research attention (Fagence, 2003; Ioannides, 2003).

Ecotourism and Community-based Tourism

In response to the types of negative impacts reported in the case study analysis, alternative forms of tourism, especially ecotourism and community-based tourism (CBT), have been proposed. The results of critical analyses of these new approaches have not, however, provided much evidence that they offer any better outcomes for the residents of the destinations. Wilson (1996), for example, concluded after a review of alternative tourism developments in the Caribbean that 'the advocacy of alternative forms of tourism serves mainly to project an image of political responsibility while supporting a marketing strategy aimed at expanding tourism' (p. 75). In a similar review of a number of alternative tourism developments in a range of developing countries, Kiss (2004) concluded that 'many projects cited as success stories actually . . . provide only a modest supplement to local livelihoods and remain dependent on external support for long periods, if not indefinitely' (p. 232).

Ecotourism in particular has come under increasing criticism. As with many concepts in tourism, there is substantial debate over the definition of ecotourism. For the purposes of this discussion, ecotourism will be defined as 'nature-based, learning-oriented tourism that has the intention of being . . . sustainable' (Weaver, 2003, p. 251). Ecotourism developments are typically small-scale, located in or near natural environments, and offer more intensive nature-based activities (Weaver, 2003). Despite the positive intentions of ecotourism proponents, Stamou and Pareskevopoulos (2003) concluded that 'ecotourism chiefly functions as a market mechanism through which consumers attenuate their guilt with respect to the environment' (p. 34). Such sentiments are becoming increasingly common as systematic evaluations are being conducted into established and emerging ecotourism programmes. More detailed evaluations and critiques of ecotourism as a development option can be found in Barkin (2003), Butcher (2006), Carrier and Macleod (2005), Cater (2003) and Kruger (2005).

CBT is the other popular alternative offered to traditional tourism development styles and it can be defined as tourism based on negotiation and participation with key stakeholders in the destination (Saarinen, 2006). In CBT, the hosts play a central role in determining the form and process of tourism development (Timothy, 2002). Although from these definitions CBT appears to have the potential to improve tourism development processes and outcomes, as with ecotourism, little evidence exists to show that this potential is being fulfilled. Indeed a number of studies have been published identifying challenges to the effective implementation of CBT. Johnson and Wilson (2000) critically analysed arguments for greater community involvement in decision making in the broader context of development in general, and concluded that proponents of community-based decision-making processes were often naive about existing political structures. Simple assumptions about the nature of political power meant that existing power structures were rarely challenged or changed, with the consequence that not all stakeholders were able to speak openly or with authority about their views on the proposed development options. According to Johnson and Wilson (2000), community participation processes can also be dominated by external consultants, government staff and development or aid agency personnel, whose knowledge of both the proposed development and of the decision-making process gives them an advantage over the local residents.

This problem of a lack of knowledge has also been noted in discussions of community involvement in tourism development planning (Timothy, 1999; Upchurch and Teivane, 2000; Chakravarty, 2003; Blackman *et al.*, 2004; Reid *et al.*, 2004). Okech (2006) uses examples from Africa to show that local residents often lack understanding of their own rights and of tourism, and this severely limits their ability to participate in tourism decision making even when community participation processes are conducted. Moscardo (2006) argues that a lack of knowledge of tourism markets has been used in many developing and peripheral regions to justify the exclusion of local residents and other community stakeholders from involvement in marketing decisions. Pearce *et al.* (1996) also note that residents in rural and peripheral regions typically have very limited experience of being tourists themselves and so lack knowledge of the potential demands of tourists or of the impacts and changes likely to be associated with tourism development. According to Hall (2005), limited awareness of tourism can contribute to false expectations about the benefits of tourism and a lack of preparedness for the changes associated with tourism, and limits opportunities for locals to benefit from tourism business opportunities.

A lack of tourism knowledge is only one challenge for CBT. Studies critically analysing CBT in practice in a range of locations have identified several barriers to the effectiveness of strategies for community involvement in tourism decisions. These barriers include:

- the costs for participants;
- increased time to make decisions, resulting in lost opportunities;
- difficulties in getting widespread representation in the processes;
- cultural and political restrictions on public expression and debate; and
- problems with conflicts over tourism (Hall, 2000; Tosun, 2000; Timothy and Tosun, 2003).

Finally, it has been suggested that CBT approaches have not yet been fully integrated into formal tourism planning processes (Butler, 1999; Burns, 2000). Timothy (1999, p. 371) states that

> most of the planning literature dealing with tourism focuses on what should be done in developing the industry at the expense of providing an understanding of what is actually being pursued and what can be done given a destination's local conditions.

In other words, many existing tourism planning models are prescriptive and start with the assumption that tourism should be developed. The option of not developing tourism is not considered and this omission is fundamentally inconsistent with CBT.

Barriers to Effective Tourism Development

The second part of Timothy's (1999) statement quoted in the previous paragraph highlights a further problem with existing approaches to tourism planning – they are rarely grounded in an understanding of actual tourism development processes (Hall, 2000; Koh, 2002; Moscardo, 2005b). The case studies of tourism development used earlier to describe the negative impacts of tourism were analysed as part of a project to understand the factors associated with different outcomes of tourism development in rural and/or peripheral regions. Table 1.1 summarizes the most commonly reported problems with, or barriers to, effective tourism development. The table also lists key results from two similar studies published in the tourism literature.

There are clear and consistent patterns in the results across all three studies with recurring themes related to local leadership, local stakeholder coordination and participation, the negative role of external agents, poor or no planning and a lack of relevant information, especially with regard to markets. Further investigation of the pattern of co-occurrence of these themes in the case study projects revealed a clear pattern linking the theme and this is presented in Fig. 1.1. This figure sets out a conceptual framework for understanding how these barriers combine to create negative outcomes from tourism development. As can be seen in the figure, there is a cumulative effect of the barriers with the ones lower in the framework contributing both directly to the negative outcomes and indirectly through the other barriers. At the bottom of the figure is the barrier of limited tourism knowledge, experience or awareness.

More specifically the analysis of the cases indicated that destination residents and other stakeholders, especially local government officials and staff, often have limited understanding of how tourism operates as a system, what the full

Table 1.1. Key dimensions of tourism development.

Barriers to effective tourism development from the case studies	Wilson *et al.* (2001) success factors	Blackman *et al.* (2004)	
		Success factors	Problems
Themes common to all studies			
Dominance of external agents Limited community involvement or control Lack of coordination of community stakeholders and conflict Limited connections to tourism distribution systems Reliance on external agents for market information Limited or no formal planning Lack of local tourism leaders Lack of local skills and capital Poor/limited infrastructure	Support from local government development Widespread community support Coordination and cooperation between stakeholders and entrepreneurs Information and technical assistance for promotion Strategic planning Good leadership Sufficient funds for development Effective local tourist association	Local government control over development High levels of community involvement Coordination and cooperation between stakeholders Good connections to tourism distribution systems Market research and planning Detailed action and implementation plans Support for local leaders Government support for education and funding schemes Investment in transport infrastructure	Community opposition to external control over development Limited or no coordination mechanisms No implementation of plans Loss of local leaders Lack of funding/ financial support Limited infrastructure, especially accomodation
Themes unique to each study			
False expectations of benefits and limited awareness of potential negative impacts	A focus on a total visitor experience in product development	Appropriate development for the setting Identification of unique experiences for visitors	A wide range of negative impacts

range of tourism development options are, what the potential impacts of tourism might be, the skills required to work in tourism and the potential markets that exist globally for tourism. While this lack of knowledge has been recognized in the tourism literature (Timo, 1999; Tosun, 2000; Burns and Sancho, 2002, 2003; Sharpley, 2002), there exists little information on how to resolve this problem. What is required are case studies and systematic evaluations of different methods

Fig. 1.1. Connections between barriers to effective tourism development.

of enhancing community knowledge of tourism. It is important to note that what is required here is not training or education to work in tourism, but knowledge about tourism to allow community residents to actively take part in tourism development decisions.

This lack of tourism knowledge is a critical barrier that not only directly limits the ability of locals to participate in tourism development, but also contributes to the next two barriers – a lack of local tourism leadership and domination of external agents. One of the few published studies of tourism leadership (Long and Nuckolls, 1994) highlighted the importance of knowledge for effective leaders. Without local leaders it becomes easier for external agents to gain power over the tourism development process. This power can be further enhanced when locals are portrayed as lacking tourism expertise and thus requiring the assistance of external agents such as marketing consultants and tour operators (Moscardo, 2006). As with tourism knowledge, while it has been recognized that tourism leadership is important, knowledge about how to identify, develop and support local tourism leaders is only just beginning to emerge (Koh, 2002). In the case studies local leaders were also often successful entrepreneurs expanding local business opportunities, suggesting that information on enhancing the effectiveness of local entrepreneurs is also likely to be important in creating better outcomes for local communities from tourism.

Where there is limited local knowledge of tourism, few, if any, local leaders emerge, and external agents hold the balance of power over tourism development decisions. Under these conditions it is not surprising to find that tourism planning is not often conducted and that little effort is made to coordinate the interests of local stakeholders. Without effective coordination mechanisms and tourism plans it becomes increasingly difficult for destination communities to get involved in either tourism development decisions or to participate in tourism businesses. This limits the potential for positive impacts from tourism and can further exacerbate negative impacts. More research and better information on different options for involving communities in tourism through better coordination mechanisms, partnerships and other cooperative ventures would be useful in assisting communities to overcome these barriers.

What Is Community Capacity?

The findings of the analysis of the 392 case studies of tourism development indicated that the most basic barrier to effective tourism development was a lack of knowledge about tourism in general. This lack of tourism knowledge was a key element contributing to limited local tourism leadership, effective planning and coordination and involvement of local stakeholders. These are all elements of community readiness or capacity to participate in tourism development. The concept of community capacity has been given only limited attention in the tourism literature (Bourke and Luloff, 1996; Reid *et al.*, 2004). This concept has, however, been extensively used in other areas of development, especially health, education and agriculture (Lavarack, 2005).

Table 1.2 provides a selection of definitions of community capacity that highlight common themes and characteristics. Two key ideas are common to all the definitions in Table 1.2: (i) that community capacity is about collective knowledge and ability within the community itself; and (ii) that this knowledge and ability is used to define problems and options from within the community. Community capacity is, therefore, a precondition for any other activity.

Table 1.2. Selection of definitions of community capacity.

Definition	Source
Community capacity refers to the levels of competence, ability and skills necessary to set and achieve relevant goals.	Balint, 2006, p. 140
Community capacity is the ability of individuals, organisations and communities to manage their affairs and to work collectively to foster and sustain positive change.	Hounslow, 2002, p. 20
Community capacity is the degree to which a community can develop, implement and sustain actions for strengthening community health.	Smith *et al.*, 2001, p. 33
Community capacity includes the assets and attributes that a community is able to draw upon in order to improve their lives. It is the ability to define, evaluate, analyse and act on . . . concerns of importance.	Lavarack, 2005, p. 267

One important characteristic of community capacity is that it is based in part upon social capital (Hounslow, 2002). According to Woodhouse (2006), social capital can be defined as the resources an individual can access and use based upon the relationships they have with others. Social capital includes the networks and relationships between people in a community, and the levels of trust and cohesiveness that exist within a community (Woodhouse, 2006). As such, it is a critical component that allows the collective action that is central to community capacity (Balint, 2006). The analysis of the 392 case studies referred to previously indicated that tourism development often erodes social capital and thus contributes to breaking down rather than building community capacity.

In addition to defining community capacity and describing its characteristics, work in health, agriculture and education has also established areas or domains that require attention in any capacity-building exercise. These are:

- knowledge and the ability to define and suggest solutions for problems;
- the ability to critically evaluate proposed projects and activities;
- local leadership and entrepreneurship;
- specific technical and managerial skills in target areas;
- networks and community cohesiveness;
- equitable partnerships with external organizations;
- resources and infrastructure; and
- motivation and confidence (Goodman *et al.*, 1998; Hounslow, 2002; Simpson *et al.*, 2003; Lavarack, 2005; Slater *et al.*, 2005; Balint, 2006; Woodhouse, 2006).

Building Community Capacity for Tourism Development

In the introduction to this book it was suggested that the key question driving all the contributions in this book was: how can we improve the process of tourism development and enhance its benefits for destinations in developing, rural and/or peripheral regions? The discussion and research presented in the previous sections suggest that one answer to this question is to improve community capacity building before the process of tourism planning even begins. This literature and research evidence from health, education and agriculture highlight the importance of key elements of community capacity building occurring before specific development options or programmes are chosen or pursued.

Figure 1.2 sets out a model for achieving this goal. On the right side is a simplified version of a standard tourism planning approach, typical of many planning texts. This approach begins with the assumption that some form of tourism is desirable and should and/or will be developed. The main steps in such an approach include identifying stakeholders and their roles in discussing and setting out tourism options, consulting with these stakeholders to identify resources available for tourism developments and then using this information to conduct strategic planning exercises. Typically these strategic plans do include discussions of infrastructure, education and community awareness needs, but these discussions are framed in the context of advocating, rather than critically assessing, tourism development proposals.

The left side of Fig. 1.2 sets out a different approach to tourism planning, incorporating concepts from the community development literature. Specifically, this model places the creation or enhancement of a tourism knowledge base before decisions are made about tourism. This approach also includes the step of critically evaluating tourism against other development options and explicitly allows for a decision to be made not to pursue tourism at all.

Once tourism is chosen as an option, the community capacity-building approach directs attention towards strategies and programmes to enhance the domains identified as critical to overall community capacity, including local leaders and entrepreneurs, coordination mechanisms, networks and equitable

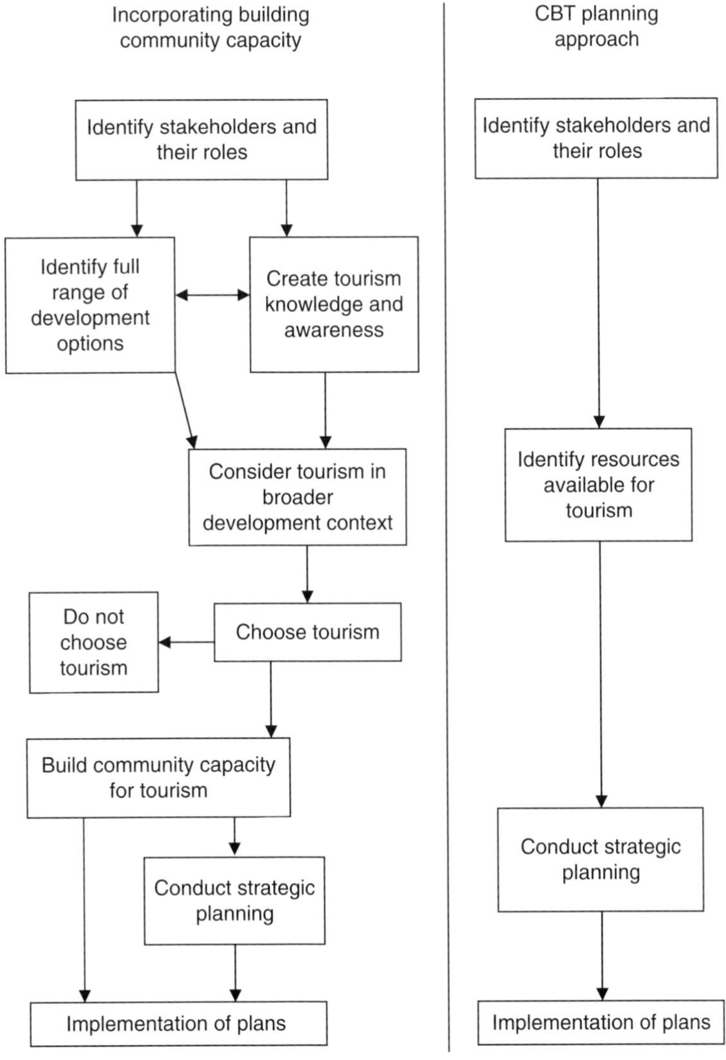

Fig. 1.2. Model for community capacity building for tourism development decisions.

partnerships. These activities run parallel to specific planning for tourism and should enhance the destination community's abilities not only to implement the tourism plans, but also to retain control over the plans themselves.

Conclusion

The challenge for this model is that there exist critical gaps in our knowledge of how to achieve the goals embedded in the community capacity-building approach to tourism development set out in Fig. 1.2. There are three main areas where our understanding of the critical phenomena could be improved:

- our understanding of the processes that result in various tourism impacts;
- our understanding of effective ways to enhance a community's collective tourism knowledge in such a way as to improve their ability to plan for, and critically evaluate, tourism; and
- our understanding of different mechanisms for improving community participation in tourism, including the development of partnerships, entrepreneurs and tourism leaders.

References

Andersen, M.J. (1991) Problems with tourism in Canada's eastern Arctic. *Tourism Management* 12, 209–220.

Apostolopoulos, Y. and Sonmez, S. (1999) From farmers and shepherds to shopkeepers and hoteliers: constituency-differentiated experiences of endogenous tourism in the Greek Island of Zakynthos. *International Journal of Tourism Research* 1, 413–427.

AusIndustry (2005) Australian tourism development program Round 2: fact sheet. Available at: http://www.ausindustry.gov.au/

Balint, P.J. (2006) Improving community-based conservation near protected areas: the importance of development variables. *Environmental Management* 38, 137–148.

Barkin, D. (2003) Alleviating poverty through ecotourism: promises and reality in the Monarch butterfly reserve of Mexico. *Environment, Development and Sustainability* 5, 371–382.

Blackman, A., Foster, F., Jewell, B., Kuilboer, A., Hyvonen, T. and Moscardo, G. (2004) Factors contributing to successful tourism development in peripheral regions. *Journal of Tourism Studies* 15(1), 59–70.

Bourke, L. and Luloff, A.E. (1996) Rural tourism development: are communities in southwest rural Pennsylvania ready to participate? In: Harrison, L.C. and Husbands, W. (eds) *Practicing Responsible Tourism: International Case Studies in Tourism Planning, Policy and Development.* Wiley, New York, pp. 277–295.

Burns, P.M. (2000) Planning tourism in a reconstructing economy: the case of Eritrea. In: Dieke, P. (ed.) *The Political Economy of Tourism Development in Africa.* Cognizant Communication, New York, pp. 98–112.

Burns, P.M. and Sancho, M. (2003) Local perceptions of tourism planning: the case of Cuellar, Spain. *Tourism Management* 24, 331–339.

Butcher, J. (2006) The United Nations international year of ecotourism: a critical analysis of development implications. *Progress in Development Studies* 6, 146–156.

Butler, R.W. (1999) Problems and issues of integrating tourism development. In: Pearce, D.G. and Butler, R.W. (eds) *Contemporary Issues in Tourism Development.* Routledge, London, pp. 65–80.

Carrier, J.G. and Macleod, D.V.L. (2005) Bursting the bubble: the socio-cultural context of ecotourism. *Journal of the Royal Anthropological Institute* 11, 315–334.

Cater, E. (2003) Spread and backwash effects in ecotourism: implications for sustainable development. *International Journal of Sustainable Development* 5, 265–281.

Chakravarty, I. (2003) Marine ecotourism and regional development: a case study of the proposed Marine Park at Malvan, Maharashtra, India. In: Garrod, B. and Wilson, J. (eds) *Marine Ecotourism: Issues and Experiences.* Channel View, Clevedon, UK, pp.177–197.

European Union (2003) Tourism: funding and instruments available. Available at: http: //europa.eu.int/comm/enterprise/services/tourism/policy-areas/instruments.htm

Fagence, M. (2003) Tourism and local society and culture. In: Singh, S., Timothy, D.J. and Dowling, R.K. (eds) *Tourism in Destination Communities.* CAB International, Wallingford, UK, pp. 55–78.

Forstner, K. (2004) Community ventures and access to markets: the role of intermediaries in marketing rural tourism products. *Development Policy Review* 22, 497–514.

Goodman, R.M., Speers, M.A., McLeroy, K., Fawcett, S., Kegler, M., Parker, E., Smith, S.R., Sterling, T.D. and Wallerstein, N. (1998) Identifying and defining the dimensions of community capacity provide a basis for measurement. *Health Education and Behaviour* 25(3), 258–278.

Hall, C.M. (2000) *Tourism Planning: Policies, Processes and Relationships.* Prentice-Hall, London.

Hall, C.M. (2005) *Tourism: Rethinking the Social Science of Mobility.* Pearson, Harlow, UK.

Hall, C.M. and Jenkins, J.M. (1998) The policy dimensions of rural tourism and recreation. In: Butler, R., Hall, C.M. and Jenkins, J. (eds) *Tourism and Recreation in Rural Areas.* Wiley, Chichester, UK, pp. 16–42.

Hounslow, B. (2002) Community capacity explained. *Stronger Families Learning Exchange Bulletin* 1, 20–22.

Ioannides, D. (2003) The economics of tourism in host communities. In: Singh, S., Timothy, D.J. and Dowling, R.K. (eds) *Tourism in Destination Communities.* CAB International, Wallingford, UK, pp. 37–54.

Johnson, H. and Wilson, G. (2000) Biting the bullet: civil society, social learning and the transformation of local governance. *World Development* 28, 1891–1906.

Kiss, A. (2004) Is community-based ecotourism a good use of biodiversity conservation funds? *Trends in Ecology and Evolution* 19, 232–237.

Koh, K. (2002) Explaining a community touristscape: an entrepreneurism model. *International Journal of Hospitality and Tourism Administration* 3, 29–62.

Kruger, O. (2005) The role of ecotourism in conservation: panacea or Pandora's box? *Biodiversity and Conservation* 14, 579–600.

Lavarack, G. (2005) Evaluating community capacity: visual representation and interpretation. *Community Development Journal* 41, 266–276.

Long, P.T. and Nuckolls, J.S. (1994) Organising resources for rural tourism development: the importance of leadership, planning and technical assistance. *Tourism Recreation Research* 19, 19–34.

Mbaiwa, J.E. and Darkoh, M.B.K. (2006) *Tourism and Environment in the Okavango Delta, Botswana.* Pula Press, Gaborone, Botswana.

Moscardo, G. (2005a) *Successful Tourism Development for Regions.* Ninth National SEGRA Conference Proceedings. Management Solutions, Brisbane, Australia.

Moscardo, G. (2005b) Peripheral tourism development: challenges, issues and success factors. *Tourism Recreation Research* 30, 27–43.

Moscardo, G. (2006) *Contested Visions of Tourism: Social Representations of Tourism Development*. Paper presented at the ATLAS Africa 2006 Conference, Mombasa, Kenya.
Munthit, K. (2006) Tourism brings hope, worry to Angkor. AAAP 20th November. Available at: http://news.yahoo.com
Okech, R. (2006) *The Role of Local Communities in the Management of Cultural Landscapes*. Paper presented at the ATLAS Africa 2006 Conference, Mombasa, Kenya.
Pearce, P.L., Moscardo, G. and Ross, G.F. (1996) *Tourism Community Relationships*. Pergamon Press, Oxford.
Reid, D.G., Mair, H. and George, W. (2004) Community tourism planning: a self-assessment instrument. *Annals of Tourism Research* 31, 623–639.
Saarinen, J. (2006) Traditions of sustainability in tourism studies. *Annals of Tourism Research* 33, 1121–1140.
Sharpley, R. (2002) Sustainability: a barrier to tourism development. In: Sharpley, R. and Telfer, D.J. (eds) *Tourism and Development: Concepts and Issues*. Channel View, Clevedon, UK, pp. 319–337
Simpson, L., Wood, L. and Daws, L. (2003) Community capacity building: starting with people not projects. *Community Development Journal* 38, 277–286.
Slater, M.D., Edwards, R.W., Plested, B.A., Thurman, P.J., Kelly, K.J., Comello, M.L.G. and Keefe, T.J. (2005) Using community readiness key informant assessments in a randomized group prevention trial: impact of a participatory community-media intervention. *Journal of Community Health* 30, 39–54.
Smith, N., Littlejohns, L.B. and Thompson, D. (2001) Shaking out the cobwebs: insights into community capacity and its relation to health outcomes. *Community Development Journal* 36, 30–41.
Snow, S.G. and Wheeler, C.L. (2000) Pathways in the periphery: tourism to indigenous communities in Panama. *Social Science Quarterly* 81, 732–750.
Southgate, C. and Sharpley, R. (2002) Tourism, development and the environment. In: Sharpley, R. and Telfer, D.J. (eds) *Tourism and Development: Concepts and Issues*. Channel View, Clevedon, UK, pp. 231–263.
Stamou, A.G. and Pareskevopoulos, S. (2003) Ecotourism experiences in visitors' books of a Greek reserve: a critical discourse analysis perspective. *Sociologica Ruralis* 43, 34–55.
Sulaiman, M.S. (1996) Islands within islands: exclusive tourism and sustainable utilization of coastal resources in Zanzibar. In: Briguglio, L. (ed.) *Sustainable Tourism in Islands and Small States: Case Studies*. Pinter, London, pp. 2–18.
Timothy, D.J. (1999) Participatory planning: a view of tourism in Indonesia. *Annals of Tourism Research* 26, 371–391.
Timothy, D.J. (2002) Tourism and community development issues. In: Sharpley, R. and Telfer, D.J. (eds) *Tourism and Development: Concepts and Issues*. Channel View, Clevedon, UK, pp. 149–164.
Timothy, D.J. and Tosun, C. (2003) Appropriate planning for tourism in destination communities: participation, incremental growth and collaboration. In: Singh, S., Timothy, D.J. and Dowling, R.K. (eds) *Tourism in Destination Communities*. CAB International, Wallingford, UK, pp. 181–204.
Tosun, C. (2000) Limits to community participation in the tourism development process in developing countries. *Tourism Management* 21, 613–633.
UNWTO (2007) About the World Tourism Organization. Available at: http://www.unwto.org/abouthwto/eng/aboutwto.htm
Upchurch, R. and Teivane, U. (2000) Resident perceptions of tourism development in Riga, Latvia. *Tourism Management* 21, 499–507.
Weaver, D.B. (2003) The evolving concept of ecotourism and its potential impacts. *International Journal of Sustainable Development* 51, 251–264.

Wilson, D. (1996) Glimpses of Caribbean tourism and the question of sustainability in Barbados and St Lucia. In: Briguglio, L. (ed.) *Sustainable Tourism in Islands and Small States: Case Studies.* Pinter, London, pp. 75–102.

Wilson, S., Fesenmaier, D.R., Fesenmaier, J. and Van Es, J.C. (2001) Factors for success in rural tourism development. *Journal of Travel Research* 40(2), 132–138.

Woodhouse, A. (2006) Social capital and economic development in regional Australia: a case study. *Journal of Rural Studies* 22, 83–94.

World Bank (2006) Tourism: an opportunity to unleash shared growth in Africa Briefing Note 16, July. Available at: http://www.worldbank.org/afr/aftps

2 Enhancing the Economic Benefits of Tourism at the Local Level

NATALIE STOECKL

School of Business, James Cook University, Australia

Introduction

As so clearly highlighted by Moscardo (Chapter 1, this volume), tourism frequently fails to live up to the unrealistically high expectations that are placed upon it. Furthermore, while tourism has the potential to bring great benefits, it also imposes costs on host communities, and since the costs and benefits associated with tourism are not distributed evenly, inevitable conflicts arise. It comes as no surprise to find that virtually all of the case studies considered by Moscardo (Chapter 1, this volume) had groups that supported tourism developments and groups that opposed them.

The strong message that arises from these observations is that those interested in promoting regional development should not simply seek to attract as many tourists as possible into their local area. Instead, they should first ask whether they ought to be promoting tourism at all.

In a theoretical, textbook world, one could answer this question by deciding whether the benefits of tourism outweigh its costs, and whether these net benefits also outweigh the net benefits of alternative development options. Yet we do not live in a theoretical, textbook world, and it is simply not possible to accurately measure *all* of the costs and benefits associated with tourism. Despite the fact that the economics literature abounds with examples of techniques that attempt to measure non-market values, too many of tourism's impacts fall outside the marketplace, making measurement an impractical option. Furthermore, it is not generally possible to measure all the costs and benefits of tourism since those impacts – indeed the impacts of any activity – are not exogenously given values that are passed down from on high. Among many other things, they depend, interactively, on the actions and activities of those within the destination community.

In other words, the overall community impact of tourism will depend, at least in part, on the way it is planned for and managed. So instead of focusing all effort on promoting tourism (without ever asking whether it *should* be promoted) or on attempting to empirically measure all of tourism's costs and benefits, those interested in regional development may find that they are able to reap greater return from their efforts if they seek to identify actions or activities that communities can undertake to increase the industry's net benefits. And that is what this chapter attempts to do.

Specifically, it aims to: (i) provide readers with background information about some of the ways in which both tourists and tourism enterprises create economic costs and benefits within rural communities; and (ii) use that information to identify 'pathways' and 'pitfalls' for planners who are keen to enhance the net community benefits of this important regional industry.

This chapter is divided into two main sections. The first focuses on 'tourists', the key message being that since different visitors interact with their host communities in different ways, regions may be able to improve the net benefits of tourism if they seek to attract the 'right' type of tourist. 'Pathways and pitfalls' for attempting to achieve this are discussed at the end of the first section. The second major section of this chapter focuses on tourism enterprises, arguing that (all else constant) the community-wide benefits of tourism can be increased if tourism enterprises can be encouraged to purchase a large proportion of their required goods and services locally, provided that community capacity to supply those goods and services is also enhanced. Here too, some of the 'pathways and pitfalls' to achieve that are discussed (at the end of the second section).

The focus of this chapter is arguably somewhat narrow because it ignores or glosses over many key 'actors' in the tourism industry, and also many of the social, cultural and environmental issues that are necessarily intertwined with the economic ones presented here. Indeed the chapter also ignores or glosses over many economic issues that are associated with tourism and regional economic development. Readers are therefore encouraged – nay urged – to consider the ideas that are presented here, alongside and in conjunction with, those presented elsewhere in this book and in the associated reference lists.

Visitors

When a tourist visits a region, he/she does not simply inject money into the economy by making local purchases. The tourist also interacts with members of the local community. Likewise he/she will use – and sometimes even abuse – local resources such as food, water and housing. Sadly, there is no guarantee that the good interactions will serve as adequate compensation for the bad, and even when a destination community is adequately compensated for the bad, those who receive the compensation will not always be those who bear the costs. As noted earlier, an inevitable outcome of this is conflict, and – perhaps unsurprisingly – much effort is expended in trying to find ways of identifying, measuring and managing the impacts of tourism so as to avoid, or at least mitigate, some of that conflict.

From an economic perspective, it is interesting to note that many of the positive impacts of tourism that are identified within the literature are financial. A more thorough discussion of these effects is contained in the second section of this chapter, but suffice to say here, when tourists spend money within local communities, they raise regional incomes – sometimes by more than the value of their spending. As might be expected, there is a substantial body of research that seeks to estimate the magnitude of this contribution in various settings (see, e.g. Kerr *et al.*, 1986; Driml, 1987; Blaine, 1992; West, 1993; Wanhill, 1994; Bureau of Tourism Research, 1999; Frechtling and Horvath, 1999; Breen *et al.*, 2001; Chang, 2001; Mules *et al.*, 2003; Dwyer *et al.*, 2004; Suh and Gartner, 2004 to name but a few), and there are also examples of studies that seek to highlight other positive side effects of that spending as when, for example, Iconic wildlife tourism provides communities with a financial incentive to preserve its environmental heritage (e.g. Hoyt, 2001; Smith *et al.*, 2005).

In contrast, relatively few of the negative impacts of tourism that are discussed within the literature are of a financial nature. Dwyer *et al.* (2004), however, do show how tourism expenditure can serve to raise local prices, thereby 'crowding out' other forms of expenditure, and researchers have noted some of the financially negative side effects of tourism – see, for example, Greiner *et al.* (2004). For the most part though, the negative impacts of tourism that are discussed are non-financial – the unintended (and unforeseen) consequence of having too many people travelling to regions that are not well prepared for them. These effects include, but are by no means limited to, the impacts associated with Moscardo's (Chapter 1, this volume) five main 'themes' of environmental degradation, conflict, cultural challenges, disruptions to daily life and disillusionment (see also Brown and Mendelsohn, 1984; Wanhill, 1997; Caserta and Russo, 2002; Egan and Nield, 2003; Greiner *et al.*, 2004; Mbaiwa, 2005; Smith *et al.*, 2005).

Of most interest here is the fact that different types of visitors have different regional impacts – be they negative or positive. This is because they behave differently and therefore contribute different resources to, and withdraw different resources from, their host communities. That different types of tourists have different tastes and motivations and reasons for travel is well documented in the literature (Pearce, 2001; Galloway, 2002; Jensen and Korneliussen, 2002; Brown, 2003; Lee *et al.*, 2004). But different visitor groups also engage in different activities and have different spending patterns (Diaz-Perez *et al.*, 2005; Stoeckl *et al.*, 2006). Furthermore, they use different facilities (Galloway, 2002), show different degrees of sustainable behaviour (Caserta and Russo, 2002) and express different levels of willingness to pay for access to congested areas (Dimara and Skuras, 1998).

Consequently, both the level and the distribution of tourism 'impacts' (positive and negative) will vary according to the aggregate number of visitors, the visitor management regime and the type of visitors that are attracted to a region. Importantly, since different regions are known to attract different types of visitors (see, e.g. the contrasting visitor characteristics of the following studies: Knapman and Stoeckl, 1995; Ryan and Mo, 2001; Prideaux, 2002; Huang and Tsai, 2003; Sorensen and Epps, 2003; Greiner *et al.*, 2004), planners cannot simply assume that what is good (or bad) for one region will also be good (or bad) for another.

Pathways and pitfalls

The preceding discussion suggests that regional communities which are able to attract the 'right kind' of visitor will accumulate greater community benefits from tourism than those that cannot – provided, of course, that the visitor impacts are managed appropriately. It is thus in a community's best interest to try and identify specific types of visitors whom they are both willing and able to attract to their region – although regions need not simply target segments whose current behaviour is 'desirable'; they can also target visitor segments that are likely to be susceptible to marketing messages that encourage them to adopt 'desirable' behaviours (Dinan and Sargeant, 2000).

On the surface, this sounds like a reasonably easy task, but it could be very difficult for small communities to identify a 'desirable' visitor mix. Part of what makes the task difficult is that there is relatively little information about the potential impacts of different types of visitors within specific regions. So planners may need to collect information about the likely impact of a range of different types of visitors (managed in different ways) prior to making judgements about their relative 'desirability'.

Another complicating factor is that visitors who are perceived as being 'desirable' to some individuals within a particular community may be perceived as 'undesirable' to others. This occurs because different types of visitors spend money on, and engage in, different types of activities; the inevitable consequence being that it will be difficult to get community consensus on what the 'desirable' visitor mix is. The owners of restaurants and cafés, for example, may want to attract visitors who spend large sums in restaurants, while the owners of caravan parks may prefer to attract visitors who like to camp. In contrast, non-business-owning local residents may prefer visitors who are unlikely to frequent, and thus congest, their favourite locations.

While it *may* be possible to identify one particular type of visitor who satisfies all the needs of those within the community, that is unlikely to occur in all situations. Some type of compromise may be necessary. So planners should not simply allocate time and resources to investigate the potential community impacts of a range of different tourist types. They should also ensure that there are resources available to: (i) arrive at a (possibly negotiated) community consensus on the 'desirable' visitor mix; and (ii) develop appropriate marketing and visitor management strategies to help minimize the negative impacts that may arise from the behaviours of their targeted visitor mix. Moreover, since one expects the mix of visitors to a particular destination to change over time (Butler, 1980), planners will need to be cognizant of the fact that the community 'impacts' of tourism will change over time, the implication being that their visitor management regime will also need to change over time.

In short, this type of planning may help raise the net benefits of tourism by ensuring that the 'right' type of visitor is attracted to the 'right' type of region. But to be effective, the planning process will need to be well resourced and should, ideally, involve ongoing, interactive engagement with the broader community. Furthermore, to be *truly* effective, the planning process should not merely consider the impact of its 'desirable' visitor mix; it should also consider the impact of its tourism enterprises and the consequent flow-on (or multiplier) effects of the tourist expenditure. It is to that important topic that the discussion now turns.

Tourism Enterprises

When new tourists are attracted to a region and enticed into spending money, the recipient of that money (hereafter referred to as a 'tourism enterprise') will see an increase in income. But that is not, necessarily, the end of the story. If the tourism enterprise spends at least some of its extra income with other, regional, businesses or households (hiring extra labour, for example), then those businesses and households will also see an increase in income. And if those businesses and householders spend at least some of their extra income on regional goods (purchasing a drink at the local hotel, for example), then still more local businesses or households will see an increase in income. The final aggregate change in regional income (i.e. the sum of all increments) will thus normally exceed the initial change in tourist expenditure (ΔE), and can, in some circumstances, be calculated by multiplying the ΔE by the *Keynesian* multiplier.

Importantly, 'feedback' effects (e.g. price increases) will tend to moderate at least some of these effects – meaning that the magnitude of the 'final' change in regional income will be somewhat less than that indicated by the multiplier. But the key point remains, namely that the final size of the economic stimulus of a tourist dollar depends upon the expenditure patterns of local firms and households. The larger the proportion of any 'extra' income re-spent within the local region, the larger are the multiplier and the greater the overall regional benefits of that initial tourist expenditure. Hence, much effort is expended in attempting to determine the size of regional tourist multipliers.

Until recently many researchers used static input–output (IO) analysis to generate regional multiplier estimates (Blaine, 1992; Wanhill, 1994; Frechtling and Horvath, 1999; Cegielski *et al.*, 2001). One of the significant advantages of this approach is that it provides a detailed picture of inter-industry links. Not only does this allow one to consider the total economic impact of a change in one part of the economy but it also allows for the identification of specific sectors within the economy that are likely to be most affected. There are, however, several problems with the technique; IO tables only provide a snapshot of a given economy at a specific and retrospective point in time, and they require researchers to accept stringent assumptions about the structure of the economy (e.g. the need to assume Leontieff technologies).

Nowadays, more sophisticated versions of IO models (dynamic IO tables, social accounting matrices, etc.) are available (see West, 1993; West and Gamage, 2001) and advances in information technology have made computable general equilibrium (CGE) models a viable, theoretically preferable and increasingly popular method of estimating regional multipliers (Dwyer *et al.*, 2004). Yet it takes many resources to develop these models and in some cases it is simply not cost-effective to build complex models of small, rural areas. Therefore, few 'off-the-shelf' models are available for regional planners to use.

Furthermore, even when 'off-the-shelf' CGE models are available, it can be difficult to use them to estimate the regional economic impact of tourism. At least part of the problem arises because tourism encompasses multiple industries including, but by no means limited to, *accommodation, restaurants and cafes*; *transport and travel*; *retail trade*; and *cultural and recreational services*. So the standard 'sectors' often used in IO and CGE models do not correspond directly to the tourism 'industry' and adjustments have to be made. Another significant problem is that businesses that provide goods and services to tourists frequently also provide goods and services to locals (e.g. cafes). Consequently, it is not always easy to determine which parts of business revenues belong to the tourism 'industry' and which parts do not.

Researchers interested in estimating the regional impact of tourism are thus frequently forced to use shortcuts and approximations and many different approaches are available (see Flegg and Webber, 1997; Baaijens *et al.*, 1998; Harris and Liu, 1998; Chang, 2001; Egan and Nield, 2003, for an overview of Archer's 1971 approach; Tohmo, 2004; Scottish Executive, 2005; Stoeckl, forthcoming). Yet, despite the diverse range of techniques employed, there seems to be widespread agreement that the economic impact of tourism is often overestimated (Egan and Nield, 2003) and that its economic impact is generally much less in small communities than across large regions.

In Australia, for example, the ABS' (2001) estimate of the multiplier associated with the accommodation, restaurant and cafes sector for all of Australia is 2.99, but Johnson (2001) estimates that the multiplier for that same sector is 2.62 for Western Australia and just 1.51 for Kimberley (a smaller part of the state of Western Australia). Similarly, Mistilis and Dwyer (1999) find that there is a concentration of economic impacts in 'gateways' (cities) rather than regional areas; West and Gamage (2001) estimate that the 'impact multiplier' across all tourists over all of Victoria (Australia) is less than 2; and Stoeckl (forthcoming) finds that tourism multipliers are generally much smaller in the remote parts of northern Australia than they are in regional centres.

This story is confirmed in other international studies: Baaijens *et al.* (1998) report that the size of a region's tourism multiplier is positively correlated with its population and geographical size; Frechtling and Horvath (1999) find that the implicit final demand multiplier for tourism in Washington, DC is just 1.2; and Mbaiwa (2005) found that tourism did little to promote economic development in rural areas. Evidently, the smaller the economy of enquiry, the smaller is the economic impact of tourism.

Sadly, many small regional communities are not aware of this, and hope (or expect?) that their multipliers will be as large as those of urban centres. Not surprisingly, they are disappointed when it does not prove to be the case, and as noted by Moscardo (Chapter 1, this volume) the most common (economic) complaint of small communities is that tourism brings less income and fewer jobs than expected.

Pathways and pitfalls

The key message flowing from the preceding discussion is that planners should be forewarned of the fact that in regional areas, small multipliers are the norm, not the exception. Nevertheless, there are ways of attempting to increase the size of local multipliers, thus raising the indirect (flow-on) effects of the tourist expenditure.

Specifically, it is clear that tourism enterprises which purchase many supplies locally provide a larger (financial) stimulus to their local community than tourism enterprises which import their supplies from elsewhere. The policy/planning implication of this is that those who wish to enhance the benefits of tourism may not, necessarily, need to attract more tourists. Instead, they may be able to increase the financial impact of their existing set of tourists by encouraging the development and use of support industries.

Members of remote communities could, for example, be encouraged to start up enterprises that seek to provide needed inputs to other existing local businesses – e.g. food and clean linen for motels. This could work particularly well in cases where there are too few visitors to support several tourism business. Instead of competing against each other for scarce customers, organizations could profit by supplying different types of goods and services along a single 'supply chain'.

Admittedly, businesses that seek to earn money by supplying inputs to other businesses will only receive a portion of the total revenues received by the businesses at the top of the supply chain. But a small portion of someone else's revenues may still be larger than other alternatives (e.g. no income at all), and some individuals may like the option of running a part-time business. Furthermore, some enterprises may be able to provide inputs to multiple businesses, thereby receiving multiple portions.

The idea of using supply chains to stimulate regional economic growth is not new: 'One of the most significant ways of ensuring that tourism contributes to fair and sustainable socio-economic development, is to build links between tourism and local economic activities via the "supply chain"' (Tapper, 2001, p. 360). But it is difficult to implement effective supply-chain strategies if regional businesses are either unwilling or unable to purchase inputs from within their local area, and it seems that many communities find that tourism brings greater benefits to those outside the region than to local residents (Moscardo, Chapter 1, this volume).

To date, there has been relatively little research into the expenditure patterns of tourism enterprises, or on their motivations for purchasing goods and services locally or otherwise (although examples do exist: see Tapper, 2001; Tyrrell and Johnston, 2001; Reichel and Haber, 2005). But in a survey of more than 400 tourism enterprises located across Northern Australia, Stoeckl (2007) found that, on average:

- Businesses disagreed with the statement that 'local goods are cheaper than non-local goods'.
- Businesses located in regional centres disagreed with the statement less vehemently than those that were located in postcodes that had been classified as remote or very remote.

At least in Northern Australia, it seems that there is a perception (or a reality?) that goods are more expensive in remote areas than in regional centres.

The key problem here, of course, is that individual tourism enterprises need to consider their profitability. They may not, therefore, be willing (or even able) to purchase local goods and services that are more expensive than their imported counterparts. Admittedly some businesses may determine that it is in their long-term interest to encourage local suppliers and may thus be willing to pay higher supply costs for an initial few years while stimulating local networks. But the owners of private businesses often have short time horizons or high discount rates and are thus unwilling to accept current, higher costs, in exchange for future benefits that are of an uncertain magnitude (Gunningham and Rees, 1997, pp. 374–375). Moreover, there is evidence to suggest that small firms have shorter time horizons than large firms (Australian Bureau of Industry Economics, 1995). Thus, 'short-termism' may prove to be a significant barrier to the effective implementation of supply-chain policies in the tourism industry, since it is dominated by small firms (Welford *et al.*, 1999).

Planners may therefore need to provide tourism enterprises with an incentive to buy (or employ) locally and the incentive will need to be large enough to overcome any real, or perceived, 'disadvantages' associated with local purchases. But they need to be careful to avoid a myopic focus on 'buy local' policies, since on their own, they cannot be guaranteed to reduce aggregate regional imports – particularly if the number of local suppliers remains constant. Nevertheless, if certain conditions hold, 'buy local' policies, which raise the number of local suppliers, can lower imports (Miyagiwa, 1991), thereby increasing the net regional benefits of tourism. It is, therefore, important to ensure that 'buy local' policies are used primarily to help stimulate the local supply chain. Once local supply chains are fully operational, discriminatory procurement policies may be neither necessary nor desirable.

That point aside, one type of 'incentive' is unlikely to suit all situations, so different regions will necessarily need to consider different incentives that suit, among other things, their culture, their tourists and their businesses (although all planners should avoid the trap of precisely specifying the types of goods and services that must be purchased locally or to specifically name preferred local suppliers, since this could stifle innovation and unfairly preclude new businesses from becoming part of the supply chain, thus defeating the entire purpose of the policy).

Some regions, for example, may decide to consider the purchasing and employment policies of businesses when deciding whether or not to give building approvals – or they may, at the very least, give preferential treatment to organizations that are *not* party to contractual arrangements which require them to purchase goods or services from outside the local area. In other regions, governments might choose to tax businesses that have 'buy (or employ) local' policies at a lower rate than those who do not and still other regions may use some form of social sanctioning to entice firms into sourcing goods and services from within their local area. But whatever the tactic, the hard reality of the 'bottom line' means that one cannot naively assume that a tourism enterprise will provide other than lip service to buy (or employ) local policies if it does not help improve their long-run profitability.

When attempting to stimulate local supply chains, planners may also need to provide training and support to aspiring suppliers. This is especially true since 'smaller firms, in particular, suffer from inadequate resources . . . [and] . . . the lack of capacity to comprehend and address a wide variety of complex issues simultaneously, may result in a failure to access or respond to information, even when it is rational (and profitable) to do so' (Sinclair, 1997, p. 551). Indeed potential suppliers may need to be provided with quite specific information about the types of goods and services required by the tourism enterprises within their region and may also need training in suitable methods of delivering or presenting those goods and services (since tourism enterprises at the 'top' of the supply chain will not simply look at the final price when deciding whether to import or buy locally – among other things, they will also consider the quality and reliability of supply).

Here too, it is important to remember that there is no 'one size fits all' solution: different communities will, necessarily, need to provide different types of training and support to the 'supply' industries within their region. But 'intermediary structures' may be important in helping to provide training and support to potential suppliers within the tourism industry, primarily because small firms are known to rely on such intermediary organizations for information and advice (Aalders and Wilthagen, 1997, p. 433).

Finally, it is worth noting that the 'buy local' incentive schemes and the training/support schemes are likely to impose at least some short-term costs on private businesses and on the community. But the schemes also have the potential to create many long-term benefits. Tourism enterprises that are able to rely on local suppliers will not need to order goods from outside the region many months in advance and may therefore save both time and money in the long term. Likewise, other non-tourism-based businesses will gain access to local workers and suppliers with a wider set of skills and these skills could raise productivity in a variety of different industries.

At the risk of becoming repetitious, it is worth reiterating that the more goods and services that tourism enterprises purchase from within their local communities, the greater will be the total financial benefits of tourism, and the more widely will those benefits be distributed. Supply-chain policies do not just serve to increase the size of the local (financial) pie – they also serve to share the pie among a broader section of the community than might otherwise be the case. Furthermore, one could also try to capitalize on these strategies if seeking to develop a 'destination image'; perhaps gaining marketing advantage from having a region that strives to make a large part of its tourism product a 'local' experience.

Conclusion

To repeat a key point from Moscardo (Chapter 1, this volume), negative tourism outcomes are most likely to occur when there is limited community involvement in tourism development. Hence, those wishing to improve community capacity to capitalize on this important industry need to consider tourism in the broader community context.

This chapter thus considered both the impact of tourists and the impact of tourism enterprises from a community perspective, noting that conflicts are likely to arise when the goals of individuals within a community are not well aligned. Specific examples raised in this chapter included the following:

- when there is little or no community consensus regarding the type of tourists (and consequent impacts) that are invited into the region; and/or
- when tourism enterprises import many goods and services from outside the region.

In both cases, the suggested pathways for improving the planning process so as to enhance community outcomes involved the adoption of strategies that broaden the level of community involvement in the tourism development.

To be more specific, in the first situation, it was noted that outcomes might be improved if planners were to allocate time and resources to:

1. Investigate the potential community impacts of a range of different types of visitors and to arrive at a (possibly negotiated) community consensus on the 'desirable' visitor mix; and

2. Develop appropriate marketing and visitor management strategies which will minimize the negative impacts of their targeted visitor mix and which are flexible enough to change in response to changes in the visitor mix that will inevitably occur over time.

In the second situation it was noted that outcomes might be improved if planners were to:

3. Provide incentives for tourism enterprises to purchase goods and services from local suppliers while attempting to develop a viable local supply chain; and
4. Provide training/support to members of the community who seek to become part of the tourism supply chain.

While these strategies are capable of improving community outcomes (at least theoretically), they are no more and no less than a list of ideas, which, by itself, will contribute nothing to community welfare. The list of ideas needs to be tailored to suit the needs and situations of specific regions, and must be implemented with the will of the community. The question of how best to do this is well beyond the scope of this chapter, but must nevertheless be addressed if one is going to transform the list into a tangible set of activities that improve the process of tourism development and thus enhance its benefits for destinations in developing, rural and/or peripheral regions.

References

Aalders, M. and Wilthagen, T. (1997) Moving beyond command-and-control: reflexivity in the regulation of occupational safety and health and the environment. *Law and Policy* 19(4), 415–443.

Australian Bureau of Industry Economics (1995) *Energy Labelling and Standards: Implications for Economic Efficiency and Greenhouse Gas Emissions: A Case Study of Motors and Drives,* Research report 57, AGPS, Canberra.

Australian Bureau of Statistics (ABS) (2001) Input–output tables Australia. Available at: http://www.ausstats.abs.gov.au/ausstats/subscriber.nsf/0/479C1745BB15388ACA256A0300022F94/$File/52090_1996–97.pdf

Baaijens, S.R., Nijkamp, P. and Van Montfort, K. (1998) Explanatory meta-analysis for the comparison and transfer of regional tourist income multipliers. *Regional Studies* 32(9), 839–850.

Blaine, T.W. (1992) Input–output analysis: application to the assessment of the economic impact of tourism. In: Khan, M., Olsen, M. and Var, T. (eds) *VNR'S Encyclopaedia of Hospitality and Tourism.* Van Nostrand Reinhold, New York, pp. 663–670.

Breen, H., Bull, A. and Walo, M. (2001) A comparison of survey methods to estimate visitor expenditure at a local event. *Tourism Management* 22(5), 473–479.

Brown, D.O. (2003) Perception differences among visitor groups: the case of horse-attraction versus other-attraction tourist markets in Lexington, Kentucky. *Journal of Vacation Marketing* 9(2), 174–187.

Brown, G. and Mendelsohn, R. (1984) The hedonic travel cost method. *Review of Economics and Statistics* 66, 427–433.

Bureau of Tourism Research (1999) *Tourism's Economic Contribution 1996–97.* Bureau of Tourism Research, Canberra.

Butler, R.W. (1980) The concept of a tourist area cycle of evolution: implications for management of resources. *Canadian Geographer* 24, 5–12.

Caserta, S. and Russo, A.P. (2002) More means worse: asymmetric information, spatial displacement and sustainable heritage tourism. *Journal of Cultural Economics* 26, 245–260.

Cegielski, M., Janeczko, B., Mules, T. and Wells, J. (2001) *The Economic Value of Tourism to Place of Cultural Heritage Significance*. Australian Heritage Commission, Canberra.

Chang, W.H. (2001) *Variations in Multipliers and Related Economic Rations for Recreation and Tourism Impact Analysis*. Dissertation submitted to Michigan State University in partial fulfilment of the requirements for the degree of Doctor or Philosophy. Michigan State University, East Lansing, Michigan.

Diaz-Perez, F.M., Bethencourt-Cejas, M. and Alvarez-Gonzalez, J. (2005) The segmentation of Canary island tourism markets by expenditure: implications for policy. *Tourism Management* 26(6), 961–964.

Dimara, E. and Skuras, D. (1998) Rationing preferences and spending behaviour of visitors to a scarce recreational resource with limited carrying capacity. *Land Economics* 74(3), 317–327.

Dinan, C. and Sargeant, A. (2000) Social marketing and sustainable tourism – is there a match? *International Journal of Tourism Research* 2, 1–14.

Driml, S. (1987) *Economic Impacts of Activities on the Great Barrier Reef*. Great Barrier Reef Marine Park Authority, Townsville, Australia.

Dwyer, L., Forsyth, P. and Spur, R. (2004) Evaluating tourism's economic effects: new and old approaches. *Tourism Management* 26(2), 307–317.

Egan, D. and Nield, K. (2003) The economic impact of tourism – a critical review. *Journal of Hospitality and Tourism Management* 10(2), 170–178.

Flegg, A. and Webber, C. (1997) On the appropriate use of location quotients in generating regional input–output tables: reply. *Regional Studies* 31(8), 795–805.

Frechtling, D. and Horvath, E. (1999) Estimating the multiplier effects of tourism expenditures on a local economy through a regional input–output model. *Journal of Travel Research* 37(4), 324–333.

Galloway, G. (2002) Psychographic segmentation of park visitor markets: evidence for the utility of sensation seeking. *Tourism Management* 23, 581–596.

Greiner, R., Mayocchi, C., Larson, S., Stoeckl, N. and Schweigert, R. (2004) *Benefits and Costs of Tourism for Remote Communities: A Case Study for Carpentaria Shire in North West Queensland*. TS CRC Project Final Report, CSIRO Sustainable Ecosystems, Canberra.

Gunningham, N. and Rees, R. (1997) Industry self-regulation: an institutional perspective. *Law and Policy* 19(4), 363–414.

Harris, R. and Liu, A. (1998) Input–output modelling of the urban and regional economy: the importance of external trade. *Regional Studies* 32(9), 851–862.

Hoyt, E. (2001) *Whale Watching 2001: Worldwide Tourism Numbers, Expenditures, and Expanding Socioeconomic Benefits*. International Fund for Animal Welfare, Crowborough, UK.

Huang, L. and Tsai, H. (2003) The study of senior traveller behaviour in Taiwan. *Tourism Management* 24, 561–574.

Jensen, O. and Korneliussen, T. (2002) Discriminating perceptions of a peripheral 'nordic destination' among European tourists. *Tourism and Hospitality Research* 3(4), 319–330.

Johnson, P.L. (2001) *An Input–Output Table for the Kimberley Region of Western Australia*. Perth, Kimberley Development Commission and The University of Western Australia, Perth, Australia.

Kerr, G.N., Sharp, B.M.H. and Gough, J.D. (1986) *The Economic Benefits of Mount Cook National Park*. Lincoln Papers in Resource Management, no. 12, Centre for Resource Management. University of Canterbury and Lincoln college, Christchurch, New Zealand.

Knapman, B. and Stoeckl, N. (1995) Recreation user fees: an Australian empirical investigation. *Tourism Economics* 1(1), 5–16.

Lee, C.-K., Lee, Y.-K. and Wicks, B. (2004) Segmentation of festival motivation by nationality and satisfaction. *Tourism Management* 25, 61–70.

Mbaiwa, J.E. (2005) Enclave tourism and its socio-economic impacts in the Okavango Delta, Botswana. *Tourism Management* 26, 157–172.

Mistilis, N. and Dwyer, L. (1999) Tourism gateways and regional economies: the distributional impacts of MICE. *International Journal of Tourism Research* 6(1), 441–457.

Miyagiwa, K. (1991) Oligopoly and discriminatory government purchasing policy. *The American Economic Review* 81(5), 1320–1328.

Mules, T., Faulks, P., Stoeckl, N. and Cegielski, M. (2003) *The Economic Values of Tourism in the Australian Alps.* Final report on work commissioned by the Australian Alps Liaison Committee and CRC for Sustainable Tourism. Queensland, Australia.

Pearce, D.G. (2001) Tourism and peripherality: perspectives from Asia and South Pacific. *Tourism and Hospitality Research* 3(4), 295–309.

Prideaux, B. (2002) Building visitor attractions in peripheral areas – can uniqueness overcome isolation to produce viability? *International Journal of Tourism Research* 4(5), 379–389.

Reichel, A. and Haber, S. (2005) A three-sector comparison of the business performance of small tourism enterprises: an exploratory study. *Tourism Management* 26(5), 681–690.

Ryan, C. and Mo, X. (2001) Chinese visitors to New Zealand – demographics and perceptions. *Journal of Vacation Marketing* 8(1), 13–27.

Scottish Executive (2005) *Economic Linkages Between Small Towns and Surrounding Rural Areas in Scotland.* Final report by the Scottish Executive, Arkleton Institute and the University of Gloucestershire, UK, March 2005.

Sinclair, D. (1997) Self-regulation versus command and control? Beyond false dichotomies. *Law and Policy* 19(4), 529–559.

Smith, A.J., Newsome, D., Lee, D. and Stoeckl, N. (2005) *The Role of Wildlife Icons as Major Tourist Attractions. Case Studies: Monkey Mia Dolphins and Hervey Bay Whale Watching – in Review.* Technical Report. CRC for Sustainable Tourism, Queensland, Australia.

Sorensen, T. and Epps, R. (2003) The role of tourism in the economic transformation of the Central West Queensland economy. *Australian Geographer* 34(1), 73–89.

Stoeckl, N. (2007) Regional expenditure patterns, remoteness and type of enterprise: which tourism businesses spend the largest amounts within their local communities? *Economic Papers* 26(1), 64–85.

Stoeckl, N., Greiner, R. and Mayocchi, C. (2006) The different socio-economic impacts of different visitor segments: an empirical investigation of tourism in North West Queensland. *Tourism Management* 27(1), 97–112.

Stoeckl, N. (2007) Using surveys of business expenditure to draw inferences about the size of regional multipliers: a case-study of tourism in Northern Australia. *Regional Studies* 41, 1–15.

Suh, Y.K. and Gartner, W.C. (2004) Preferences and trip expenditures – a conjoint analysis of visitors to Seoul, Korea. *Tourism Management* 25(1), 127–137.

Tapper, R. (2001) Tourism and socio-economic development: UK tour operators' business approaches in the context of the new international agenda. *International Journal of Tourism Research* 3(5), 351–366.

Tohmo, T. (2004) New developments in the use of location quotients to estimate regional input–output coefficients and multipliers. *Regional Studies* 38(1), 43–54.

Tyrrell, T. and Johnston, R. (2001) A framework for assessing direct economic impacts of tourist events: distinguishing origins, destinations, and causes of expenditures. *Journal of Travel Research* 40, 94–100.

Wanhill, S. (1994) The measurement of tourist income multipliers. *Tourism Management* 15, 281–283.

Wanhill, S. (1997) Introduction. In: *Tourism Development and Sustainability.* Wiley, New York.

Welford, R., Ytterhus, B. and Eligh, J. (1999) Tourism and sustainable development: an analysis of policy and guidelines for managing provision and consumption. *Sustainable Development* 7, 165–177.

West, G. (1993) Economic significance of tourism in Queensland. *Annals of Tourism Research* 20, 490–504.

West, G. and Gamage, A. (2001) Macro effects of tourism in Victoria, Australia: a non-linear input–output approach. *Journal of Travel Research* 40, 101–109.

3 Understanding How Tourism Can Bring Sociocultural Benefits to Destination Communities

Philip L. Pearce

School of Business, James Cook University, Australia

Introduction

This chapter is concerned with the broad-scale analysis and nurturing of the sociocultural benefits of tourism. It can be suggested that there are few easy generalizations about tourism's sociocultural consequences. There are likely to be even fewer universal mechanisms to develop and enhance such sociocultural benefits since, both for the purposes of analysis and action, tourism can be an unwieldy phenomenon. By way of example, the social and cultural benefits of having backpackers in a community are different in Australia to the effects of the same travel group in Thailand (Cohen, 2004; Richards and Wilson, 2004). Factors affecting these tourism differences include the biophysical and cultural settings in which the tourism operates, the behaviour and travel patterns of the visitors, the skills of the tourism personnel involved and the role of tourism in the community's options for development (Dredge and Jenkins, 2007).

This chapter builds an understanding of tourism's social and cultural benefits by initially paying attention to issues of tourism's diversity as discussed above. It focuses particularly on cultural relativism, language use, social networks and the concept of well-being. These concerns are seen as a necessary and informative preface to capturing a rich understanding of the variety and scope of tourism's social and cultural effects. The central part of the discussion then presents an organizing model of sociocultural benefits. This approach, it will be argued, holds some promise of enriching the more traditional discussions which tend only to itemize tourism's costs and benefits. A compilation of the mechanisms to enhance tourism's benefits in the sociocultural domain is provided using the insights generated by the organizing model.

Sociocultural Benefits: an Overview

The sociocultural benefits which tourism may bring to destination communities are principally determined by the perceptions and values of those who influence and are affected by the development process. It is especially clear from previous studies that the worth of most sociocultural outcomes may be largely a matter of stakeholder perspective (Rocharungsat, 2004). At the broadest and cross-national level, possible sociocultural benefits such as 'exposure to outside influences and contact', 'awareness of other societies' and 'seeing how other people live' may be seen positively in some settings and less so in others. In a study of farm tourism in New Zealand, Pearce (1990) noted that the farm hosts thought of these kinds of items as beneficial to the well-being of their children. By way of contrast, such demonstration effects were seen as a source of threat and indeed a negative influence among the more closed Amish farming communities in the USA studied by Fagence (2003). Such differences in opinion and appraisal of sociocultural outcomes prevail not just across cultural and national groups but within communities themselves. Robinson (1997) examined the growth of tourism and recreation infrastructure, such as museums and heritage centres, in regional English cities. He noted that previously passive citizens were beginning to contest the positive views held by city planners and political change agents. In particular, the residents asked whether the money could be better spent and questioned the use of a heritage focus as a social and cultural benefit. Such concerns link to a widely held cultural concern that the process of displaying heritage has the goals of empowering some and disenfranchising others (Kirshenblatt-Gimblett, 1998).

These divisions and perspectives concerning the benefits of tourism's sociocultural consequences alert researchers to the inappropriateness of using standardized scales for tourism's impacts, particularly if those scales contain an implicit evaluation by the researchers (cf. Lankford and Howard, 1994). A major starting point in assessing sociocultural benefits is thus one of adopting a position of social and cultural relativism where the benefits of tourism have to be gleaned from the stakeholders directly rather than imposed by researchers.

A second perspective worthy of initial consideration in reviewing the development of the positive sociocultural benefits of tourism derives from carefully examining the language of impact studies. Language in tourism has occasionally been a focus of interest for mainstream tourism scholars with considerable efforts made to locate tourist talk and the languages serving tourists in a broader sociolinguistic context (Dann, 1996). As Flyvbjerg (2001) and Gergen (1997) both argue, researchers too have distinct languages, and in this instance the kinds of language and phraseology used to describe tourism's impacts are of particular concern. Some phrases from the research titles in the impacts literature which are powerful and potentially insightful include 'in the wake of the tourist', 'tourist ghettos', 'pathologies' of the tourist presence, 'blight', 'cultural arrogance' and 'sex paradise' (Lambert, 1966; Young, 1973; Farrell, 1977; Bosselman, 1979; Pearce, 1993). Within the actual text of many studies a similar emotive language to that described by Jafari's (1990, 2005) reactionary platform persists, with not infrequent references to the erosion, destruction, collapse and even the tragedy of tourism's social and cultural legacy. An alternative lexicon using terms such as accretion, integration, rebuilding, broadening and coexistence is, arguably, less frequent. The use of modifiers such as modest, minor or partial to describe the sociocultural impacts of tourism does exist but rather infrequently in the corpus of sustainability studies in tourism (Bramwell and Lane, 2005). It can be suggested that careful attention to the use of language should accompany an assessment of tourism's sociocultural benefits and a pathway found to use graduated and subtle terms rather than a simple dichotomy of success and failure (cf. Gould, 2004). A four cell model in which the sociocultural benefits of tourism are presented along two graded dimensions represents a particular response in this chapter to the somewhat overstated dichotomies sometimes found in this language of tourism analysis.

A central question for studies of tourism's sociocultural benefits revolves around the level or span of these benefits. At the broad level, sociocultural impacts are linked to such global concerns as the human development index (HDI), the gross national happiness scores and the happy planet index (Leigh and Wolfers, 2006; Stanton, 2007). The HDI, which was first developed in 1990, computes a single measure of national well-being derived from equally weighted contributions from three domains. There is a one-third contribution from the measure of life expectancy. There is another one-third contribution related to the topic of knowledge which itself is assessed by adult literacy rates (two-thirds of the knowledge score) and educational enrollment figures (one-third of the knowledge score). The final component making up the HDI is described as a decent standard of living, which is assessed in terms of gross domestic product and purchasing power per capita.

There is plenty of noise in these scores, a fact readily acknowledged by Amartya Sen, one of the co-founders of the index, when he describes the scores as a 'vulgar measure' (Sen, 2000). Many researchers have become embroiled in debates about the adequacy and subtlety of the measures. For example, Blanchflower and Oswald (2005) report that Australia has a very high HDI but very low levels of job satisfaction and relatively poor scores on a range of happiness indicators. Leigh and Wolfers (2006) contest this set of results and using a broader measure of life satisfaction find that Australians do report levels of well-being consistent with a high HDI.

The HDI and similar measures of community well-being may also be described as assessing what Elkington (1997) has called one of the shear zones in the triple bottom line approach to sustainability. The term shear zone refers to the areas where the main dimensions of sustainability, which are consistently represented as separate economic, sociocultural and environmental domains, do effectively overlap. In the case of the HDI, the shear zone of interest is that between sociocultural dimensions of well-being and economic measures of development. It is appropriate to extend the discussion of tourism's sociocultural benefits to this shear zone, since such features of communities as their literacy levels and knowledge competencies are important social and cultural resources, influencing ongoing and future tourism capabilities.

Following this line of reasoning it can also be noted that there is a shear zone in the triple bottom line sustainability formulation between the sociocultural domain and the environmental domain. In addition to supplying the physical resources which sustain life, environmental benefits matter in the intersection with sociocultural benefits for such items as recreational amenity, the aesthetics of living spaces and human health.

Two further frameworks are useful in concluding this broad overview of the considerations which help frame an understanding of the levels or span of sociocultural benefits. One of these concerns is the large volume of work on social capital and social networks (Portes, 1998; Harris, 2005). The social capital literature effectively asserts that a full treatment of the benefits of any enterprise for a community must consider the links, connections and working relationships among community members. The term social capital, it can be argued, is pivotal to understanding intragroup interactions and hence helps define a community's capacity to undertake and maintain tourism projects. In this view, communities with little social capital will struggle to initiate tourism enterprises and are likely to be badly affected by externally imposed tourism developments which generate social and cultural impacts.

Glover and Hemingway (2005) distinguish two dominant meanings of the term social capital and note that these interpretations reflect the somewhat different emphases in the use of the term by the pioneering authors Bourdieu (1986), Coleman (1990) and Putnam (2000). One approach considers the resources and information available to individuals because of their social relationships. In a tourism context this may be illustrated by one agritourism family business providing information and knowledge concerning how to host tourists to others who seek to operate such a business (Carlsen *et al.*, 2004). A second approach to social networks focuses less on the resources available from social networks and more on civic links developed in formal and informal associations. An illustration here applicable to tourism lies in the development of a local community development group, such as a bed and breakfast association, which constitutes a form of civic leadership and engagement (Morrison *et al.*, 1996). Glover and Hemingway observe that unlike other forms of capital, social capital enlarges with use but dissolves without continuous investment. This perspective points to the possible stimulation and management of social capital by governments and civic initiatives, since the construct is malleable and dependent on opportunities for communication to build the trust, reciprocities and obligations formed by positive human interaction.

A second special topic of interest provides for an expanded and comprehensive treatment of tourism's sociocultural benefits. Ideas derived from the literature on happiness and human flourishing supplemented by conceptual work in positive psychology on subjective well-being also have a role to play in considering tourism's consequences. Many philosophers and social commentators have been concerned with how communities can work well and how individuals can lead lives which are fulfilling and happy (Seligman and Csikszentmihalyi, 2000; de Botton, 2002). Some comments by one prominent intellectual, the 17th-century figure Rene Descartes, can be used to straddle the concerns of the ancient philosophers and the more contemporary social science attempts to assess well-being. Descartes, whose ideas reflected earlier traditions set by Aristotle, observed in 1645: '[I]f we regard everyone's contentment as the full satisfaction of his desires, duly regulated by reason, I do not doubt that those who are poorest and least blessed by fortune, can be as fully contented and satisfied as anyone else, even though they do not have as many good things' (in Grayling, 2005, p. 237).

To modern sensibilities the phraseology may sound a little pompous but the perspective that happiness and actual financial well-being are not necessarily linked is of enduring value. Such comments are relevant to assessing sociocultural well-being since individual and group contentment are only weakly linked to the fruits of consumerism and material wealth (Kahneman *et al.*, 1999; Diener, 2000; Myers, 2000; Harris, 2005).

Sociocultural Benefits: a Business-derived Model

The principal contribution of this chapter, bearing in mind the previous caveats concerning relativism, language style, social capital and well-being, lies in the development of a four cell model to classify and foster sociocultural benefits. The four cell model is defined by two dimensions and is used to outline a comprehensive view of the sociocultural benefits of tourism for destination communities. The source of the model lies in the writing of Esty and Winston (2006), but there are a number of adaptations to their formulation for the purposes of an interest in tourism and its sociocultural consequences. The *y*-axis in the model is defined by its two poles, where the positive gains are on one end of the dimension and the control of negative consequences is at the other extreme of this construct. In this context, avoiding negative consequences can be seen as either avoiding risks or reducing losses. The *x*-axis in the model is represented by a time dimension with a short time frame at one pole and a longer more extended set of benefits fitting the other end of this construct. This structure gives rise to four cells which are characterized by the axes as follows: tangible benefits and social capital revenue are short-term and positive gains; community reputation gains are positive but longer-term; savings through reducing losses is often shorter-term while forestalling and delimiting risks is a somewhat longer-term but is still a loss-minimization approach. Examples of sociocultural benefits which fit these descriptions are presented in Fig. 3.1

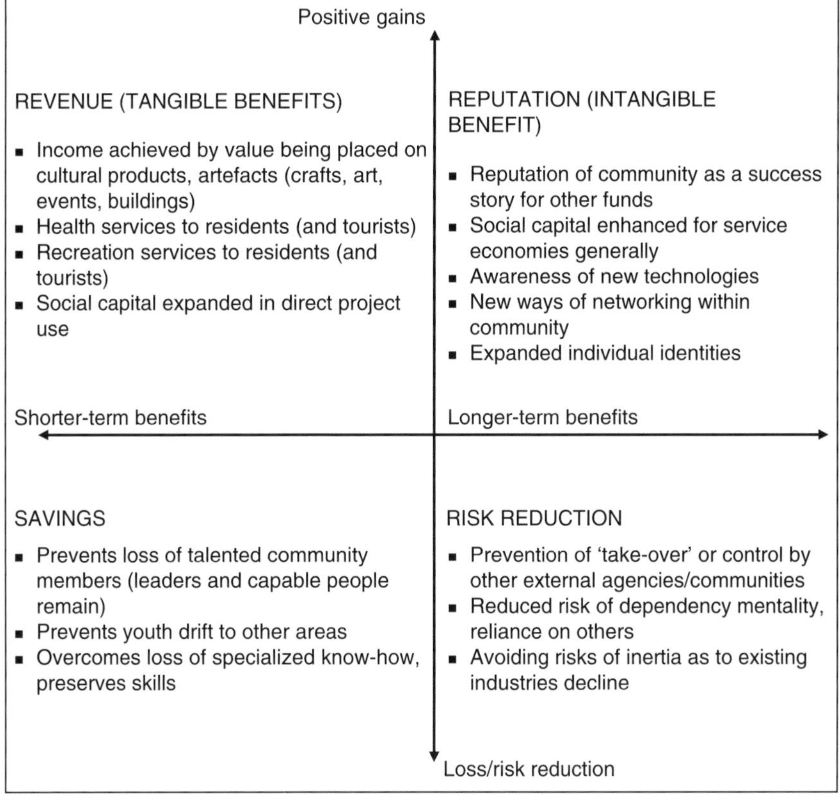

Fig. 3.1. A business-derived model to identify the sociocultural benefits of tourism in a destination community.

Box 3.1. Strategies and measures to maintain or develop sociocultural benefits of tourism in a destination community.

Revenue – tangible benefits

- Grants and loans to community groups by government
- Subsidies and tax incentives by government
- Seed money and grant schemes for establishing networks to support social and cultural concerns
- Certified users of cultural products and icons leading to price premiums
- Quality control mechanisms to look after copyright and authorized use of images with paid benefits to community or individuals
- Tradable licences and permits to operate social and cultural activities monitored by government
- Development of social contracts where external investor must provide social services such as:
  - Access for residents to health service
  - Access for residents to some recreational services shared with visitors
  - Training and educational subsidies and opportunities for local community

Savings and cost reductions

Tax relief and subsidies to emerging businesses:

- Free or low-cost technical assistance and resources supplied to enterprises (e.g. market information, training)
- Destination marketing partnerships lowering the cost of promotional efforts
- Government schemes to co-fund employment of local people in strategic positions
- Linkage with volunteer organizations and workers to provide supportive skills and labour

Reputation – intangible benefits

Monitoring, documentation and reporting to support reputation:

- Collecting data and providing audits of outcomes for internal and external appraisal of benefits (e.g. number of people in training courses, community networks and social links)

External marketing:

- Presenting and promotion of community through diverse outlets as willing to adopt innovation and change
- Reports by visitors on community well-being

Internal marketing:

- Presentation and promotion within the community of the management and delivery of sociocultural benefits
- Creation of associations and networks by business groups for self-promotion and identity

Risk reduction

- Rebates and surety bonds – arrangements to ensure compliance with good practice
- Strong planning laws extending beyond land-use planning and involving contracts to employ quotas of local workers and use of local products
- Prosecution of tourists for illegal and undesirable activities
- Participation in international agreements and charters on human rights and well-being
- Interpretation and public education to influence visitor behaviour

The information provided in Fig. 3.1 asserts that there are four kinds of benefits to be realized in relation to the sociocultural benefits of tourism. These advantages are presented here as a corrective to the dominant writings on the sociocultural consequences of tourism which tend to emphasize the less-favourable outcomes. It would be naive and inappropriate to claim that the benefits listed in Fig. 3.1 frequently occur. To adopt such a perspective would be to engage in the kind of boosterism and tourism advocacy which Jafari (2005) among others has noted. Instead, the information provided in Fig. 3.1 itemizes targets or goals for the management of better community futures.

It is, however, not simply adequate to itemize and categorize the potential positive sociocultural benefits of tourism. Steps towards achieving these targets represent a more complete picture of managing tourism which can benefit a community in social and cultural terms. Box 3.1 provides a complementary tool kit for the management and delivery of the sociocultural components of tourism.

Discussion

The practices and strategies provided in Fig. 3.1 and Box 3.1 involve a range of stakeholders. Some of the parties affected by, and who effect changes to, tourism include community associations and organizations within a destination. Additionally, at times leading individuals in a community can act almost autonomously to induce change. Further, regional and national governments may be involved in a number of the strategic and tactical approaches to influence tourism's sociocultural impact, and tourism businesses, both local and external to the community, have roles to play. Some examples of stakeholder involvement are provided in a consideration of each cell of the model.

Savings and Cost Reduction

This cell of the model emphasizes that some of the sociocultural benefits of tourism lie in the form of savings and cost reductions, notably avoiding the loss of personnel and hence the capacities which exist in a community. It may be that in a regional destination, tourism employment can prevent the drift to urban centres and in this process preserve the skills, enthusiasm and capability to continue and embellish local traditions and practices. The strategies and measures to facilitate this process include government schemes to co-fund employment, to provide tax relief to emerging businesses, to support low-cost training and to offer marketing assistance. Such efforts can create more efficient business and community development operations (Dredge and Jenkins, 2007; Hall, 2007). A New Zealand example of this assistance is the provision of a course entitled Certificate in Jade and Hand Stone Carving which underpins the development of a number of craft galleries and jade outlets in the west coast town of Hokitika. The government-sponsored provision of the course through the local technical college represents a savings in training costs for businesses and further provides publicity for the Hokitika Craft Gallery, which functions as a cooperative for local artists and craftspeople (http://www.hokitikacraftgallery.co.nz/about.asp).

Revenue: Tangible Benefits

The tangible benefits and revenue cell of the model emphasize new income which can support the social and cultural life of the destination community. A long-standing tradition in the anthropological and sociological traditions of tourism study has emphasized a range of dangers and changes attached to the commercialization of cultural community practices (Greenwood, 1978; Smith, 1978). It is therefore necessary to build locally appropriate self-determination mechanisms into the commercialization process. Examples of these mechanisms include certification and community approvals of practices, often through the development of copyright-style controls involving the authorized use of images and products. This latter set of practices actually combines two cells of this model: risk reduction and revenue generation.

In addition to the direct income to destination communities and their members, the revenue perspective on the sociocultural benefits of tourism can be considered in terms of the advantages of obtaining government grants and loans linked to tourism initiatives (Dredge and Jenkins, 2007). For example, seed money can support and even regenerate social and cultural concerns. Establishing a premium or high price for special cultural products may be a valuable strategy to enhance revenue in some contexts. Alternatively revenue may be thought of not in such a direct commercial way but rather as heightened understanding and tolerance.

These revenue-earning practices may involve direct sales to tourists but can include consortia, traders and organizations which accredit local products such as the fair trade groups. An example of an organization providing revenue for such products as African masks, statues and art objects is African Art gallery, a group based in the Netherlands but with a marketing and distribution system meeting the needs of tourists who have been to the locations (http://us-africa.tripod.com/art/index/html). Revenue for locally made and distinctive products may extend beyond arts and crafts to food products, furniture and certain categories of home ware and electronic goods. The ability to provide transport and shipping services rather than have tourists transport such products in their luggage has expanded the possibilities for destination communities to benefit from the tourist shopping behaviour and consumerism (cf. Harris, 2005).

Risk Reduction

A number of practices working at different levels have been employed and are included in a risk-reduction view of tourism's sociocultural consequences. The establishment of strong legal frameworks, which permit the prosecution of those who seek to exploit members of a destination community, represents one form of risk reduction. Examples of this kind of risk reduction include international agreements preventing and legislating against slavery, child sex tourism and drug use. A less formal but widely used form of risk reduction lies in good communication and powerful interpretation, which can influence visitor behaviour in areas where the actions of outsiders may offend or endanger local cultural groups and activities.

One of the better-known organizations working in the risk-reduction context is the anti-child sex and slavery group known as ECPAT. This group with national sub-branches in a number of countries has stimulated the development of strong laws, such as the UK Sexual Offences Act, 2003, which permit the prosecution of travelling sex offenders in their countries of origin. The most successful outcomes achieved by these groups appear to lie in multiple stakeholder attempts to reduce the risk of exploitation. This cooperation involves businesses, community members and policing together with the provision and wide distribution of interpretive and explanatory warning material (http://www.ecpat.org.uk/protecting.html).

Reputation: Intangible Benefits

It has been recognized for some time that sustainable tourism must be linked to the wider concept of sustainable development (Bramwell and Lane, 2005). One longer-term consequence of successful tourism in a destination lies in the building and development of the social capital of the community which may gain the area a reputation that can help stimulate other developmental initiatives. There is of course a core question central to the fundamental premise of this book that community capacity must be adequate before tourism itself can be developed. Nevertheless, if a view is taken that the construction of social capital is an iterative process with feedback from small successes, then a valuable role in terms of the reputation of the community can be suggested. In more developed tourism destinations the success of a destination in staging a major tourism-linked initiative such as the Olympic Games or major sporting fixtures may generate a reputation which sees other communities seeking to employ members of the successful community and emulate their operations. In the Australian context the Tjapukai Cultural Park, a tourist attraction built around the history, stories and dance performances of a local indigenous group, has been a moderately successful commercial venture (Moscardo and Pearce, 1999). Its success, however, reaches beyond revenue and has involved the national tourism body, Tourism Australia, frequently using members of Tjapukai to spearhead international marketing campaigns. This has benefited the image and reputation of the performers and the company, both expanding the number of workers and giving rise to parallel groups keen to build their own reputation and success stories (The Didgeridoo Hut and Art gallery, http://didgeridoohut.com.au; Tjapukai Cultural Park, http://tjapukai.com.au).

Conclusion

An attempt has been made in this chapter to adopt a broad view of the possible range of tourism's sociocultural benefits and how to influence them. In taking this approach it has been necessary to collate rather different mechanisms of influence at varying scales of operation and hence the discussion encompasses legal approaches, tax incentives, public education and marketing perspectives.

The discussion has placed more emphasis on the behaviour and practices of organizations rather than focusing on the interaction of individuals. There is an extensive literature which considers and treats the topic of how the interacting parties influence one another, which in part determines the micro-sociological impacts of tourism (Cohen, 2004; Pearce, 2005). While recognizing the additional contribution of this literature to tourism's influence on the well-being of the local destination, the broader ambit of concerns adopted in this chapter speak to the larger issues of overall socio-economic well-being and the opportunities generated by tourism for community development and self-determination. In particular, by looking at the four cells of a sustainability and business-derived model to classify and nurture tourism's sociocultural effects, it is proposed that analysts and practitioners may have a useful tool to consider thoroughly tourism's role in the future of diverse destination communities.

References

Blanchflower, D.G. and Oswald, A.J. (2005) Happiness and the human development index: the paradox of Australia. Available at: http://www.nber.org/papers/W1146

Bosselman, F. (1979) *In the Wake of the Tourist: Managing Special Places in Eight Countries.* The Conservation Foundation, Washington, DC.

Bourdieu, P. (1986) *Distinction: A Social Critique of the Judgment of Taste.* Routledge, London.

Bramwell, B. and Lane, B. (2005) From niche to general relevance? Sustainable tourism, research and the role of tourism journals. *Journal of Tourism Studies* 16(2), 52–62.

Carlsen, J., Getz, D. and Morrison, A. (2004) *Family Business in the Tourism and Hospitality Industries.* CAB International, Wallingford, UK.

Cohen, E. (2004) *Contemporary Tourism.* Elsevier, Amsterdam.

Coleman, J.S. (1990) *Foundations of Social Theory.* Belknap Press, Cambridge, Massachusetts.

Dann, G.M.S. (1996) *The Language of Tourism: A Sociolinguistic Perspective.* CAB International, Wallingford, UK.

de Botton, A. (2002) *The Art of Travel.* Penguin, London.

Diener, E. (2000) Subjective well-being: the science of happiness and a proposal for a national index. *American Psychologist* 55, 34–43.

Dredge, D. and Jenkins, J. (2007) *Tourism Planning and Policy.* Wiley, Milton, Queensland, Australia.

Elkington, J. (1997) *Cannibals with Forks. The Triple Bottom Line of 21st Century Business.* Oxford, Capstone.

Esty, D.C. and Winston, A.S. (2006) *Green to Gold.* Yale University Press, New Haven, Connecticut.

Fagence, M. (2003) Tourism and local society and culture. In: Singh, S., Timothy, D.J. and Dowling, R.K. (eds) *Tourism in Destination Communities.* CAB International, Wallingford, UK, pp. 55–78.

Farrell, B. (1977) *The Tourist Ghettos of Hawaii.* Center for South Pacific Studies, University of California, Santa Cruz, California.

Flyvbjerg, B. (2001) *Making Social Science Matter.* Cambridge University Press, Cambridge.

Gergen, K.J. (1997) The place of psyche in a constructed world. *Theory and Psychology* 7/6, 723–746.

Glover, T.D. and Hemingway, J.L. (2005) Locating leisure in the social capital literature. *Journal of Leisure Research* 37(4), 387–401.

Grayling, A.C. (2005) *Descartes.* Pocket Books, London.

Greenwood, D.J. (1978) Culture by the pound: an anthropological perspective on tourism as cultural commoditization. In: Smith, V.L. (ed.) *Hosts and Guests.* Blackwell, Oxford, pp. 129–138.

Gould, S.J. (2004) *The Hedgehog, the Fox and the Magister's Pox. Mending and Minding the Misconceived Gap Between Science and the Humanities.* Vintage, London.

Hall, C.M. (2007) *Tourism in Australia. Development, Issues and Change*, 5th edn. Pearson education, Frenchs Forest, NewSouthWales, Australia.

Harris, D. (2005) *Key Concepts in Leisure Studies.* Sage, London.

Jafari, J. (1990) Research and scholarship: the basis of tourism education. *Journal of Tourism Studies* 1(1), 33–41.

Jafari, J. (2005) Bridging out, nesting afield: powering a new platform. *Journal of Tourism Studies* 16(2), 1–5.

Kahneman, D., Diener, E. and Schwartz, N. (eds) (1999) *Well-being: The Foundations of Hedonic Psychology.* Russell Sage Foundation, New York, pp. 3–5.

Kirshenblatt-Gimblett, B. (1998) *Destination Culture. Tourism, Museums and Heritage.* University of California Press, Berkeley, California.

Lambert, R.D. (1966) Some minor pathologies in the American presence in India. *Annals of the American Academy of Political and Social Sciences* 368, 157–170.

Lankford, S.V. and Howard, D.R. (1994) Developing a tourism impact attitude scale. *Annals of Tourism Research* 21(1), 121–139.

Leigh, A. and Wolfers, J. (2006) Happiness and the human development index: Australia is not a paradox. Available at: http://www.nber.org/papers/W11925

Morrison, A.M., Pearce, P.L., Moscardo, G., Nadkarni, N. and O'Leary, J.T. (1996) Specialist accommodation: definitions, markets served, and roles in tourism development. *Journal of Travel Research* 35(1), 18–26.

Moscardo, G. and Pearce, P.L. (1999) Understanding ethnic tourists. *Annals of Tourism Research* 26(2), 416–434.

Myers, D.G. (2000) The funds, friends and faith of happy people. *American Psychologist* 55, 56–67.

Pearce, P.L. (1990) Farm tourism in New Zealand: a social situation analysis. *Annals of Tourism Research* 17(3), 337–352.

Pearce, P.L. (1993) The importance, incidence and interpretation of the social impacts of Australian tourism. In: Faulkner, B. and Kennedy, M. (eds) *Australian Tourism Outlook Forum 1992: Contributed papers.* Bureau of Tourism Research, Canberra, pp. 9–16.

Pearce, P.L. (2005) *Tourist Behaviour. Themes and Conceptual Schemes.* Channel View, Clevedon, UK.

Portes, A. (1998) Social capital: its origins and applications in modern sociology. *Annual Review of Sociology* 24, 1–24.

Putnam, R.D. (2000) *Bowling Alone: The Collapse and Revival of American Community.* Simon & Schuster, New York.

Robinson, M. (1997) Tourism in de-industrializing centers in the UK. In: Robinson, M. and Boniface, P. (eds) *Tourism and Cultural Conflicts.* CAB International, Wallingford, UK, pp. 129–159.

Richards, G. and Wilson, J. (2004) The global nomad: motivations and behaviour of independent travellers worldwide. In: Richards, G. and Wilson, J. (eds) *The Global Nomad: Backpacker Travel in Theory and Practice,* Channel View, Clevedon, UK, pp. 14–42.

Rocharungsat, P. (2004) *Community-Based Tourism: Perspectives and Future Possibilities.* Unpublished PhD thesis, School of Business, James Cook University, Townsville, Australia.

Seligman, M.E.P. and Csikszentmihalyi, M. (2000) Positive Psychology: an introduction. *American Psychologist* 55, 5–14.

Sen, A. (2000) A decade of human development. *Journal of Human Development* 1(1), 17–23.
Smith, V.L. (ed.) (1978) *Hosts and Guests.* Blackwell, Oxford.
Stanton, E. (2007) The human development index: a history. Political economy research institute. Working paper Series number 127. University of Massachussetts, Amherst, Massachusetts.
Young, G. (1973) *Tourism, Blessing or Blight?* Penguin, Harmondsworth, UK.

4 Linking a Sense of Place with a Sense of Care: Overcoming Sustainability Challenges Faced by Remote Island Communities

KAYE WALKER

School of Business, James Cook University, Australia

Introduction

This book recognizes that remote communities have numerous challenges to overcome with respect to understanding, developing and managing sustainable tourism in their region. This chapter proposes a way that tourism, especially ecotourism operators may enhance communities' awareness of negative and positive tourism impacts as an inherent function of their own operational sustainability and accreditation processes. The proposed approach can also provide a community with greater capacity to be more integrated into the tourism process by having their values incorporated into the functional aspects of the operation, while increasing the operator's and tourist's awareness of the challenges facing remote communities. This approach is especially relevant to remote island communities who demonstrate their own distinctive set of challenges to understanding and managing tourism development and their own sustainability. The aim is to contribute to a community's greater appreciation of the potential negative impacts of tourism while capitalizing on the potential for positive impacts.

A particular challenge to enhancing a community's awareness of tourism development issues is to address the negative impacts of tourism, which Moscardo describes in five key areas (Chapter 1, this volume). The first of these areas is environmental degradation, which includes the depletion of natural resources in the local environment. In response to these types of negative impacts, ecotourism was proposed as a potentially more suitable form of tourism, but it was suggested that there is little evidence that it offers any better outcomes for the residents of the destinations. This is especially relevant to remote island communities who often have limited natural resources. Additionally, these communities may be remote not only from potential tourism and resource markets but also from their own central or regional government bodies. These communities may be even more isolated from their own national government, resources and assistance by fate of tribalism, race and minority status, historical national boundary manipulation

 Building Community Capacity for Tourism Development (ed. G. Moscardo)

and imperialism. Examples of these situations impacting upon the resources and assistance provided to remote islands abound in the Asia-Pacific Region, and the author would like to briefly consider one example in order to highlight the distinctive nature of some of the challenges facing these remote communities.

The example is the delay in the provision of aid by the Solomon Island government to one of its most remote island communities in the aftermath of the Category 5 Cyclone Zoe in 2002. The cyclone rendered the population of Tikopia (~1000) without freshwater or shelter and devastated the tiny island's self-sustaining cultivated food-producing gardens and coconut groves. While the Solomon Islands is 95% Melanesian, the people of Tikopia are of Polynesian descent, indicative in their culture and language. Historically, they pushed out the Melanesian population of Tikopia and surrounding islands around 1200 AD, raiding and eliminating whole Melanesian populations during that period. However, the British proclaimed an extended protectorate over the Melanesian archipelago's southern islands in the 1890s, which were renamed the Solomon Islands in the 1970s and independence granted in 1978. Thus, Tikopia represents the traditional enemies of the vast majority of the Solomon Island people, and an ethnic minority in a country whose government is predominantly Melanesian and experiencing political turmoil. Tikopia is, however, a highly sought destination (but infrequently visited due to its remote location) for the more adventurous of the Expedition Cruise itineraries. Expedition Cruising is a form of ecotourism specializing in environmental and cultural tourism expeditions conducted from small cruise vessels with a maximum capacity of approximately 120 passengers (see Walker and Moscardo, 2006, for a more detailed description of this type of cruising operation). But, despite its tourism attraction and potential for tourism development in the Solomon Islands, Tikopia did not appear to represent any inherent value to the Solomon Islands community, nor did it seem that the community was incorporated into any political or administrative process that ensured adequate awareness, concern and support for their well-being.

The author had just visited Tikopia the month before the cyclone, while working on board an Expedition Cruise vessel as an environmental interpreter, experiencing the last destination in the Solomon Islands before ending the cruise in Fiji. In retrospect, upon hearing of the Tikopians' cyclonic predicament, waiting more than 5 days for anyone, any country or aid organization to come to their assistance, it begged the question of what sustainable or capacity-building value had the ecotourism experience brought to that isolated community. If the ecotourism operations had not been able to facilitate a sense of awareness and care for this special island population, and the money paid for the experience could not help the Tikopians in their plight, in what significant way did ecotourism contribute to the island's community capacity for sustainability?

In this situation, it appeared to the author that one way the ecotourism experience could have been of some benefit is to have facilitated a sense of care regarding the sustainability of this population among the ecotourism operators and participants (representing a global population), which in turn may have been appreciated by the Solomon Islands government, if only in a purely economic sense. In ecotourism operations, the participants' understanding and awareness of their environmental and cultural experiences is principally facilitated through the process of interpretation. Thus, there was an incentive to investigate the capability of the interpretive process to facilitate in participants an awareness of the challenges faced by the community and a sense of care for its well-being. The aim being to create a model for the interpretation conducted in ecotourism operations that effectively facilitated, or at least provided, the basis to create a psychological environment for the participants to consider their sense of care for the communities they encountered. It also seemed apparent that this model would be far more effective if it could be incorporated into the ecotourism process, integrating the community into an operational and administrative framework. This could potentially improve the community's capacity to ensure its sustainability because it had become a component formally embedded in the tourism process.

Both a model of interpretation (referred to as the Value Model of Interpretation-I (VMI-I), see Fig. 4.1) and an operational framework (referred to as a Sustainable Tourism Framework, see Fig. 4.2) were developed (a more detailed discussion of their theoretical and applied construction is discussed by Walker in Chapter 7, this volume). The present chapter intends to explore two particular aspects of their application in remote destinations.

The first aspect to be discussed involves investigating the interpretive capacity of Expedition Cruises to facilitate a sense of care among its participants. This discussion focuses primarily upon the results of a case study of another remote, but more accessible island involving a marginalized community, Easter Island. It also draws from a study involving the Traditional Owners (TOs) of a remote group of islands in the Great Barrier Reef called the Flinders Island Group. The second aspect to be examined in this chapter considers how by utilizing an ecotourism accreditation process in the scope of the proposed operational framework, a community may be provided a greater capacity for involvement in the sustainable tourism development process. Both aspects may contribute to overcoming some of the more distinctive challenges faced by remote and marginalized island communities to ensure their involvement in the tourism process and potentially their own sustainability.

Ecotourism in Remote Communities: a Link Between a Sense of Place and a Sense of Care

The VMI-I (see Fig. 4.1) was developed while investigating the personal value-based outcomes for participants experiencing a type of ecotourism operation referred to as Expedition Cruising. These personal values were facilitated by the interpretation provided as an integral function of these operations (and other types of ecotourism), and in this research elicited by the subsequent participant questionnaires regarding the interpretive experience. These questionnaires relied upon a ladder of abstraction approach adapted from the means-end analysis technique (Klenosky *et al.*, 1998). The application of this technique provided the identification of the most important interpretive attributes (staff expertise and dedication, experiential activities and the facilitation of tourists participation in these activities) and benefits (cultural and environmental awareness, environmental immersion and experiential enhancement), as determined by

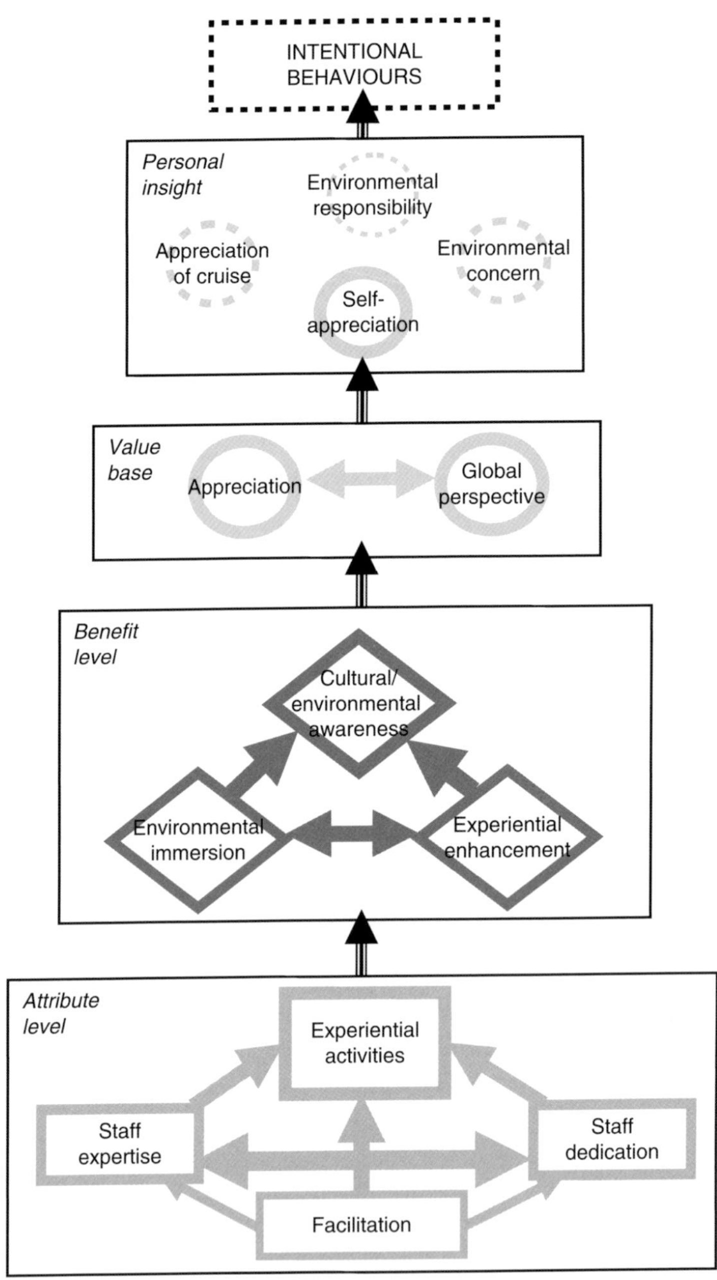

Fig. 4.1. The Value Model of Interpretation-I.

the participants. These were also the most important elements in facilitating the recognition and identification of the personal significance of the interpretive experience to the participant, representing values such as a deeper level of appreciation for the people, environment or culture, and the placement of this aware-

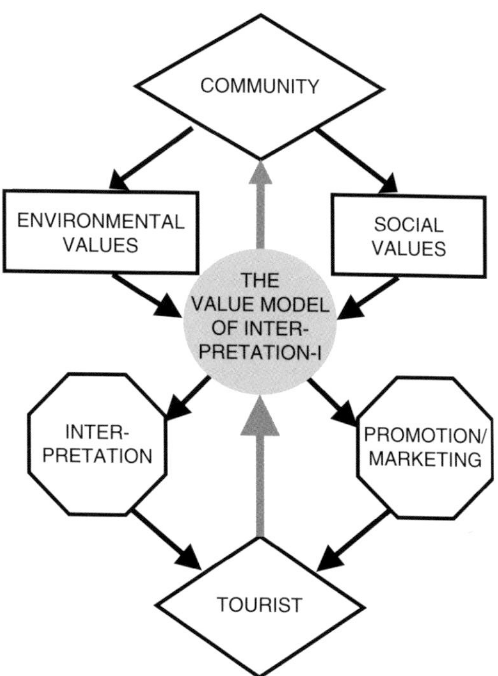

Fig. 4.2. A Sustainable Tourism Framework – linking the community to the tourist.

ness into a global perspective of personal importance to the participant. These initial value-based responses were then linked to a greater personal insight of some significance referred to as 'self-appreciation'. This level of responses often included references to environmental concern and responsibility for the place and people visited, and a more insightful appreciation of the value of this type of tourism. This higher-level value-based response appeared to be the one most likely to lead to an intentional behaviour of the participant as an outcome of their ecotourism interpretive experience. In other words, in an ideal Expedition Cruise situation, the use of experiential activities guided by dedicated and expert staff facilitates a visitor's access to a particular setting. These attributes of the interpretation support a range of benefits perceived by the visitor which can include experiential enhancement, environmental immersion and awareness. In turn, these benefits support the development of values such as appreciation and then, through this appreciation and the ability to take a broader or global perspective, personal insights. These personal insights then support the development of pro-environmental behavioural intentions.

The theoretical premise of this research was that intentional pro-environment behaviours, occurring as an outcome of ecotourism experiences, were unlikely to be facilitated by increased environmental learning alone (Orams, 1996), but required the facilitation of the participants' own identification of the personal significance of the experience (Ham and Krumpe, 1996; Beck and Cable, 1998; Ballantyne and Uzzell, 1999; Moscardo, 1999; Ham and Weiler, 2002; Knapp and Benton 2004). The term 'environmental' in this discussion includes the participants' perceptions of the social and cultural aspects of the experience and their global environment. One of the value-based concepts that was identified as being significant in the interpretive process to both the host community and tourist in the earlier stages of the research was a 'sense of place'. This concept is considered to be a community-embedded value which could be beneficial to community capacity building if recognized by the visitor and sustained by the host, and as an interpretation concept it has been discussed with respect to its importance in interpretive programmes and community sustainability (Beck and Cable, 1998; Moisey and McCool, 2001; Armstrong and Weiler, 2002; Walker, 2007).

Sense of place is a holistic concept, which is said to incorporate the social, cultural, environmental, psychological, geographic and demographic dimensions of people's lives in relation to their place of residence or other significant place, and thus attempting to identify the meaning a people attach to a place helps researchers to understand the people's culture, values and concerns (Tuan, 1977; Raitz, 1987; Jackson, 1994; Bricker, 1998; Bricker and Kerstetter, 2006). Historically, sense of place with respect to tourism has been addressed through research on the host community with the suggestion that

> understanding the relationship between local community members and the place in which they live assists tourism planners, operators, and marketers in their development of sustainable quality tourism experiences.
>
> (Bricker and Kerstetter, 2006, p. 100)

It is suggested this understanding assists those involved in tourism development in three ways:

1. Determining the appropriateness of the tourism product;
2. Contributing to understanding the aspirations and desires of the local tourism impact strategies; and
3. Responding to the value people assign to the place in which they live, which minimizes potential negative impacts on local cultures (Bricker and Kerstetter, 2006).

It is the sense of place concept and its potential relationship to developing a sense of care and concern in the ecotourism participants for the place and people that will be explored in the following results of this research. It is also the prospective reciprocal nature of this concept when applied to interpretive programmes in ecotourism operations that is intriguing. Does it have the capacity to increase not only the tourists' and tourism developers' understanding and awareness of the inherent value of a place and the associated community values, but also the community's awareness of these values? Thus, potential negative impacts may become more apparent to both host and guest. Is it even a concept that can be effectively conveyed to the tourist, especially a passenger on board an Expedition Cruise vessel which provides all their accommodation and meals, and hence destinations are often visited for just a short period of time? The chapter is then finalized by considering how the community's involvement may be more fully integrated into the tourism process utilizing the concepts within the context of ecotourism accreditation.

Two Case Studies of Remote Communities Visited by Expedition Cruises

The Easter Island, or Rapa Nui (as the island is called by the indigenous population), case study is the main focus of this chapter because it demonstrates most closely the set of distinctive challenges faced by remote, marginalized island communities. It is about as far away from any other land mass as any other place in the world (3700 km from the nearest mainland, Chile). It is a small island (180 km^2) with extremely limited natural resources due to previous over-exploitation. It was annexed under Chilean territory in 1888 after its remnant Polynesian population (the Rapanui) had also been exploited and ravaged by introduced European diseases. Its current population is approximately 3000, with one-third being from Chile and Europe. At the time of this research (October 2004), the Rapanui had no centralized government or representation that was considered to be officially recognized by the Chilean national government. There was a supply vessel provided by the Chilean government, but it did not take commuting passengers, and although there is an international airstrip on the island, all flights are provided by LanChile (Chile's national airline), which is expensive and, depending on the time of year, may only fly a couple of times a week from Santiago. Yet again, it is also considered a prime but difficult cruise ship destination, as it has a fascinating history with significant archaeological edifices (most renowned being the Moai), and most of the island is a National Park (UNESCO World Heritage recognized), which is managed exclusively by the Chilean National Forest Corporation. But it represents days of sea travel from anywhere in the Pacific, and landing passengers on the island called the 'the navel of the world' is dependent upon weather and sea conditions.

The author arrived at Rapa Nui on board an Expedition Cruise vessel which unusually spent more than 1 day or a few hours at the island, as its passengers were being flown out from the island and the next passenger group being flown in. The author was one of the Expedition Cruise guides and a participant observer, and stayed on for a period of 10 days after disembarkation to conduct community interviews for this research. During one consultation, the self-appointed council representatives of the local indigenous population (the Rapanui) were asked if they had a tourism development plan for the island. Yes, but it was only in their heads at this point in time. That is, it was not written in any document form as they lacked the resources, support and administrative capacity for formulating such. There were two main tourism guiding companies on the island offering tours and guides, with whom representatives were interviewed. One was owned and operated by a European married to a local Rapanui, and the other managed by a Chilean married to a local (noting that the whole Expedition Cruise ship itinerary on the island was arranged and coordinated by a Chilean representative of this tour company, who flew from Santiago to meet and supervise the passengers' tours). The guides were a mixture of people born in Europe and Chile, as well as some local community members of the Rapanui.

Additionally, there were new restaurants and other small tourism handicraft entrepreneurs starting up to cater for the growing tourism drawn by more frequent flights and special deals at certain times of the year. Yet, while most of the land is National Park (mainly to protect the archaeological aspects), none of the marine environment was protected at that time, and already the island's local fishing was being exploited as the local lobster (crayfish) was considered to be a prime meal for tourists. According to informants, fishing for other species was already being pushed further away from the island as fish stocks were depleted. Live coral was also being collected indiscriminately to dry and sell to the tourists. Thus, there were some obvious negative environmental impacts occurring that were perceived by the visitors, and by some locals who felt there was reason to be concerned about their marine resource sustainability. Personal communication with residents revealed there were some pushing for a dedicated Marine Park to be declared, as well as the implementation of officially managed fishing and marine collection limits. However, there appeared to be little government support to even discuss this situation.

Thus, we witness a disenfranchised indigenous population, marginalized by its non-indigenous government, with no representation in the Chilean government's tourism development plans or the management of its major tourism attractions, remote and isolated, or with at least limited access to and from tourism and resource markets, its main guiding companies managed by non-indigenous operators, and potential negative tourism-orientated environmental impacts upon their extremely limited natural resources being largely ignored by the Chilean government. Therefore, the relevance of the sense of place concept to the challenges faced by this remote community appears to be validated, if its application can in fact contribute to the three aspects of tourism development proposed by Bricker and Kerstetter (2006), as described previously.

The following is a brief description of the other case study in the context of the community's situation and involvement with Expedition Cruises, in order to provide the background for its contribution to the research results being discussed in this chapter. The Flinders Island Group, of which Stanley Island is the most well known for its spectacular and culturally significant rock art sites (aboriginal cave paintings), is situated in the Far Northern Great Barrier Reef Marine Park Management Area in north-eastern Australia. It is now an uninhabited group of islands after the aboriginal people were removed during the Second World War, and with the closest remaining TO representatives residing in the nearest coastal town of Hopevale or thereabouts. The situation of the Expedition Cruise ship's visit to Stanley Island within which the research was conducted had been facilitated some years previously by the author when she was employed by the Queensland Department of Environment and Heritage, and was responsible for rewriting the Cruise Ship Visitation Policy to the Northern Great Barrier Reef region. When the management authority was approached by the Expedition Cruise company wishing to obtain a permit to visit these islands as part of their Great Barrier Reef itinerary, liaison was initiated with the Hopevale community with regard to the appropriateness of this sort of tourism activity on Stanley Island. Discussion involved how these visits could be conducted in accordance with the community's goals for this island group and the impending Joint Management Agreement they had forged with the Australian Federal government.

There was a strong desire in the community to be able to inform others (i.e. non-traditional peoples such as tourists) about the cultural significance of these islands. They contain some of the most significant aboriginal rock art in the country, as well as other places culturally and historically important to the traditional community. The flora and fauna are considered to be culturally significant as the predominantly native species represent traditional resources and connections to their environment. Middens containing marine shells are quite evident near the landing places of Stanley Island. Thus, the community wished to increase awareness and appreciation of this place, its cultural and natural environment, and the connections these represent, as well as creating an element of care, support and responsible behaviour, particularly with respect to preserving the condition of the rock art and native flora and fauna.

It was felt that if officially permitted visits by groups were accompanied by TO guides this may be achieved, as well as providing scope for investing younger members of the community in their cultural way of life and guiding practices. Due to their lack of access to these islands, the elders felt that the young were no longer aware themselves of the islands' significance. Thus, this opportunity could also provide scope for instilling the significance of the site in the young members of their community, so they could not only continue to be custodians of the sites, but also be inspired to be more culturally and environmentally interactive with the sites, and by being so create a setting to which others may respond positively. Accordingly, it was decided the policy for visits by Expedition Cruise ships who wished to land passengers on Stanley Island should include the requirement that groups are accompanied by two TO guides from the Hopevale community, and this had been occurring since its inception in 2001. Additionally, a TO guide could accompany groups consisting of a maximum of 20 passengers at a time on location, thus requiring a rotation system of passengers disembarking and landing on site so there were never more than 40 passengers on shore at any time.

Both of these case studies were conducted while on board and on location, during or after two different and unconnected Expedition Cruise ship itineraries in the Pacific Region in 2004, though utilizing the same Expedition Cruise ship as the research platform. Questionnaires were voluntarily completed by the Expedition Cruise participants at the end of each cruise. These case studies represent the third and fourth progressive elements of an inductive qualitative research programme based on a grounded theory approach. Approximately half of the passengers on board participated in the Flinders Island Group case study (representing 30 completed questionnaires) and 65% in the Easter Island case study (representing 62 completed questionnaires). The major differences between the two case studies in reference to the interpretive experience are that the two guides for the Flinders Island Group visit were TOs and accompanied the cruise passengers on board for a day before the visit to the islands and the day after (due to access issues to this remote location), but the visit on the island itself was of a short duration (approximately 2 hours for most passengers). Whereas the ten or so guides on Easter Island included indigenous, Chilean and expatriate representatives, the passengers had approximately 2 days on the island (one and a half of these spent on tour with the tour guides), but the passengers stayed on board the vessel for the first night of their visit and spent the next night onshore in hotels prior to flying out the following day, and the guides did not accompany the passengers on board at any time.

Results and Discussion

Stanley Island case study

Sense of place, as a potential tourist value arising from the interpretive experience, had been identified in research prior to these two case studies (Walker and Moscardo, 2006). But its definition proved to be elusive with respect to its relationship to participants' value-based responses. It was originally defined as representing the development of a more abstract value beyond that of a personal value, to recognizing the inherent significance or meaning of a place and expressing this in a perspective or context of its own value. Thus, by its definition, it did not express a personal value or significance for the participants of the ecotourism experience, which is what the ladder of abstraction questionnaires sought. Consequently, most passenger responses referring to the significance of a place either fell under the value of 'appreciation', or went further to express care or concern for a place or culture and thus fell under the value of 'cultural/environmental concern'. But could a sense of place approach be important for the guides in order to lead a visitor to a 'sense of care' for a place?

Thus, it was interesting to find in the Stanley Island case study that it was the attribute of 'facilitation' that most strongly aligned with the participants' awareness of a sense of place, particularly as the actual time spent on location was less than 2 hours (refer to Fig. 4.1 for the position 'facilitation' in the model at the Attribute Level). 'Facilitation' is defined as the recognition of the facilitation of participation in a particular experience or activity in a manner in which the passenger desires, enjoys or feels comfortable. It was within these categorized responses that passengers described how fundamental the guides' sense of place approach was to their understanding and appreciation: that is, the dedication and ability of the guides to convey their own cultural and environmental connection, care and concern for these islands and presenting the islands' intrinsic value and cultural significance. This was not all achieved in the 2 short hours on Stanley Island however, as the participants indicated it was enhanced by the opportunity to interact with the guides on board and their willingness to discuss many issues of their aboriginality and current lives in Australia. The resulting major value-based response for participants in this study was 'cultural/environmental concern', which was defined as the actual expression of concern or care for the current status or future implications of a place or culture. The major cognitive linkage to this value was the benefit of 'cultural/environmental awareness', which was defined as the recognition or understanding of environmental or cultural issues, concerns, balances, connections or concepts.

Thus, these results appear to demonstrate the connection between considering the concept of a 'sense of place' approach in an interpretive programme and its connection to facilitating a 'sense of care ' in the tourists. It also describes the community's own appreciation of the intrinsic value of presenting their own sense and care of place in the interpretive programmes of an ecotourism operation. They recognized this opportunity to limit the potential negative impacts of environmental and cultural degradation on the islands, while capitalizing on the opportunity the interpretive experience allowed them to enhance the potential positive impacts of ecotourism in their region. This involved not only the tourists, but also their own community, particularly the younger members as each time the guides accompanied an expedition, one experienced guide would bring an inexperienced member of the community with them as the second guide. The sense of place approach reciprocally increased the awareness and sense of care of both the TOs of the place and the visitors, including the eco-operators who had to implement the visitation restrictions in their operational procedures for cruises in this region of the Great Barrier Reef. The findings of the Easter Island case study, however, provided quite different insights into the function and outcomes of a sense of place approach.

Easter Island case study

The Easter Island community's interpretive aims were identified as being most closely connected with the value-based outcomes of 'appreciation', 'cultural/environmental concern' and 'cultural/environmental responsibility', along with the benefit of 'cultural/environmental awareness'. 'Appreciation' was defined as the development beyond mere enjoyment or understanding of a place to include the discussion of the significance of a place or culture in a personal context. 'Environmental responsibility' was defined as the literal expression of actions or feelings of responsibility for the culture, people or environment. These were determined from formal interviews with nine representatives of the Easter Island community, including Rapanui, Chilean and expatriates. All but one were involved in tourism on the island, which was considered to be the main source of income, employment and development potential. The Rapanui interviewees wanted tourists to recognize the indigenous people as distinct from Chileans, their Polynesian ancestry and cultural way of life, their current societal orientation and values based on an open community (extended family) providing a safe environment for family development and, in particular, their still existent ancestral connections to the archaeological sites of their forebears. This included protection of and respect for the sites representing the community's cultural integrity and values which included being culturally identified and recognized as Rapanui, and appreciation of their need and right for more autonomy from the Chilean government with respect to management decisions regarding their cultural sites and island development. Both Rapanui and expatriates talked about wanting the tourists to 'feel' the 'spirit' of the sites and the island, and all wished the current population would also respect the significance of the island, in particular that the Rapanui children have the opportunity to learn, experience and demonstrate such.

When the Rapanui interviewees were asked what values they felt were important to their community identity and needed to be sustained, it was mentioned numerous times that it was imperative that the Rapanui language be preserved. It was as if the terms 'language' and 'values' were indistinguishable. Indeed, language has been described as 'a carrier of a people's culture', and that 'culture is a carrier of a people's values', with values being the 'basis of a people's self-definition' (Ngugi wa Thiong'o cited in Freeman, 2006). Yet, there was no mention of wanting the tourists to recognize the existence of the Rapanui language; however there were numerous references to the need for more Rapanui guides to be involved in the tour operations. Likewise, there was no mention of the need for tourists to recognize the pride felt by some of the interviewees: proud to be the descendants of a nation of people who were able to build such a successful society with such great artisans, and then to survive such great catastrophes as the collapse of their society, the ravages of disease and other Western forces intentionally or not inflicted upon them.

There was a connection made between tourism and sustaining the traditional Rapanui language and cultural pride. At the time of these interviews, all official schools on the island were taught in Spanish. Only one school that taught classes in the Rapanui language had been established by a local woman in the past 2 years. It was often expressed that the only way for the community to acquire money to fund such ventures to sustain language and culture and their own development needs was through tourism. Although there were also negative impacts identified, particularly with the way the cruise tourism operations were managed currently on the island, most interviewees considered tourism to be a positive development for the community. Many had suggestions as to how the cruise tourism operations on the island could be improved both for the tourists' enjoyment and satisfaction, and for the purposes of more effectively conveying the previously discussed values the interviewees felt were important, as well as increasing the income from tourism to remain within the community for community use. It appeared to be generally agreed that the vehicle for achieving their community goals for development, management and autonomy was tourism. However, it was not indicated that the tourists should recognize this fact necessarily, but it was often suggested as an improvement that more time be allowed in tours for local interaction with local community elders and children. It was generally felt that the little time allocated to each cruise tourism visit to the island (usually half a day, or perhaps a whole day) meant that the cultural significance of the island, its history, its monuments and its people could not be effectively interpreted by the guides or appreciated by the visitors.

While the guides' interpretive aims overall appeared to reflect most of those of the community, their aim to facilitate 'cultural/environmental concern' was not literally conveyed to the researcher. However, through participant observation of their guiding styles it was evident they encouraged the visitors to behave with respect towards the sites not only to prevent physical degradation, but also for their inherent cultural significance, simultaneously contributing their personal passion and feeling for the place. The guides' desire to facilitate a 'sense of place' was clear and coincided with the community's goals for tourism with regard to feeling the spirit of the archaeological sites, and thus potentially reflecting the Stanley Island study in encouraging not only a 'cultural/environmental awareness', but also a deeper 'appreciation' leading to 'cultural/environmental concern'. However, the guide interviewees felt the duration of most tours was too short to adequately allow the contemplation time required at sites to facilitate a sense of place, and intriguingly the outcomes of the interpretive experiences in this study were quite different from Stanley Island, where passengers had only 2 hours on site.

While 'cultural/environmental awareness' was predominantly achieved as a benefit of the interpretive experience and linked to the expression of a higher level of 'appreciation', it was the identification of the personal value of a 'global perspective' which linked most strongly with the predominant higher-level value of 'self-appreciation'. The expressions of 'cultural/environmental concern' and 'cultural/environmental responsibility' were the least identified in the results. Yet, over all the studies and as indicated in the VMI-I, it is the value of 'self-appreciation' that potentially links most compellingly with participant 'intentional behaviours' as an outcome of the interpretive experience, and environmental concern and responsibility are considered to be potential components of that value-based set (see Fig. 4.1). Consider the examples of participant responses provided below for the values of 'global perspective' and 'self-appreciation'. Both could be considered to implicate intentional behaviours by the participants.

First, the definition of 'global perspective' was a more abstract placement of the experience or place into a global perspective of personal significance, and the definition of 'self-appreciation' was the recognition of a personal insight or ability. For example, one of the participant's responses with respect to 'global perspective' was:

> A society can overuse their resources and in effect destroy their society. This happened on EI and can happen to other societies or the world at large if we don't manage our resources and environment carefully.

While a response with respect to 'self-appreciation' was:

> ... [t]hat I want to relate the things I've learned to the island of Hawaii, especially the early Polynesian history and the current situation.

Furthermore, even though the interviewees did not state any desire that tourists should recognize their perceived importance of tourism to their community goals, just as one could expect feelings of cultural pride and connection to a place to emanate in a guide's interpretation, their political, personal and community-orientated aspirations may also be reflected. And this appeared to be the case, for a new participant benefit subcategory was significantly determined within 'cultural/environmental awareness' and referred to as 'cultural tourism awareness'. Although not an apparent thematic goal of the guides' interpretation, it appeared that the community's aspirations revolving around tourism development were indicated as an outcome of the interpretive experience. Perhaps this could be considered to be part of the community's sense of place as they perceive tourism to be intrinsically connected to maintaining their cultural integrity. This subcategory benefit was defined as the understanding or awareness of the role cultural tourism is playing or may play in maintaining or developing the culture, their interactions with their land and others, or the socio-economic base of the people and place being visited. Some examples of participant responses in this category were:

> The culture of EI is still alive and thriving and tourism is significantly helping fund the refurbishment of the culture.
>
> EI not really ready for mass influx of more tourists, fragile artefacts at risk from insensitive tourists, infrastructure (toilets for instance), roads etc. could be overwhelmed.
>
> They need to balance preservation of environment and cultural for the benefit of tourists *and* locals with the desire of the locals to live a higher standard of living.

This category, in particular, indicates the recognition by the tourist of the potential negative and positive aspects of tourism, and the challenges faced by the community. The community had also recognized some of the negative impacts regarding natural resources, but was in particular focused upon maximizing the potential positive impacts of tourism in overcoming the challenges they faced as a politically marginalized community and improving their potential for cultural sustainability. The differences in the participant benefit and value outcomes between the two studies constitute a more detailed discussion for another time regarding the different approaches and situations the ecotourism experiences offered at these destinations and the interconnectedness of the community goals with the guides' functional role and individual interpretive aims. How the sense of place approach is facilitated in experiential timing, and in particular the interactive opportunities provided with community representatives appeared to influence the scope of interpretive outcomes. However, despite the different outcomes of the two studies, they both indicate that a sense of place approach in the interpretive function of the ecotourism operation did appear to contribute to the three aspects described earlier by Bricker and Kerstetter (2006) in:

1. Determining the appropriateness of the tourism product as the guides and others involved in tourism on the islands recognized the limitations of the tour experience and were able to suggest improvements or operational imperatives to enhance the outcomes;
2. Understanding the aspirations and desires of the local community prompted their own suggestions and the development of practices for appropriate impact management, and the communication and liaison of these with tourism operators; and
3. Responding to the value the community assigned to places in which they live enabled tourism participants to consider the negative impacts upon cultures and environments in a global perspective.

It additionally appeared to reciprocally increase the participants' and communities' awareness of the potential positive outcomes tourism provided, as well as the challenges faced by remote communities in regard to tourism development. And depending on the experiential and interpretive situation involving the place and the guides, it seems a participant's sense of care could be facilitated, in conjunction with other personally significant value-based outcomes that linked with intentional environmental behaviours. Through their own identification of the important values to sustain and which they desired tourists to recognize and appreciate in the interpretive process, communities also made the connection between tourism and their cultural integrity and sustainability. If this sense of place approach is incorporated as the basis for the interpretive component of these ecotourism operations and facilitated through the utilization of the VMI-I within the context of the Sustainable Tourism Framework, which is placing the importance upon identification and facilitation of community-based values, then this becomes an integral component of the sustainable tourism process. How can we ensure, though, that the community and its values are incorporated into the administrative process of sustainable tourism, thus achieving one of the earlier stated aims to integrate remote island communities into an administrative or operational process in order to contribute to the capacity for sustainability? The proposed answer is to link this approach into already established operational agendas for ecotourism operators through their accreditation processes.

Operational Agenda: Ecotourism Accreditation

Although Bricker and Kerstetter (2006) also identified the ecotourism accreditation processes as an appropriate avenue for the facilitation of a sense of place approach to developing appropriate and quality tourism experiences for remote communities, there was no operational agenda developed to integrate this into the process. The interpretive strategy discussed in this chapter has operational implications from both the perspective of the sustainable tourism process as well as its implementation into ecotourism accreditation programmes.

If the Sustainable Tourism Framework (Fig. 4.2) is considered as an operational framework and its application coordinated with the use of the VMI-I (Fig. 4.1) as an assessment tool as well as an interpretive tool, then it is possible to compare the personal values and environmental awareness identified by the tourists with those identified by the community as being significant. This takes the environmental accreditation programmes currently in place to an extended level of application and usefulness. Take, for example, the International Ecotourism Standard which has been developed by Ecotourism Australia in conjunction with the Cooperative Research Centre for Sustainable Tourism of Australia. This Standard is based on the Australian Nature and Ecotourism Accreditation Programme (NEAP), Agenda 21 and the guiding principles for sound ecotourism certification based on the Mohonk Agreement (Mohonk Mountain, New York State, USA, in November, 2001). Green Globe 21 has the exclusive licence for the distribution and management of the International Ecotourism Standard. Green Globe 21 is the global Affiliation, Benchmarking and Certification programme for sustainable travel and tourism. According to the Tourism Australia web site, its brand signifies better environmental performance, improved community interactions, savings through using fewer resources and greater yields from increased consumer demand (Tourism Australia, 2007).

Green Globe 21 has four separate standards regulating compliance in their accreditation scheme: a Company Standard; a Community/Destination Standard; the International Ecotourism Standard; and a Precinct Planning and Design Standard. The International Ecotourism Standard defines Ecotourism Tours as those that involve being taken on an excursion with a guide (or guides) for the purpose of viewing and interacting with the natural environment, and typically combine activities such as driving, walking or riding with viewing and interacting with the environment (Green Globe, 2006). Although the definition does not include any reference to interacting with the local community, the principal objectives of this standard are:

- to assist operators of Ecotourism products to protect and conserve natural and cultural heritage;
- to respect social and community values, contribute to an improved environment and improved ecotourism experiences; and
- to achieve better business through meeting responsible ecotourism performance standards.

Thus, there is a clear objective to respect social and community values which would suggest that the operator needs to have either ascertained or been made aware of these values. Under the Interpretation and Education section of this standard the Ecotourism product is required to provide interpretation and/or education opportunities for visitors to learn more about the natural and cultural heritage of an area via an Interpretation Plan, which includes (among other requirements):

- goals and objectives in terms of educational and/or conservation outcomes;
- details of interpretive content, including the conservation significance of the area, appropriate minimal impact methods and appropriate behaviour in culturally sensitive regions/sites;

and for an Advanced Ecotourism product includes:

- monitoring and evaluation techniques, including performance benchmarks.

The Ecotourism product must also demonstrate that ecotour guides have awareness of (among other requirements):

- interpretation and communication; and
- environmental and conservation management issues of the product area.

Despite a required respect for local social and community values, which would indicate an awareness of such, there is no mention of their interpretation in this section, or specifically being part of the guides' awareness requirements. The focus is mainly upon environmental conservation issues. These issues could be considered in most situations to be inextricably entwined with the local community values. Of course, these community-orientated interpretive goals could be included into the Interpretation Plan's objectives, but it is only the Advanced Ecotourism product which requires monitoring and evaluation techniques and performance benchmarks, and these techniques and benchmarks are not described.

So how does this process ensure the community's values regarding their region and their cultural presence are being facilitated if this is the overriding, current, global sustainable tourism benchmarking accreditation process? According to this standard, the operator is aware of these values and is respecting them. This does not imply a communication of these values to the tourist to increase their awareness; nor does it appear to comply implicitly with sustainable tourism development goals to ensure the cultural integrity and social cohesion of communities. It would appear that under the Green Globe 21 accreditation process this is the responsibility of the community. The Green Globe Community/Destination Standard's principal objective is to facilitate responsible and sustainable environmental and social outcomes for communities, providing them with a framework to benchmark, certify and continuously improve their environmental and social performance (Green Globe, 2006). The first requirement of this standard is that the community provide an authority who is properly constituted and has a mandate to provide leadership for the management of Green Globe sustainable environmental and social outcomes for a community, and shall prepare an environmental and social sustainability policy which incorporates considerations listed, such as taking account of relevant international and national agreements and policies relating to sustainability. On this basis, many of the communities I have been involved with in the South Pacific, including Easter Island, will be waiting a long time for their accreditation, as this level of policy creation is currently beyond their capacity for various reasons related to the distinctive challenges they face and have been discussed in this chapter, including adequate representation and involvement in regional development, administrative capacity and economic opportunity. In the mean time, Green Globe may be accrediting the tour operators visiting their community who are meant to be aware of and respect their values but who are not provided with operational guidelines to incorporate them into their interpretive programmes or measure their facilitation, along with their purely environmental considerations.

This seems like an enormous prospect to contribute significantly to enhancing community capacity for cultural sustainability going largely unaddressed, when in fact a potentially incorporative accreditation process is already established. If the ecotourism operator has an awareness of the community's values, then these could be incorporated into the interpretive plan's objectives along with the environmental values. The programming and function of the interpretive plan can follow the approach recommended in the VMI-I and utilizing the Sustainable Tourism Framework facilitate comparison of the participants' interpretive outcomes with the community's values. In this way the community is intrinsically incorporated into the Sustainable Tourism/Green Globe accreditation process. The community is also provided with a functioning framework that is being implemented by the ecotourism operator that can be reciprocally contributed to, coordinated, continually assessed and communicated, while requiring little or no more requirement than the operator currently complies with under the Green Globe Standard.

This approach could be particularly significant in contributing to community capacity if adopted by the large conglomerate tourism companies such as First Choice, which is ever expanding into more regions of land and sea, and managing many different types of tourism including ecotourism. As of 2007, this company had expanded its operations to take on board three Expedition Cruise companies whose operations rely upon teams of guides, and their interpretive skills and programmes, while they visit many remote regions of the world. First Choice made a commitment to sustainable development in 2002 and in 2005 produced their first Environmental and People Report (First Choice, 2007). With such a vast array of interpretive components involved in their many operations, such a standard approach could minimize the complexity and provide an operational framework to guide their internal and external accreditation processes. It would also allow for internal comparison of their sustainability achievements between operations overall. This approach would also aid the new or small ecotourism operators who desire to implement sustainable tourism goals and gain accreditation. Running a business, particularly one potentially reliant upon multiple environmental management compliance regulations and necessary permits, is demanding enough. The ability to standardi ze their interpretive planning with the sustainable tourism accreditation process will serve to minimize unnecessary duplication of effort. It will also contribute to improving their performance, which ultimately contributes to sustaining our global cultural and ecological environment.

The standardization of this process for interpretation in all ecotourism operations and incorporation into global sustainable tourism accreditation programmes describes the operational agenda for the VMI-I and the Framework. A standard assessment form, standard sustainable value-based tourism indicators or 'benchmarks', standardization of community and environmental value incorporation into ecotourism operations and a standard guide for interpretive planning will make it a far less complex and more productive process for all companies wishing to gain accreditation, or to operate under sustainable development motivations while contributing to community capacity. It also ensures that remote communities are part of an administrative and operational process which may contribute to overcoming sustainability challenges they face regarding their remoteness and possible political marginalization. It does this by ensuring ecotourism operations do contribute significantly to the values and tourism development aspirations of remote communities.

References

Armstrong, E.K. and Weiler, B. (2002) Getting the message across: an analysis of messages delivered by tour operators in protected areas. *Journal of Ecotourism* 1(2&3), 104–121.

Ballantyne, R. and Uzzell, D. (1999) International trends in heritage and environmental interpretation: future directions for Australian research and practice. *Journal of Interpretation Research* 4(1), 59–75.

Beck, L. and Cable, T.T. (1998) *Interpretation for the 21st Century*, Sagamore Publishing, Champaign, Illinois.

Bricker, K.S. (1998) Place and preference: as study of whitewater recreationists on the South Fork of the American River. *Unpublished doctoral dissertation*, The Pennsylvania State University, University Park, Pennsylvania.

Bricker, K.S. and Kerstetter, D. (2006) Saravanua ni vanua: exploring sense of place in the rural highlands of Fiji. In: Jennings, G. and Nickerson, N.P. (eds) *Quality Tourism Experiences*. Elsevier, Oxford, pp. 99–111.

First Choice (2007) *First Choice – Environment and People Report 2005*, First Choice Holidays. Available at: http://www.fcenviromentalandpeople.com/fcenviro

Freeman, J. (2006) Resistance fighter. *Review in Weekend Australian* 2 (12), p. 8.

Green Globe (2006) *Green Globe Standards*. Green Globe Asia Pacific. Available at: http://www.ggasiapacific.com.au

Ham, S.H. and Krumpe, E.E. (1996) Identifying audiences and messages for nonformal environmental education: a theoretical framework for interpreters. *Journal of Interpretation Research* 1(1), 11–23.

Ham, S.H. and Weiler, B. (2002) Interpretation as the centrepiece of sustainable wildlife tourism. In: Harris, R., Griffin, T. and Williams, P. (eds) *Sustainable Tourism: A Global Perspective*. Butterworth-Heinemann, Oxford, pp. 35–44.

Jackson, J.B. (1994) *A Sense of Place, a Sense of Time*. Yale University Press, New Haven, Connecticut.

Klenosky, D.B., Fraumand, E., Norman, W.C. and Gengler, C.E. (1998) Nature-based tourists' use of interpretive services: a means-end investigation. *Journal of Tourism Studies* 9(2), 26–36.

Knapp, D. and Benton, G.M. (2004) Elements to successful interpretation: a multiple case study of five National Parks. *Journal of Interpretation Research* 9(2), 9–25.

Moisey, R.N. and McCool, S.F. (2001) Sustainable tourism in the 21st century: lessons from the past; challenges to address. In: McCool, S.F. and Moisey, R.N. (eds) *Tourism, Recreation and Sustainability: Linking Culture and the Environment*. CAB International, Wallingford, UK, pp. 1–15.

Moscardo, G. (1999) *Making Visitors Mindful: Principles for Creating Sustainable Visitor Experiences Through Effective Communication*, Sagamore Publishing, Champaign, Illinois.

Orams, M.B. (1996) Using interpretation to manage nature-based tourism. *Journal of Sustainable Tourism* 4(2), 81–94.

Raitz, K. (1987) Commentary: place, space and environment in America's leisure landscapes. *Journal of Cultural Geography* 8(1), 49–61.

Tourism Australia (2007) *Sustainable Tourism – Benchmarking Environmental Performance*, Tourism Australia. Available at: http://www.tourism.australia.com

Tuan, Y. (1977) *Space and Place: A Perspective of Experience*. University of Minnesota Press, Minneapolis, Minnesota.

Walker, K. (2007) The role of interpretation in sustainable tourism: a qualitative approach to understanding passenger experiences on expedition cruises. PhD thesis, James Cook University, Townsville, Queensland, Australia.

Walker, K. and Moscardo, G. (2006) The impact of interpretation upon passengers of expedition cruises. In: Dowling, R.K. (ed.) *Cruise Ship Tourism*. CAB International, Wallingford, UK.

5 Community-based Tourism in Asia

PIMRAWEE ROCHARUNGSAT

Tourism Industry Development and Management Division, Phetchaburi Rajabhat University, Thailand

Introduction

> In contemporary tourism, a consideration of economic development alone provides an incomplete picture of the complexity of the phenomenon. Since tourism is now an integral part of modern societies, its broad study and analysis is imperative if its potential economic and social benefits are to be maximised and developed in a manner consistent with society's goals.
>
> (Murphy, 1985)

The above statement indicates the importance of community involvement in tourism as the destination community is a key element of any society. A number of tourism-related organizations around the world promote 'people' in the 'community' as the 'centre' or 'heart' of tourism development. In the academic context, Pearce and Moscardo (1999) pointed out that the concept 'tourism community relationship' is frequently cited in research planning documents and often given priority status in the list of global, national and local tourism research agendas. From these forces, the concept 'community-based tourism' (CBT) has arisen.

The growth of community tourism perspectives is based on a growing awareness of the need for more resident-responsive tourism, that is, more democratic participation in tourism decision making by grass-roots members of a destination society (Dann, 1999). The development of such tourism is not, however, an easy route to follow due to several factors. Diverse community attitudes towards tourism development and growth raise concerns that community-driven tourism planning may be an unachievable ideal (Jamal and Getz, 1995; Kneafsey, 2001). Mostly, the 'culture and economy' approach is not applied by any one actor, but rather emerges from the combined actions of various players operating at different spatial scales with sometimes conflicting agendas (Kneafsey, 2001). Experience has shown that tourism may not always be the most appropriate form of investment for regions, especially in the developing world which includes most of the countries in Asia. As suggested above, a range of economic, sociocultural, environmental and political questions have been raised which serve to both challenge and yet include tourism as a strategy for development in the countries (Son *et al.*, 1999). CBT is seen as a corrective style since earlier tourism planning has failed to deliver development to the community at large, especially where parts of the latter are poor or particularly disadvantaged (Burns, 2004).

To successfully manage CBT, community participation is a core requirement. In addition to community participation there are other issues that need to be clarified in this emerging topic area, including:

- the identification of measures which ensure that tourism development is in harmony with the sociocultural, ecological and heritage goals of the local community;
- the search for creative approaches towards fostering citizen participation in the economic benefits of tourism development; and
- the understanding of resident perceptions, values and priorities regarding tourism's role in the community (Hawkins, 1993).

The discussion in this chapter will focus on CBT, especially in the case of countries in Asia. In particular, this chapter will present the results of several research studies conducted by the author. Suggested successful criteria and steps towards CBT development will be described so that they may guide the development of more effective community tourism. A particular focus will be given to understanding what a community wants and is concerned about, to remind practitioners that without real community participation and input, CBT cannot be successful.

The Importance of Community Participation

Community involvement in tourism has been receiving increasing attention because the success and sustainability of the development depends on active support of the local populations since higher levels of integration lead to enhanced socio-economic benefits for the community (Mitchell and Eagles, 2001). In the years since the publication of Murphy's *Tourism: A Community Approach* (written in 1985), the concept of community involvement in tourism development has moved nearer to the centre of the sustainability debate (Taylor, 1995). Central to the debate on tourism development are the issues of how benefits to destinations can be maximized at the local level and this is one of the main principles of sustainable tourism development. CBT planning, therefore, can introduce not only new management tools, but also a 'language of management' and new ways of thinking (Wearing and McDonald, 2002). It has been argued that the communities should participate in planning decisions regarding tourism development in order to better handle the impacts (Li, 2004). This view is congruent with the notion that the sustainable growth of tourism cannot be achieved without the support from the destination community (Wu, 2000 cited in Li, 2004). The success of tourism depends upon the active involvement of locals who are able to communicate aspects of local culture to the tourists (Kneafsey, 2001). Therefore, the development of dynamic and collaborative planning processes is crucial in those destination communities that are experiencing growth and change due to tourism (Jamal and Getz, 1995).

Tosun and Timothy (2003) also argue that community participation is a vital element in the implementation of tourism plans and strategies and provide several benefits of community participation in tourism development, including:

- increasing tourist satisfaction;
- helping tourism professionals to design better tourism plans;
- contributing to a fairer distribution of costs and benefits among community members;
- assisting in satisfying locally identified needs; and
- strengthening the democratization process in tourist destinations.

Support for community involvement in tourism is also evident in several major programmes for sustainable tourism development. For instance, following the appearance of 'Our Common Future, the Brundtland Report' (World Commission on Environment and Development, 1987), many individuals, communities and other organizations have been attempting to convert the intentions of sustainable development into practice (Sharpley, 1997; Ko, 2001). The World Tourism Organization and World Travel and Tourism Council have conducted a series of regional seminars to increase awareness and to adapt the programme for local implementation (Brunet *et al.*, 2000). Agenda 21, which was adopted by 182 countries at the Rio Earth Summit in 1992, provides a comprehensive programme of action. These programmes are supported by new research in this field which argues that approaches to tourism, particularly in rural areas, must be inclusive and emphasize meaningful public participation and bring the community on board (Reid *et al.*, 2004).

The support for CBT is also evident in the form of cooperation, conferences and projects (Harrison, 2003). In the Asia-Pacific region, the 'First Tourism Ministerial Meeting' of the Asia-Pacific Economic Cooperation (APEC) was held in July, 2000, in Seoul, Korea. The main theme was 'APEC Tourism 21/21: Challenges and Opportunities for Tourism in the APEC Region' (Lee *et al.*, 2001). The Seoul Declaration on the APEC Tourism Charter reflected a collective commitment to improve the economic, cultural, social and environmental well-being of APEC member economics through tourism (Lee *et al.*, 2001).

If the active participation of locals can be achieved, it can minimize the challenges of community tourism in issues of ownership, economic leakage, local employment, benefit distribution, social and environmental impacts and dependency (Goodwin *et al.*, 1998). Important trends that support the growth of CBT are an expanding global market, marketing and promotion, the emphasis on responsibility in tourism, the increase of interconnectedness and better information, easier access/transportation and better infrastructure and a growing number of public–private partnerships (Rocharungsat, 2005; UNWTO, 2007a).

It is important to note that this concept of community tourism has been developed and refined in the context of Western countries in search of sustainable approaches to tourism development. However, the applicability of such a concept to Asian countries seems not to have been considered in detail (Tosun, 2000). For instance, Li (2004) observed that although scholars have explored community tourism issues in China, they have mainly focused on community involvement in the economic benefits of tourism and not yet covered the complexity of applying the concept. There remains, therefore, a much needed and important discussion on the implementation of community tourism in Asia which is in the present interest (Li, 2004).

Community-based Tourism in Asia

In Asia, tourism is one of the most rapidly growing economic sectors. It is also a major source of income for many countries in the region. Tourism is now affecting the lives of rural people and is often seen as a tool for development (Ashley and Roe, 1998; Neto, 2002; Harrison, 2003; UNWTO, 2007b). In 2007, from January to April, global figures showed that international travel worldwide rose by over 6% to 252 million, representing an additional 15 million arrivals as against the same period in 2006 (UNWTO, 2007a), and Asia and the Pacific region achieved the strongest growth of more than 9%. According to World Tourism Organization Report in 2007, although Europe is the world's most visited and most mature destination, Asia and the Pacific stands out as the best performing region in the world in the first 4 months of 2007. The highest increase in arrivals was recorded by South Asia (+12%), while South-east Asia and North Asia were both at +9% (UNWTO, 2007a). UNWTO's Tourism 2020 Vision forecasts that international arrivals are expected to increase to nearly 1.6 billion by 2020 and Asia will be one of the top three receiving regions of tourist arrivals (UNWTO, 2007b). Additionally, the past crisis in Asian economies demonstrates the advantage of tourism during crises because if a currency collapses, tourism is likely to suffer less than other economic sectors as the cheaper exchange rate may attract more tourists (Ashley and Roe, 1998). Tourism is likely to grow and be emphasized in depressed economies because its income potential is highlighted (Neto, 2002). Thus, the growth rates for foreign arrivals in Asia clearly support this position (Roe *et al.*, 2004).

One reason for the rapid growth of tourism in Asia is the abundance of cultural and natural resources. This growth is also fuelled by the development of new markets and changes in consumer taste. Mitchell and Eagles (2001) indicated that since 1980 several countries have been promoting sustainable tourism to take advantage of their unique ecosystems and to attempt to reduce negative impacts. Jenkins (1997) also noted that countries such as China, India, Indonesia and Pakistan will largely remain tourist receiving countries into the foreseeable future. The following statement clearly explains why tourism has become the 'hope' of communities, especially in this region:

> Tourism seems tailor-made for the world's poorer nations, and a growing number of developing countries have placed emphasis on tourism in their development plans. Reasons are because a ready market is available for the attractions these destinations can offer; many of them have an appealing climate, combined with exotic scenery and a rich cultural and historical heritage. Land and labour costs are comparatively low and, in the absence of significant mineral production or an export-oriented agricultural sector, tourism is a potential source of foreign exchange and can generate new opportunities for employment and stimulate demand for local products and industries.
>
> (Son *et al.*, 1999, p. 211)

Tourism is therefore viewed as a community and economic development tool that serves certain ends (McCool *et al.*, 2001; Davis and Morais, 2004; UNWTO, 2007a). Roe *et al.* (2004) identified examples in Laos, Vietnam and Cambodia where tourism is the best available export opportunity. However, the empirical evidence from Andereck and Vogt (2000) suggests that while locals support tourism development, they are aware of the potential for tourism to result in negative impacts.

A number of questions have been raised about whether or not community tourism will effectively work in developing countries like some in Asia (WTO, 1983). The development of community tourism industry is a growing phenomenon as communities respond to the opportunities and, in some cases, the threats of tourism (Hatton, 2002). In the past, prior to the age of European exploration and colonization, natural resource management in much of the world – including Asia – was largely village- and/or descent-group-based, and therefore was heavily reliant on de facto community-based resource management processes (World Resources Institute, 2001). The key benefit of this community-based management system was that it was highly adaptable to local socio-economic, biological and physical conditions. During the colonization period, there was a change from local control to top-down management. CBT approaches have tried to reassert and re-establish local input.

In many cases, tourism is initially welcomed as a springboard to economic development, contributing to the conservation of nature and providing employment for destination communities. Later, following the onset of large-scale tourism, the less desirable impacts of the industry have become apparent (Twining-Ward, 1999). A study by Walker *et al.* (2001) in Molas, Indonesia, which examined the implementation of a livelihood strategy for community planning, noted that the villagers initially identified short-term personal economic opportunities through selling their land to speculators and developers, but failed to establish potential long-term personal economic benefits from tourism development. Hall (2000) pointed out that there is a false but common assumption made that tourism easily generates income and jobs. A local study team of tourism in Laos supported by UNESCO (UNESCOBKK, 2000) explained: 'It is true that some of the local people have sold their pieces of land, or teak garden to buy taxis, buses, tuk tuks to serve in the tourism sector and they have thought it might bring them good income and better living condition' (p. 23). There is no guarantee that the benefits of tourism will trickle down to the poorest groups; nor does tourism necessarily reduce inequalities (Ayres, 2002).

Wearing and McDonald (2002) argued that using the concepts of power and knowledge leads us to regard the tourist destination site as an interactive space supporting a continuous process where different social values meet and new meanings are created. Therefore, community tourism brings opportunities to a community as well. However, all new forms of tourism should not automatically be seen as ethically and morally superior to mass, conventional tourism (Mowforth and Munt, 1998). Critically it is the process of how tourism is implemented. The most fundamental objectives of tourism deal with its role in enhancing economic opportunity, protecting cultural and natural heritage, and achieving a desirable quality of life. The extent to which we do not understand how tourism helps communities accomplish these goals serves as a barrier to their accomplishment and may lead to a misallocation of scarce human and financial resources (McCool *et al.*, 2001). Recently tourism organizations have placed more emphasis on the successful practice of community tourism in destinations as a corrective to the traditional patterns of tourism impact. New streams of community tourism literature focus more on partnership and collaborative approaches (Reed, 1997) rather than on blaming the outsiders or private sector who bring traditional patterns of negative impacts to tourism. In addition, it can be argued that the study of community tourism also needs to direct more attention to these issues in developing countries rather than in the developed world. In particular, there has been very little research conducted in Asia.

Success Criteria for Community-based Tourism Development

While there have been some research studies that have sought to find the success criteria for CBT (i.e. Brown, 1998; Tosun, 2001; Li, 2004), this is still an area that requires more research, particularly in Asia. In order to address these gaps a series of studies were conducted evaluating different aspects of successful CBT in the case of Asia (Rocharungsat, 2005). The first study examined the perspectives of 113 tourism academics and professionals who had written about community tourism in the major tourism journals between 1992 and 2002, on different aspects of CBT through an e-mail survey. This survey sought information on their experiences of successful CBT and the factors used to evaluate successful CBT.

The results indicated that, overall, recent CBT approaches to tourism in many destinations in Asia were still struggling to be successful. Despite this the sample believed that the practice of CBT was not totally unrealistic. According to the professionals in this study, careful planning to suit each community destination is a challenging process that requires several factors and the involvement of key stakeholders. Understanding the criteria used to evaluate successful CBT destinations is very important. The criteria to evaluate successful CBT suggested by the professionals were summarized into six main factors:

- CBT should practically involve the broad community.
- Benefits gained from CBT should be distributed equally throughout the destination community.
- Good and careful management of tourism is significant.
- CBT should have strong partnerships and support from within and outside a community.
- Uniqueness of the place should be considered to sustain the destination.
- Environmental conservation should not be neglected.

Of the six factors identified by the respondents for successful CBT destinations, *'local involvement and support'* was the most frequently stated. To develop and manage CBT, broad local involvement and commitment was considered important. The respondents provided examples of communities forming legal non-profit entities, which is one aspect for successfully controlling tourism in their communities. In practising this, it was suggested that communities should focus on opportunities to participate in tourism projects through planning, giving input or managing their own tourism business.

Local gaining of 'benefits' was the second important factor. Distribution of profits was important, and benefits should reach all sections of a community. Benefits can be both economic and social. Examples of benefits stated by the professionals were new money injected into a community, improving local lives, bringing new opportunities to the area, uplifting a community from poverty and job creation.

Good management of tourism was also one of the key success criteria. Some examples given here were good process, good planning and management, good publicity and good marketing. Most professionals suggested slow and careful development so that the local community will have time to adjust. *Partnership and support* for tourism from both within and outside a community was also considered to be important. Successful CBT destinations may gain assistance from professional support such as business people, political and economic support, and media. These partnerships can provide advantages like financial and human resource improvement.

Uniqueness of the place was also seen as significant for success. CBT destinations should have their unique attractions. For instance, cultural events, man-made attractions, historical value places or even outstanding information distribution could create uniqueness for community tourism. The last factor stated was *environmental conservation*. Professionals agreed that CBT development should also develop environmental awareness for a community. Some destinations have environmental organizations or provide education for both community and visitors. This is believed to promote sustainable development, which is the main strategy for CBT.

It should be noted that 'community involvement' and 'community benefits' were stated most often as the main criteria for successful CBT. In other words, community involvement in tourism development can be viewed from at least two perspectives: involvement in the decision-making process and involvement in the benefits of tourism development (Timothy, 1999). Brown (1998) supports this argument providing evidence that small-scale tourism using cooperatives has a greater potential for improving rural living standards, reducing rural–urban migration, rejuvenating rural communities and countering structural inequities of income distribution. Therefore, the community involvement should simultaneously come with community benefits in order to be considered successful.

The researcher also asked other stakeholders (decision makers, operators, visitors and communities) to state their success criteria for CBT. The results were very consistent with those previously reported, and this consensus confirms that successful CBT destination must involve community members in the process and distribute benefits widely to the community. In addition, the stakeholders' criteria suggest that successful CBT should maintain and conserve community culture and environmental resources as well as satisfying tourists. These respondents also emphasized the value of cultural exchange. These suggested success criteria could be used as a guide to monitor the progress of CBT initiative.

Steps Towards Community-based Tourism Development

Following the examination of CBT success criteria, a study exploring more in-depth perspectives from the main stakeholders' experiences and expectations was implemented (Rocharungsat, 2005). McCool *et al.* (2001) suggested that a broad description of perspectives would help determine stakeholder differences and similarities and form the basis of dialogue for the future of the tourism industry. Additionally, several researchers have advocated joint decision making by key stakeholders and consensus in this process as important for attaining appropriate tourism development. This literature suggests that better practice in CBT management must be derived from linking different stakeholders' perspectives.

Based on this stakeholder theory, the second study examined the groups of decision makers, operators and visitors in Thailand, Indonesia and Malaysia using a self-administered questionnaire. The research explored overall attitudes towards, and expectations of, CBT and views on the future of CBT development.

The stakeholders who participated in the present research reported that the 'community-centred' emphasis of the CBT concept was important. One respondent stated that '[i]f members of the community have not yet taken the first step towards CBT themselves, then the first step an outsider should take should not be focused on tourism development'. Instead, planners should focus on 'social assessment' and 'active participation'.

The surveyed stakeholders were also asked to prioritize nine steps recommended to develop CBT. These prioritized views are presented in the following diagram (Fig. 5.1) and can assist in decisions about what should be emphasized in the process. After this, respondents gave details of what could be gained from community input. These benefits are described in Fig. 5.2.

Although there was general agreement about these steps from most of the respondents of the research, one respondent saw some limitations to community consultancy and stated that:

First priority	- Understand what resources the community can offer - Get all people involved to work together
Second priority	- Make community aware of costs and benefits of tourism - Develop a tourism plan with clear goals and objectives - Form organizational structure - Get community input and support in tourism development - Identify key leader to do the work
Third priority	- Develop education and training program for community - Get the leading institutions to give expert assistance to local people

Fig. 5.1. Prioritized steps for community involvement.

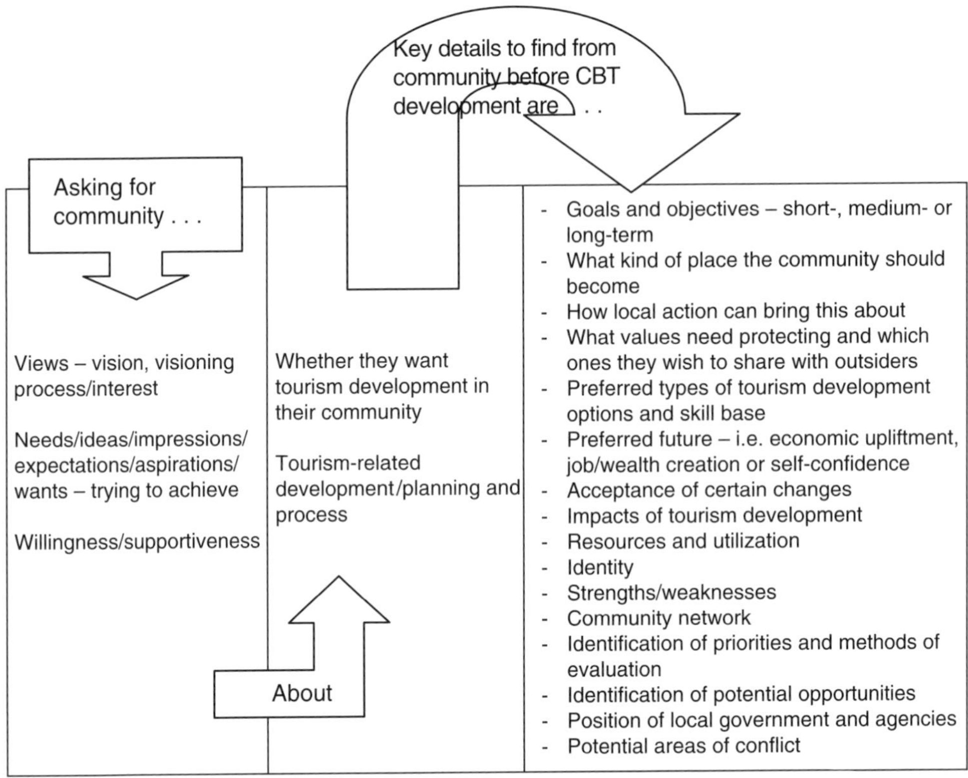

Fig. 5.2. First steps recommended: consultancy and support of community.

> There may be no consensus or political culture/framework which encourages participation in the decision making process (especially in the developing world) and a reluctance to express opinions. Some residents may not be interested in taking part, unless they perceive themselves to be personally affected by any tourism development, so it is difficult to secure adequate representation.

Understanding Community Perspectives

Emphasizing the community's view and input, McGehee and Andereck (2004) argued that no matter what future direction resident-attitude research takes, the most important goal must be to assure that the varied voices of the community are heard. Theoretically, residents who view tourism as potentially or actually valuable and believe that the costs do not exceed the benefits will favour and support tourism development. Jurowski and Gursoy (2004) noted that the evaluation of the costs and benefits differs within a set of residents and residents' perceptions may vary according to their characteristics (Faulkner and Tideswell 1997). This is supported by recent research findings, which reported heterogeneity of community responses and diversity of resident attitudes about tourism development (Williams and Lawson, 2001; Sirakaya *et al.*, 2002; Andriotis and Vaughan, 2003; McGehee and Andereck, 2004; Rocharungsat, 2005). Gursoy and Rutherford (2004) demonstrated that some residents view tourism as having both positive and negative impacts; some are likely to perceive it as having negative social and cultural ones; and some view it as having positive economic, social and cultural impacts. Their findings suggested that perceptions of impacts are not independent because the most salient perceived impact is likely to influence the perception of all other impacts. Given the centrality of community attitudes in the development of CBT, it is important to examine methods for gathering information on these perspectives.

The implementation of community participation is needed at all stages, or in other words continuously, to reach sustainable tourism goals. At each stage, awareness and education should be important elements. Findings in the study of Gursoy and Rutherford (2004) suggested that community leaders and developers thinking of growing tourism need to consider the perceptions and attitudes of residents before they start investing scarce resources. Awareness of residents' perceptions of tourism development and its impacts can help planners and developers to identify real concerns and issues for appropriate policies and action to take place, optimizing the benefits and minimizing the problems (Sirakaya *et al.*, 2002; Andriotis and Vaughan, 2003). Hatton (2002) suggested that contact among the participants will not only keep people interested and supportive, but it will also prepare them to take advantage of opportunities that tourism might offer. This is the essence of CBT.

CBT planning should consider the uniqueness of a particular community; the structure, goals and themes from different environments; and the growth patterns, cultural values and stages of development in each community. Quite simply, communities are different (Hatton, 2002), and this needs to be considered in the planning process. In order to clarify what communities want to be fulfilled from CBT, the communities' voice should be understood. There are several options to achieve this. The following discussion describes one of them.

A study using techniques of 'open to question' or 'asking questions for the future' was conducted to gain input from the four communities in Thailand and Indonesia (Rocharungsat, 2005). This study attempted to complete the multiple stakeholder perspectives by focusing on communities' overall attitudes and expectations towards CBT. The four communities were: Desa Wirun, Indonesia, and Koh Pratong, Thailand, with low levels of tourism development; and Seloliman, Indonesia, and Mae Kampong, Thailand, with medium levels of tourism development. Community members were asked to state their concerns about tourism development in their area. The results from the analysis of these responses can be presented as three layers of concerns (Fig. 5.3). The nearest layer to 'CBT' represents the agreement from all four communities about the questions, the second layer gains consensus from the three communities and the outside layer gains support from two communities.

It could be interpreted that the core issues of CBT that are central to all are the community benefits and involvement. Again, there is support for the argument that, without creating opportunities for local people to take part in the decision-making process, it can be very difficult for local people to get adequate benefits from tourism

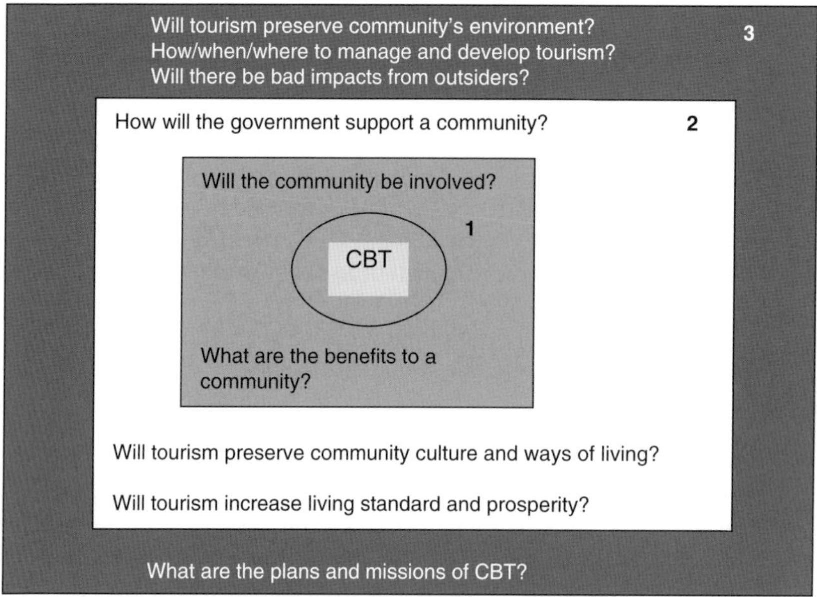

Fig. 5.3. Questions from communities.

development. The second layer of issues of concern to these communities involves government support, preservation of culture and ways of life and improving living standards. These are also not new issues of concern. There is clear documentation accumulated over more than two decades that suggests that the nature of some forms of tourism in parts of the developing world is leading to an unacceptable destruction of social structure and cultural values (Lea, 1993). No community would like this to happen and all would like tourism to be reconciled with their culture. Other related factors included questions about levels of local ownership and control, the use of local resources, the extent to which local amenities are impacted, and marketing strategies. This could be linked to the next layer of concern towards environmental destruction and bad impacts from outsiders that the communities aim CBT to prevent. They therefore would like information about the development and management plan and missions of the CBT before its implementation in their community.

In a study by King *et al.* (1993) it was noted that although the residents support tourism in their community, they are aware of the negative impacts and that support is not based on a belief that it causes only positive impacts on host communities. One of the operational limitations in tourism development is the limit of information being communicated to a community. It is important to understand a community's concern and level of acceptance before tourism development begins. Pearce (2000) argued that the need to reflect on what has been achieved, to assess what the present situation is and to re-evaluate future directions is particularly important in small developing countries. According to Inskeep 'host communities must have a voice in shaping their future community as their right' (1991, p. 616).

Conclusion

CBT in Asia is now growing rapidly along with concerns about whether it will actually benefit communities. Although most countries in Asia foster and support this form of tourism, some are struggling when it comes into practice. Directions, successful cases and guidelines for effective implementation are still required for CBT in Asia.

While it is clear that CBT should involve and benefit destination communities, one thing we have to keep in mind is that every community is unique and the challenge is to find ways which can lead each community to success. There is no one solution that fits all for CBT development and it is likely that successful applications in Europe may not be applicable for Asian communities. Of particular importance is the problem that communities must have an awareness of tourism to be able to decide about its development. Therefore, support from other involved stakeholders such as government or the private sector may be important for countries in Asia where some communities are still remote from education and communication. However, the hope that CBT could be an effective tool for Asian community development is not unrealistic, and we can improve our understanding of what positive and negative impacts may occur from tourism development.

References

Andereck, K.L. and Vogt, C.A. (2000) The relationship between residents' attitudes toward tourism and tourism development options. *Journal of Travel Research* 39(1), 27–36.

Andriotis, K. and Vaughan, R.D. (2003) Urban residents' attitudes toward tourism development: the case of Crete. *Journal of Travel Research* 42(2), 172–185.

Ashley, C. and Roe, D. (1998) *Enhancing Community Involvement in Wildlife Tourism: Issues and Challenges*. International Institute for Environment and Development (IIED), UK.

Ayres, R. (2002) Cultural tourism in small-island states: contradictions and ambiguities. In: Apostolopoulos, Y. and Gayle, D.J. (eds) *Island Tourism and Sustainable Development: Caribbean, Pacific, and Mediterranean Experiences* Praeger Publishers, Westport, Connecticut, pp. 145–160.

Brown, D.O. (1998) In search of an appropriate form of tourism for Africa: lessons from the past and suggestions for the future. *Tourism Management* 19(3), 237–245.

Brunet, S., Bauer, J. and Lacy, T.D. (2000) Green Globe 21: certifying sustainable tourism in heritage cities in Asia/ Pacific. Available at: http://www.unescobkk.org/culture/archives/brunet_day5.pdf

Burns, P.M. (2004) Tourism planning: a third way? *Annals of Tourism Research* 31(1), 24–43.

Dann, G. (1999) Theoretical issues for tourism's future development: identifying the agenda. In: Pearce, D.G. and Butler, R.W. (eds) *Contemporary Issues in Tourism Development*. Routledge, London and New York, pp. 13–30.

Davis, J.S. and Morais, D.B. (2004) Factions and enclaves: small towns and socially unsustainable tourism development. *Journal of Travel Research* 43(1), 3–10.

Faulkner, B. and Tideswell, C. (1997) A framework for monitoring community impacts of tourism. *Journal of Sustainable Tourism* 5(1), 3–28.

Goodwin, H., Kent, I., Parker, K. and Walpole, M. (1998) *Tourism, Conservation and Sustainable Development: Case Studies from Asia and Africa*. International Institute for Environment and Development (IIED), UK.

Gursoy, D. and Rutherford, D.G. (2004) Host attitudes toward tourism: an improved structural model. *Annals of Tourism Research* 31(3), 495–516.

Hall, D. (2000) Identity, community and sustainability: prospects for rural tourism in Albania. In: Richards, G. and Hall, D. (eds) *Tourism and Sustainable Community Development*. Routledge, London and New York, pp. 48–60.

Harrison, D. (2003) Working with the tourism industry: a case study from Fiji. Available at: http://www.devstud.org.uk/studygroups/tourism.htm

Hatton, M.J. (2002) Community-based tourism in the Asia Pacific. Available at: http://www.community-tourism.org/

Hawkins, D. (1993) Global assessment of tourism policy: a process model. In: Pearce, D. and Butler, R. (eds) *Tourism Research: Critiques and Challenges*. Routledge, London, pp. 175–200.

Inskeep, E. (1991) *Tourism Planning, an Integrated and Sustainable Development Approach*. Van Nostrand Reinhold, New York.

Jamal, T.B. and Getz, D. (1995) Collaboration theory and community tourism planning. *Annals of Tourism Research* 22(1), 186–204.

Jenkins, C. (1997) Impacts of the development of international tourism in the Asian region. In: Go, F.M. and Jenkins, C. (eds) *Tourism and Economic Development in Asia and Australia*. Cassell, London and Washington, DC, pp. 48–66.

Jurowski, C. and Gursoy, D. (2004) Distance effects on residents' attitudes toward tourism. *Annals of Tourism Research* 31(2), 296–312.

King, B., Pizam, A. and Milman, A. (1993) Social impacts of tourism. *Annals of Tourism Research* 20, 650–665.

Kneafsey, M. (2001) Rural cultural economy: tourism and social relations. *Annals of Tourism Research* 28(3), 762–783.

Ko, J.T.G. (2001) Assessing progress of tourism sustainable. *Annals of Tourism Research* 28(3), 817–820.

Lea, J.P. (1993) Tourism development ethics in the Third World. *Annals of Tourism Research* 20, 701–715.

Lee, Y.T., Kim, D.K. and Kim, C. (2001) Tourism in the APEC Region. *Annals of Tourism Research* 28(4), 1063–1064.

Li, Y. (2004) Exploring community tourism in China: the case of Nanshan cultural tourism zone. *Journal of Sustainable Tourism* 12(3), 175–193.

McCool, S.F., Moisey, R.N. and Nickerson, N.P. (2001) What should tourism sustain? The disconnect with industry perceptions of useful indicators. *Journal of Travel Research* 40, 124–131.

McGehee, N.G. and Andereck, K.L. (2004) Factors predicting rural residents' support of tourism. *Journal of Travel Research* 43(2), 131–140.

Mitchell, R.E. and Eagles, P.F.J. (2001) An integrative approach to tourism: lessons from the Andes of Peru. *Journal of Sustainable Tourism* 9(1), 4–28.

Mowforth, M. and Munt, M. (1998) *Tourism and Sustainability: New Tourism in the Third World*. Routledge, London.

Murphy, P.E. (1985) *Tourism: A Community Approach*. Methuen, New York.

Neto, F. (2002) *Sustainable Tourism, Environmental Protection and Natural Resource Management: Paradise on Earth?* The International Colloquium on Regional Governance Sustainable Development in Tourism-driven Economies, Mexico.

Pearce, D.G. (2000) Tourism plan reviews: methodological considerations and issues from Samoa. *Tourism Management* 21, 191–203.

Pearce, P.L. and Moscardo, G. (1999) Tourism community analysis: asking the right questions. In: Pearce, D.G. and Butler, R.W. (eds) *Contemporary Issues in Tourism Development*. Routledge, London and New York, pp. 31–51.

Reed, M.G. (1997) Power relations and community-based tourism planning. *Annals of Tourism Research* 24(3), 566–591.

Reid, D.G., Mair, H. and George, W. (2004) Community tourism planning: a self-assessment instrument. *Annals of Tourism Research* 31(3), 623–639.

Rocharungsat, P. (2005) Community-based tourism: perspectives and future possibilities. Unpublished PhD thesis, James Cook University, Australia.

Roe, D., Ashley, C., Page, S. and Meyer, D. (2004) *Tourism and the Poor: Analysing and Interpreting Tourism Statistics from a Poverty Perspective* (Working Paper No. 16). The UK Department for International Development (DFID), London.

Sharpley, R. (1997) Sustainability: a barrier to tourism development? In: Sharpley, R. and Telfer, D.J. (eds) *Tourism and Development: Concepts and Issues*. Cambrian Printers, UK, pp. 319–337.

Sirakaya, E., Teye, V. and Sonmez, S. (2002) Understanding residents' support for tourism development in the Central region of Ghana. *Journal of Travel Research* 41(1), 57–67.

Son, N.T., Pigram, J.J. and Rugendyke, B.A. (1999) Tourism development and national parks in developing world: Cat Ba Island National Park, Vietnam. In: Douglas, G.P. and Butler, R.W. (eds) *Contemporary Issues in Tourism Development*. Routledge, London and New York, pp. 211–231.

Taylor, G. (1995) The community approach: does it really work? *Tourism Management* 16(7), 487–489.

Timothy, D.J. (1999) Participatory planning: a view of tourism in Indonesia. *Annals of Tourism Research* 26(2), 371–391.

Tosun, C. (2000) Limits to community participation in the tourism development process in developing countries. *Tourism Management* 21, 613–633.

Tosun, C. (2001) Challenges of sustainable tourism development in the developing world: the case of Turkey. *Tourism Management* 22, 289–303.

Tosun, C. and Timothy, D. (2003) Arguments for community participation in the tourism development process. *Journal of Tourism Studies* 14(2), 2–14.

Twining-Ward, L. (1999) Towards sustainable tourism development: observations from a distance. *Tourism Management* 20, 187–188.

UNESCOBKK (2000, April) Cultural heritage management and tourism: models for cooperation among stakeholders: a case study on Luang Prabang Lao PDR. Available at: http://www.unescobkk.org/culture/norad.tourism/pilot_sites.htm

UNWTO (2007a) Press Release: Strong World Tourism Growth in 2007. Available at: http://www.world-tourism.org/newsroom/news/en/ press_det.php?id=971&idioma=E

UNWTO (2007b) Facts & Figures: Tourism 2020 Vision. Available at: http://www.world-tourism.org/facts/eng/vision.htm

Walker, J., Mitchell, B. and Wismer, S. (2001) Livelihood strategy approach to community-based planning and assessment: a case study of Molas, Indonesia. *Impact Assessment and Project Appraisal* 19(4), 297–309.

Wearing, S. and McDonald, M. (2002) The development of community-based tourism: re-thinking the relationship between tour operators and development agents as intermediaries in rural and isolated area communities. *Journal of Sustainable Tourism* 10(3), 191–206.

Williams, J. and Lawson, R. (2001) Community issues and resident opinions of tourism. *Annals of Tourism Research* 28(2), 269–290.

WTO (1983) *The Framework of the State's Responsibility for the Management of Tourism.* World Tourism Organization, Madrid, Spain.

World Commission on Environment and Development (1987) *Our Common Future.* Oxford Press, London.

World Resources Institute (2001) Management of the coastal resources. Available at: http://www.wri.org/reefsatrisk/management_01.html

Wu, B. (2000) *Local Tourism Development and Management.* Science Press, Marrickville, Australia.

6 Examples of Effective Techniques for Enhancing Community Understanding of Tourism

Joy Sammy

School of Environmental Design and Rural Development, Ontario Agricultural College, University of Guelph, Canada

Introduction

For communities faced by the absence of significant economic alternatives, community-based tourism (CBT) focused on the local environment and culture appears as a straightforward solution that has the potential to alleviate poverty and environmental stress. CBT encompasses the desire to encourage empowerment, gender equity, capacity building, education and the strengthening of cultural identity and traditions. There is a wide range of academic research that explores the planning, implementation and outcomes of CBT (Costa and Ferrone, 1995; Brohman, 1996; Joppe, 1996; Mowforth and Munt, 2003; Reid, 2003; Burns, 2004; Blackstock, 2005) and, as stated by Moscardo in Chapter 1 (this volume), it is recognized that the participation of key stakeholders, in particular the host community, is vital for the long-term success of CBT (Arnstein, 1969; Little, 1994). Several challenges exist, however, that hinder community participation in particular in the initial stages of planning a CBT project.

First, a fundamental yet often overlooked barrier to community participation is a lack of understanding, within the community, of what tourism actually is. What is tourism for a country or culture that has no equivalent concept? As stated by Berno:

> There is much debate in the literature on the conceptualization of 'tourism' and 'tourist'. This, however, is often confined to a theoretical debate and the research literature often neglects to consider that the many researchers and participants may define tourism and tourist differently. Even within the Western literature there is little agreement about what exactly tourism is in any given context.
>
> (Cohen, 1974, 1984, from Berno, 1999, p. 656)

In addition, non-Western societies may have different views of hospitality and of the boundaries of their community or may have no equivalent concept of tourism at all (Taylor, 1995; Berno, 1999). For example, from my personal experience while living in Ghana, I was often asked during holidays in the country if I was travelling to visit family, going to a funeral or travelling for work. The idea of travelling as a tourist was a foreign concept. Eventually, the conclusion in many of these conversations was that I was 'just going to see the place', in essence the local definition of tourism. By no means do I intend to imply that all Ghanaians define tourism in this same way; however, I do want to illustrate that tourism must be understood as a culturally defined concept, that is quite often very different from 'Western' notions of tourism.

The second challenge for communities in understanding CBT is the balance that the community must play as both 'host and attraction'. CBT often offers the opportunity for tourists to stay within rural communities and even within the homes of local people; community members will act as guides, friends and cultural ambassadors for tourists. It has been noted that in the context of mass tourism, the commoditization of the community–tourist relationship has affected the traditional host–guest relationship such that hosts become the provider of services and guests become customers (Aramberri, 2001). The host–guest relationship within the context of CBT, however, has hardly been discussed (Maoz, 2006) and, moreover, the simplicity of the host–guest relationship that is frequently used as an analogy when explaining the community–tourist relationship does not adequately capture the complexity of the interactions that occur. The community needs to be aware that they are not only participants in CBT, as planners and managers, but are also a part of the tourism product itself (Taylor, 1995; Reid, 2003). How can non-governmental organizations (NGOs), governments and individual consultants create an understanding within a community of the often difficult balance that occurs for communities as both the host and attraction?

The challenges of defining the concepts of 'tourism and tourist' from different cultural perspectives and of understanding the diversity of the community–tourist relationship must now move from theory to application in the planning process. Traditional methods of CBT planning have moved from top-down to participatory approaches but remain one-sided in that they encourage communities to understand Western notions of 'tourism and tourist' but do not encourage partners in CBT development to understand the community's perspective. Communities and their partners in CBT, however, need to be familiar with each others understanding of tourism, laying the foundation for local tourism leadership development and addressing the need to 'create tourism knowledge and awareness' as indicated in the *community capacity-building approach* to tourism development illustrated by Moscardo in Fig. 1.2 (this volume). Thus, the purpose of this chapter is twofold: first, to explore different techniques for enhancing community understanding of tourism encompassing both a local and a 'Western' perspective as well as the host–guest relationship; and second, to provide opportunities for partners in CBT development to understand the community's perspective. This will be illustrated by exploring three practical techniques, drama, field trips and drawing. It is prudent at this time to acknowledge that, at least initially, CBT is often facilitated by the staff of governments or NGOs and it is within this context that these activities are suggested.

Drama: 'Playing Tourist'

The purpose of the 'playing tourist' drama activity is to encourage community members to show what *their* understanding of CBT is. This activity is best facilitated early on in the process of developing CBT. This will help to establish how the community perceives CBT based on their own experiences, cultural norms, beliefs, practices and ideas. The facilitators' role is to 'set up' the role play and then stand back and observe, it is important that the facilitator does not try to influence the outcome of the role play but instead treat the activity as a learning experience.

Initially, the tourism context for the role play should be established through an open discussion, suggestions should be recorded. There are no right or wrong suggestions and the participants should be encouraged to discuss what kind of tourism they think might take place within their community. If there are several different ideas, for example, day tours including a guided nature walk, home stays for a longer duration or the establishment of a hostel, several role plays could be enacted.

Next, the facilitator discusses with community participants the different characters that will be present in the role play, for example, the tourists, the tour guide, local community leaders, government officials, taxi drivers, accommodation personnel and regular community members (farmers, fisher people, teachers, etc.). Depending on the size of the group some participants may need to remain as audience members. There are no irrelevant characters for this activity. Depending on the resources available, name tags and props can be used to enhance the role play, for example, cameras, backpacks and sunglasses are useful in distinguishing the tourists from other role-play characters.

Depending on cultural norms and group dynamics, a rehearsal may be required before performing; however, it is the diversity of the initial thoughts of the participants that is desired, so rehearsals which have the potential to oust ideas ought to be kept short. If required, particulars such as a time limit, physical space for the skit and language of performance may need to be discussed.

As the skit(s) is/are being performed the facilitator should observe and record as much information as possible, video recording is useful at this point but note taking is also adequate. The community participants should be informed that the facilitator will act as an observer for the duration of the role play. If there is an audience they too should be involved in active observation and asked to think about what they would add to the role play, their likes and dislikes, and critiques of the conclusions derived from the role play.

In order to debrief the role play it is important to ask the participants for more details concerning their portrayal of CBT. Why did they show the tourist staying at someone's home instead of at a hostel? Why did the tourist get a pizza for lunch instead of a local dish? By asking *why* a more robust understanding of how the community 'sees' tourism will surface. Table 6.1 provides a list of common themes and questions that may surface as a result of the role play.

In 1999, I facilitated a role play in the rural village of Kapatura, in the Okavango Delta of Botswana. Eight communities had formed a community organization called Teemachane Community Development Trust with the aid of

Table 6.1. Common themes and facilitator questions to ask for the debriefing of community tourism role-play activity.

Common themes	Questions to ask
Accommodation	What type of accommodation is included in the skit, for example, hostel, lodge, campsite or home stay?
Food	What kind of food do the tourists eat, for example, local foods, foreign/Western foods? How are the foods prepared and by whom?
Activities	What do the participants think the tourists will find interesting? How long are tourists involved in different activities? What happens when they are not on a guided tour or in a cultural centre? Do they 'hang out' in the community or get on a bus and leave?
Money	How do those employed directly by CBT get paid and do other community members receive any monetary benefits? What happens to the money that tourists spend? How much money do community members expect from CBT?
Interactions	Who interacts with tourists? In what capacity? What qualifications do community members need in order to be involved in CBT?

Kuru Development Trust (now ToCADI), a local NGO. Kuru Development Trust was involved in a range of community development activities and in the initial stages of CBT planning. Two of the interesting outcomes of the role play were:

- The tourists would sleep in a traditional grass hut on a grass mat directly on the ground, no toilet facilities would be provided and only one candle would be allotted. The lack of 'creature comforts', such as a cot and latrine were important to note, considering that most tourists, even backpackers, expect or at least appreciate a clean bed and washroom facilities. In the follow-up discussion it was discovered that the community participants had understood that the tourists wanted to experience their 'traditional way of life', which was exactly what had been communicated to the community. 'Traditional way of life' had been translated very literally by the community and therefore included many of the hardships that the community had experienced such as the lack of water, lighting and toilet facilities. As the development of CBT progressed the accommodation requirements of tourists were discussed in more detail in order to create a fair representation of traditional housing, yet provide good quality accommodation.
- In the role play the community participants portrayed the tourists paying guides directly in cash for each item of information that was imparted concerning the local environment or culture. Therefore, in the course of one guided nature walk, each time a new species of bird or plant was pointed out the guide would ask all the tourists for money. This enactment in the role play brought to light the differences in how the NGO and the community viewed the financial structure around the collection and distribution of benefits from

tourism. In addition, it was realized that the 'norms' around money and tourists needed to be discussed. Most tourists expect to pay a lump sum for a tour, perhaps providing a tip for guides, but would be uncomfortable if asked for money at regular intervals.

Ideally, the outcome of the role play is that the facilitator and those parties encouraging CBT, be it private tour operators, NGOs or governments, can compare *their* CBT to the *community's* CBT and discover to what degree their versions coincide. This enables misconceptions, such as the payment of fees discussed above, to be addressed early on and gives the facilitating organization the opportunity to understand and manage the expectations of the community. The role play also serves to explore the diversity of ideas within a community and can contribute to potential CBT development plans.

Field Trip

Many communities on the verge of becoming involved in CBT are rural and often isolated. Few if any members of the community may have experienced tourism before or may have experienced only one type of tourism, for example 'mass' tourism in resorts or exclusive lodge tourism. In order to facilitate an understanding of CBT, an effective method of learning is to expose community members first hand to CBT and the expectations created by its implementation. This may be achieved through a field trip to another CBT programme. The field trip experience is multi-purpose: first, community members are provided with a first-hand experience of being a tourist; second, community members are exposed to all aspects of implementing a CBT programme from management structures to maintenance of the facilities; third, through discussions, community members are able to learn directly from their peers about both the positive and negative impacts of CBT. Field trip destinations will often depend on what is accessible; however, a more robust experience is provided if other locations that support different kinds of tourism, perhaps mass tourism resorts or exclusive high-end lodges, are visited in addition to CBT sites. This allows community participants to compare CBT to other forms of tourism and understand the costs and benefits of both.

In order to facilitate an understanding of what a tourist is, community members should be provided with a first-hand experience of being a tourist themselves. Participants can go on a tour to the CBT destination site, take a meal from the restaurant and/or stay in the hotel or guest house provided. The participants can be asked to discuss what their expectations are before the experience and after the tour the participants should be asked how it felt to be a tourist. Did they enjoy the experience? Is that what they thought it was going to be like to be a tourist? Recently, I aided in the facilitation of a training programme for the Nature Conservation Research Centre, a Ghanaian NGO working in CBT. The participants included CBT staff from all over the county with varying levels of experience. A component of the workshop was for participants to go on a guided tour themselves. During the debrief discussions many interesting issues arose for the participants. As tourists the participants had a variety of concerns that included anxiety over the potential physical difficulty faced by the walking trails, concerns over religion while visiting an animist shrine and the duration of time required for the tour. The experience gave the participants a window into what it feels like to be a tourist and understand some of the concerns a tourist might have. It also proved to be very enjoyable for the participants and provided some exposure as to why tourists travel and seek out new experiences. This activity also illustrated the cultural differences in how tourism is defined. It was interesting for the facilitators and participants to discover that in some instances, the interests of local Ghanaian tourists (the participants themselves) are quite different from the interests of foreign 'Western' tourists. The outcome being that CBT projects should develop tour content that is appropriate for the various audiences they may receive.

During the field trip, participants should not only be exposed to the tourists' side of CBT but also to the communities' role. It is important that all features of CBT, detailed in the table below, are explored during the field trip. Each CBT programme is unique; consequently it is impossible for the table below to be inclusive of all features of CBT development and implementation. Table 6.2, however, does

Table 6.2. Different features of CBT and learning objectives to be addressed during field trip.

Features of CBT	Learning objectives
Physical site and infrastructure	• To become familiar with the maintenance and upkeep of accommodation, bathroom facilities, information signs, visitor centres, trails and grounds, etc. • To discuss the construction of infrastructure and use of local materials, as well as, the technical knowledge required for maintenance
Protocols and procedures	• To become familiar with record keeping (visitor numbers and accounts), visitor surveys and feedback, community feedback and emergencies procedures and problem-solving protocols
Activities and services	• To become familiar with and have practical experience with food preparation, cleaning and reception duties
Organizational structures and management	To address the questions: • *What are the organizational structures required?* Financial management boards, decision-making structures and traditional organizations • *Who participates?* Representation of community diversity within management (ethnic groups, religious groups, gender) • *What are the boards responsible for and how do the structures function?* Distribution of benefits, association with other local government and private organizations that may be stakeholders in CBT, regular meetings, written reports
Attractions	• To become familiar with the potential diversity of tours and sites, including nature tours, cultural tours, significant local sites, specialized tours (birds, medicinal plants) that can be offered

encompass the range of features that bring together CBT and suggests learning objectives that can be explored to enhance community understanding of CBT.

The interactions and discussions between the experienced community and field trip participants should encourage learning about practical issues such as food preparation and ground maintenance and it should also include discussions about the process that the more experienced community went through in planning and implementing CBT. A discussion should occur concerning how the community members of the established CBT programme feel about the tourists who visit and discuss what they *thought* CBT would be like at first and how their ideas have *changed*. This aims to avoid the common 'trap' during debrief discussions, of 'but that will never happen to us', with reference to the negative impacts of CBT. In my experience field trip participants obtain a greater understanding of the common pitfalls and misconceptions associated with CBT, as well as, the benefits when delivered by their peers.

Prior to the field trip, the participants should be asked to define or describe CBT as they understand it. This can be done individually or as a group. During the field trip the participants should be encouraged to be critical and asked to keep a record of their observations. Depending on the duration of the field trip, debriefing discussions with the field trip participants can be held daily or reserved until the end of the trip. Participants should be asked to review their initial definition of CBT and to think about and discuss whether or not their definitions have changed. This can be followed by a group discussion where participants list what they learned, both positive and negative, about CBT (either as a group or individually and then presented to the group). All participants should be asked to share what they think and asked questions such as:

1. Was there anything you saw that surprised you?
2. What was your favourite part of the field trip?
3. Was there anything you saw that you would like to do in your community?
4. Was there anything you saw that you think is not good or that you did not like?
5. What did you learn from the community members we visited?

The questions and observations concerning CBT are almost unlimited but the discussion should focus on understanding CBT from both the tourist and community perspective. The field trip experience leads to several learning opportunities. First, community members are provided with the opportunity to be tourists and gain an understanding of tourist motivations. Second, the field trip enables the community to move beyond the 'rosy image' of CBT to understand both the positive and negative impacts that may occur. Third, the nuts and bolts of running a tourism project are revealed from the diversity of employment opportunities provided to the financial management structures and physical site maintenance requirements. Fourth, the field trip provides an opportunity for the community to witness and discuss the changes that transpire as CBT changes and grows. With this exposure and knowledge the community has a more realistic understanding of the complexity of the host–guest relationship and therefore has the opportunity to be proactive in planning their own CBT programme. The community can discuss what they feel would be appropriate and inappropriate for their community and create a list of goals that encompass both short-term and long-term objectives. Specific issues can be identified, for example, the community may learn that home stays, although profitable, are also very intrusive for the families providing the accommodation. The community participants having gained this knowledge are better equipped to make a decision about including home stays as an option or providing other accommodation choices.

Commonly, field trip participants are limited to the local traditional and government leaders, who are very often men. In order to fairly represent the diversity of a community, however, it is important to encourage a range of participants, including different ethnic and religious groups and women. Upon returning to the community at large, field trip participants should be given a forum in which to share with the community what they have learnt from the field trip. If the equipment is available it is useful at this point to have video or photographs available as visual aids.

Drawing: 'What Is a Tourist?'

The purpose of the drawing activity is to create an understanding of tourism from within a local context by illustrating the similarities and difference between tourists and community members. A significant part of creating an understanding of what CBT is, is to understand who the tourists are, their motivations for travel and expectations once at a destination. Potential conflicts and frustrations between community members and tourists can be averted if misconceptions are realized and addressed. This activity depends on drawing and visual images and is therefore excellent for communities with several different languages and/or low literacy levels. This activity can be facilitated as a large group activity or in smaller focus groups; large chart paper with a variety of drawing tools is best suited for this activity.

To begin the facilitator will describe the purpose of the activity as stated previously. The participants can be asked a series of questions concerning travel and why they would travel. For example: if you were going to leave your village, where would you go, why would you go, how would you dress, what would you take, would anyone come with you, how would you travel (bus, walk, bicycle, fly, personal car), how long would you go for, when you come back would you bring anything with you back home? The aim is to begin with the familiar in order to generate discussion. A 'bare bones' picture of a man and woman from the community should be provided and the responses to the questions added to the image (as pictures). For example, in Ghana when people travel outside of their village they are often formally dressed, women frequently travel for market and trading purposes and everyone travels for funerals. The picture can be drawn by the facilitator or participants can be invited to add their own images.

The second part of the activity is to repeat this exercise but now ask the participants to think of a foreign tourist. Similar questions should be posed concerning the tourist. For example: why do you think this person is travelling, what are they wearing and carrying, what kind of transportation are they using, where are they from? The outcome is an image that represents 'the tourist' through local eyes. Many community members will have only seen foreigners but never interacted directly as individuals with them, and therefore this exercise is particularly interesting in that it reveals what ideas have been developed based solely on visual observations. The pictures that the community creates, of not only themselves, but also of the tourists, will illustrate the perceptions and in many cases the values of the community.

The pictures of the local traveller and the foreign traveller, as shown in Fig. 6.1, can then be discussed drawing on similarities and differences. The notion of travelling may be one that is familiar to the local community, but not thought of in the context of tourism per se. By discussing why people travel, both local and foreign, a greater understanding of tourist motivations, what tourists' behaviour might mean and what they desire from CBT is created. In addition, by providing a local context for tourism it is hoped that community members will begin to understand the concept of tourism.

In Ghana, as illustrated in Fig. 6.1, a common difference between a local person travelling and a tourist is the formality of dress. Tourists are often dressed casually and are thought to look messy or dirty. In particular, the footwear of tourists is frequently noted by locals, as many foreigners wear 'flip-flops' which in Ghana are considered to be bathroom slippers and therefore inappropriate for outside of the home. Ghanaians commonly dress very formally for travelling, wearing traditional dress and jewellery. However, the Ghanaian practice of bringing gifts, commonly bread, home for friends and family can be compared to the tourist bringing home pictures and souvenirs to show their friends and family where they have been. Therefore, the reason behind why tourists carry cameras and are always taking pictures is given a context that is comparable to local practices.

In addition to the two pictures of the local and foreign travellers that are created by the community for this activity, it may be useful for the facilitator to

Fig. 6.1. Drawing of a community member prepared to travel and a tourist, providing a basis for discussion of the similarities and differences between the people in the drawing, and also the local and foreign concepts of travel and tourism.

have a picture on hand of the 'typical tourist' that may visit the CBT site being planned. This can be used to fill in the knowledge gaps of the community if they have had very little exposure to tourists. By discussing the similarities and differences between the local traveller and the foreign traveller an understanding will emerge about who the tourists are that is grounded in local knowledge and experience. Not only will the local community become more familiar with tourists but they can also begin to discuss 'codes of conduct' that they may want to provide for tourists.

Conclusion

CBT has the potential to have a significant impact on the social, political and cultural state and development of a community, in particular in rural communities where CBT may be the only economic activity outside of subsistence agriculture and natural resource use. Communities, however, are rarely the only stakeholders involved in CBT development and are often left out of the early stages of CBT planning due to a lack of understanding of what tourism is both for tourists and for themselves. A 'lack of awareness is one of the factors which acts as barriers to effective communication at community level tourism development' (Tosun, 2000, p. 626) and combined with poverty a lack of understanding can result in apathy towards participation in the tourism development process (Tosun, 2000). It is therefore vital that communities understand what CBT actually is.

The techniques discussed in this chapter aim to address this need for understanding by exploring both Western and local concepts of tourism encompassing the host–guest relationship and the balance the community must maintain as both the host and attraction. In addition, the activities encourage partners in CBT development such as donor agencies, government and NGOs to recognize that 'tourism' is a culturally defined concept that must be examined prior to CBT development thus enabling active community participation in CBT planning. The activities can be used individually but are very effective when used together. The drama activity can be used initially to establish a common understanding between the community and facilitator of how the community comprehends tourism. The field trip can be used virtually at any time to provide a first-hand experience of being a tourist for community members and expose community members to the working reality of CBT. The drawing activity can be used to provide a context for tourism based on local experiences of travel. The practical outcomes of these activities are, first, to address misconceptions concerning tourism at an early stage in CBT development aiming to reduce potential conflicts or misunderstandings in the future; second, to provide an understanding of both the positive and negative impacts of CBT from first-hand experience and peer education; and third, to generate a more detailed understanding of the similarities and differences between tourists and community members from a local context, including motivations for travel. The knowledge gained by the community, from these experiences, can then be brought to decision making in order to represent the communities own ideals, values and interests in the tourism planning process.

References

Aramberri, J. (2001) The host should get lost: paradigms in the tourism theory. *Annals of Tourism Research* 28, 738–761.

Arnstein, S. (1969) A ladder of citizen participation. *Journal of American Institute of Planners* 35, 216–224.

Berno, T. (1999) When a guest is a guest: Cook Islanders view of tourism. *Annals of Tourism Research* 26, 656–675.

Blackstock, K. (2005) A critical look at community based tourism. *Community Development Journal* 40, 39–49.

Brohman, J. (1996) New directions in tourism for Third World development. *Annals of Tourism Research* 23, 48–70.

Burns, P.M. (2004) Tourism planning a third way? *Annals of Tourism Research* 31, 24–43.

Cohen, E. (1974) Who is a tourist? A conceptual clarification. *The Sociological Review* 22, 527–555.

Cohen, E. (1984) The sociology of tourism: approaches, issues, and findings. *Annual Reviews in Anthropology* 10, 373–392.

Costa, J. and Ferrone, L. (1995) Sociocultural perspectives on tourism planning and development. *International Journal of Contemporary Hospitality Management* 7, 27–35.

Joppe, M. (1996) Sustainable community tourism development revisited. *Tourism Management* 17, 475–479.

Little, P.D. (1994) The link between local participation and conservation. In: Western, D. and Wright, M. (eds) *Natural Connections: Perspectives in Community-based Conservation.* Island Press, Washington, DC, pp. 347–370.

Maoz, D. (2006) The mutual gaze. *Annals of Tourism Research* 33, 221–239.

Mowforth, M. and Munt, I. (2003) *Tourism and Sustainability: Development and New Tourism in the Third World.* Routledge, London.

Reid, D.G. (2003) *Tourism, Globalization and Development: Responsible Tourism Planning.* Pluto Press, London.

Taylor, G. (1995) The community approach: does it really work? *Tourism Management* 16, 487–489.

Tosun, C. (2000) Limits to community participation in the tourism development process in developing countries. *Tourism Management* 21, 613–633.

7 Tools to Enhance Community Capacity to Critically Evaluate Tourism Activities

Kaye Walker

School of Business, James Cook University, Australia

Introduction

Moscardo in Chapter 1 (this volume) highlighted the gaps in our knowledge and literature regarding the community capacity-building approach in her model for tourism development. One of the areas identified for which there is very little information was how to enhance a community's collective tourism knowledge in such a way as to improve their ability to plan for, and critically evaluate, tourism.

It was also identified that governments of developing nations and other agencies involved in funding and consulting in tourism development have considered in particular two types of tourism for their proposed greater potential to involve and build community capacity. Sammy has addressed one of these in Chapter 6 (this volume), community-based tourism (CBT), while discussing examples of effective techniques for enhancing community understanding of tourism. These techniques fit well into the early stage of Moscardo's proposed model for community capacity building, to create tourism knowledge and awareness, prior even to the decision to choose tourism as a development option.

While fully supporting the premise of Moscardo's model, it is this author's experience, particularly with the small nations and island communities of the Pacific region, that this initial phase of the proposed capacity-building process has already been supplanted. This is not to suggest that these early phases and techniques should not or could not be conducted or introduced post tourism initiation. But it is suggested that many of these island communities have already had tourism either thrust upon them via external tourism operators or local agents, or have actively sought ways to attract such from their observation of nearby island tourism activities, and have therefore already formed their own concepts of tourism and tourists, however limited these may be. The type of tourism the more remote island communities are experiencing is often in the form of ecotourism operations. This is a proposed type of tourism identified by Moscardo in Chapter 1 (this volume) which supposedly has the potential to involve and build community capacity.

Though in concurrence with Moscardo's observations about the potential of ecotourism to build community capacity, this author has not witnessed in her past 5 years of research and involvement in a form of ecotourism operation, predominantly in the Pacific region, the potential community capacity-building benefits proposed with the introduction of this type of tourism to small island communities. The author has worked as a guide and lecturer on Expedition Cruises, in environmental impact management and as an academic researcher in numerous peripheral communities. In many cases it is apparent that these small communities have not been able to develop their own sustainable tourism, often benefiting only a minimal economic return from externally owned and operated tourism with little or no enhancement of their environmental or social conditions. In fact, a stimulating factor for the author's research investigating the relationship between a particular type of ecotourism and the concept of sustainability has been the recognition by various communities of their incomprehension of the tourists' behaviour and conduct of the operations. The following story exemplifies the lack of understanding of both the communities regarding the tourists and the ecotourism operators regarding the communities:

> Some small South Pacific island community members would ask why the visitors did not want to return to their island after the morning welcome ceremony, in order to sit and talk to the locals, or to see how they lived and to partake in their hospitality. Instead, the visitors went snorkelling or diving on their reefs, or even stayed on the vessel, in which neither activity the locals were invited to be involved. Many community members had come from other neighbouring islands to participate in this interaction and all were hoping to learn more about their visitors, and to experience a social and cultural exchange. These people wished to understand more about their visitors so they could make the experience more rewarding, for both visitor and host.
>
> (Walker, 2007, p. 1)

It is suggested by this author that the reason this situation occurs is because ecotourism operators are more often focused upon enhancing the tourists' or the participants' experience, while it is assumed this sort of tourism merely via its activity and objective to increase participants' environmental and cultural awareness is inherently beneficial to the community, especially when a continued relationship of visitation is achieved. However, rarely is the ecotourism operation's focus upon how to enhance the tourism experience for the local community, or what the community or community participants could learn from the tourism experience in order to increase their understanding, and therefore their capacity to evaluate, manage, plan and contribute more to subsequent tourism opportunities. Even when operators attempt to build community capacity, perhaps through the establishment, training and engagement of local guides and building of continuing relationships with community representatives, the lack of available tools along with their ignorance of how to contribute to the communities' understanding of the tourism process and the tourists prevents this type of tourism from achieving its supposed potential for sustainability by building truly inherent community capacity, i.e. contributing to the community's own ability to evaluate the appropriateness of the outcomes of the ecotourism activity, based on their own community values.

Within the context of a tourism operation's accordance with the social and environmental aspects of the sustainability concept, this extends beyond the suggested facility of current ecotourism accreditation processes and their criteria as prescribed in certification and tourism guideline programmes such as the Green Globe 21 International Ecotourism Standard and National Ecotourism Accreditation Programme (Bricker and Kerstetter, 2006). In the remote island communities of the South Pacific region in particular, the tourism operations that wish to visit and do visit, sometimes without prior arrangement, are owned and conducted by external companies. Thus, any assessment of their operation with respect to current tourism sustainability indicators does not necessarily signify the measurement of inherent community capacity building, particularly with respect to increasing the community's understanding of the tourism process or the tourists themselves. In these cases, the sustainability indicators are more focused on measuring the potential of the tourism activity to continue within a place or region without negatively impacting upon its sustained operations with respect to the local environment and community.

This position is supported by the initial definition of sustainable development and the subsequent expressions of sustainable tourism definitions in the literature. The definition of sustainable development in the Bruntland Report (WCED, 1987, cited in Wearing and Neil, 1999) is development that meets the needs of the present without compromising the ability of future generations to meet their own needs. The World Tourism Organization's (WTO) reinterpretation of this definition with respect to tourism has been cited as the starting point for the realization of sustainable tourism (Stabler, 1997). The extended definition appears in *Steps to Sustainable Tourism*, Australia's Department of the Environment and Heritage guide for planning sustainable tourism (2004, p. 1):

> Sustainable tourism development meets the needs of present tourists and host regions while protecting and enhancing opportunities for the future. It is envisaged as leading to management of all resources in such a way that economic, social and aesthetic needs can be fulfilled while maintaining cultural integrity, essential ecological processes, biological diversity and life support systems.

Butler (1991, cited in Wearing and Neil, 1999, p. 6) had previously defined sustainable tourism as 'tourism that is developed and maintained in an area (community, environment) in such a manner and at such a scale that it remains viable over an indefinite period and does not degrade or alter the environment'. Thus, it can be seen that while sustainability of the community and environment is paramount, there is no explicit reference to contributing to inherent capacity building within the community to achieve or manage their own sustainability. However, since the WTO's definition, Ham and Weiler (2002, p. 36) have adopted and adapted it to include additionally to the aim that tourism development will not undermine the physical and human environment, but that it will also 'sustain and nurture it'. By 'nurture' one could assume it is meant that the community is helped to be able to help itself, a fostering mentality of nurturing inherent talents or capacity. It is this inherent capacity-building role within the sustainable tourism process and related practices, such as ecotourism, that has yet to be given adequate investigation, and so we lack knowledge as to how to facilitate this dimension of sustainable tourism.

Accordingly, this chapter discusses a new approach and framework in sustainable tourism and associated ecotourism development. This approach provides the community with the opportunity to evaluate the outcomes of a tourist activity with respect to the tourists' recognition and incorporation of, and accord with, the community's own values. It does this by providing communities and ecotourism operators, local governments and tourism agencies and consultants with a tool to enhance their understanding of the personal outcomes and significant values of the tourists participating in the ecotourism experience. This subsequently provides a link between the community and the tourist, while utilizing the involvement of the external tourism operators. Thus, this approach provides the opportunity for communities already experiencing ecotourism to better understand and evaluate the tourism activity and experience. By utilizing the ecotourism operations already functioning within their community and region, it takes advantage of their current potential for community capacity building and effectively provides a feedback loop in Moscardo's model between the latter stage of *building community capacity for tourism* with the earlier stage to *create tourism knowledge and awareness* (see Fig. 7.1).

This approach is intended to be incorporated as part of the sustainable tourism process, clearly integrating the community capacity-building potential with the conduct of ecotourism. It exploits the interpretive component of ecotourism operations as the conduit and linkage between the tourist and the community through the facilitation, assessment and comparison of social values. Because of the fundamental nature of the interpretive component in ecotourism operations, it is suggested this approach can be further encouraged and implemented via ecotourism and sustainability accreditation programmes. In this chapter, the theoretical premise for this approach will be discussed and the development of the framework linking the community to the tourist. This establishes the importance of the identification of community values to community capacity building within the sustainability concept. This is followed by considering the potential development of the framework as a tool for community capacity building if used in conjunction with ecotourism operations already or potentially occurring and involving remote communities who have little other resources from which to learn about tourism and tourists.

Community Understanding of the Tourist in the Sustainable Tourism Process

The following discussion investigates the place and importance of community values in the sustainability concept. It is pertinent to establishing the linkage between the potential for community capacity building as proposed in the introductory chapter of this book, with the sustainable tourism process. It is suggested these linkages are particularly relevant to the gaps in our knowledge regarding how to achieve the goals of community capacity building, such as:

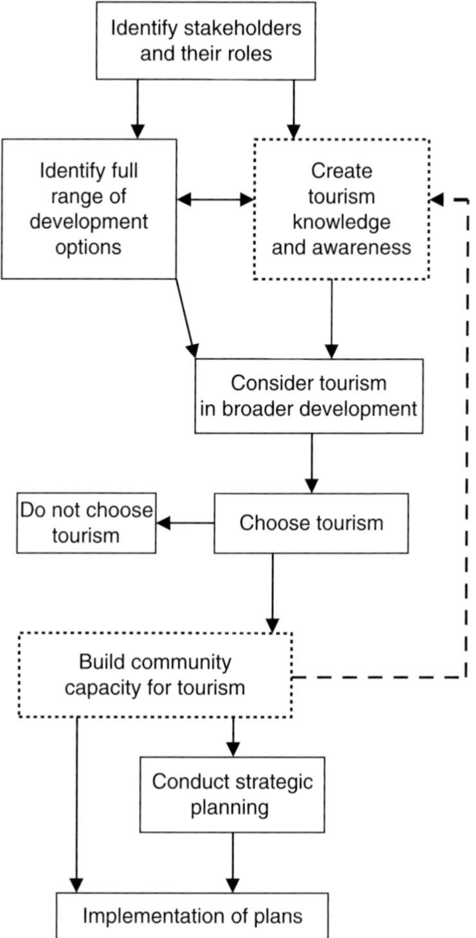

Fig. 7.1. Model for community capacity building for tourism development decisions – with feedback loop.

- enhancing a community's ability to critically evaluate tourism outcomes and understand the tourist; as well as
- enhancing community participation in tourism and developing effective partnerships with external agents.

It is proposed that in order to encourage, enhance and facilitate community capacity-building opportunities with respect to already established tourism operations, identifying and affiliating with currently advocated tourism concepts and practices such as sustainability and ecotourism will assist the integration and recognition of the greater incorporative potential of these for the operators and the community representatives, local, regional and national governments and tourism associated agencies.

At the Rio Earth Summit (1992, cited in Smith, 2001, p. 191) the 179 participating governments endorsed Local Agenda 21, which 'challenges action on the part of local authorities to adopt ways to involve their communities in defining their own sustainable futures'. This agenda suggests that sustainable development can only be achieved 'through planned, democratic, cooperative means including community involvement in decisions about the environment and development' (Jackson and Morpeth, 1999, cited in Smith, 2001, p. 191). Smith (2001) believes the sustainability of culture, especially indigenous culture, to be the further challenge in sustainable tourism. She quotes McLaren (1999, cited in Smith, 2001, p. 200) who feels the globalization of tourism threatens indigenous values and basic rights to informed understanding, potentially 'reducing indigenous peoples to simply another consumer product that is quickly becoming exhaustible'.

McCool and Moisey (2001) also support the need for more consideration of social goals and values and consider the processes of integrating tourism into a broader social and economic development picture. They identify a linkage in need of construction between tourism development and promotion. They discuss how these processes are usually conducted independently, referring to this as 'compartmentalised decision making' (McCool and Moisey, 2001, p. 6). This approach obstructs the sustainability principle of holistic or integrated planning and strategy making as described earlier and recommended by the Brundtland Report (WCED, 1987). These authors suggest there is a predominant focus on promotion rather than responsible marketing that should take into account product development and protection. They suggest that tourism development and promotion should be collective decisions within which public knowledge and the identification of goals and attitudes of the public are important considerations.

There are numerous publications composed of case studies and articles reiterating the need for greater understanding of community values and attitudes, and processes to acquire this information and integrate it with the sustainability concept (Murphy, 1985; Pearce *et al.*, 1996; McCool and Moisey, 2001; Smith and Brent, 2001; Singh *et al.*, 2003). This literature describes models that often address the negative impacts of tourism upon communities and the deterioration of community attitudes to tourism over time (Doxey, 1975 in Pearce *et al.*, 1996; Smith, 2001). Moisey and McCool (2001) constructed a model to demonstrate the connections between the major participants in tourism development with respect to their shared goals and opportunities for sustainability. However, while it includes the environmental management agencies, the local residents and the tourism industry, it fails to include the tourist.

The previous review of sustainable development and tourism definitions firmly established the individual tourist as a vital component in the sustainability concept. Additionally, if indigenous values are being threatened by tourism, and community or public attitudes are to be incorporated into the sustainability decision-making process, then not only must tourists be an integral part of the process but also there must be facilitation of community understanding of the tourist in order to develop representative public attitudes to tourism as an instrument of development. In other words, any model of sustainability involving tourism should incorporate a mechanism of inherent community capacity building with respect to contributing to the local's understanding of the tourist within their own community context, that of their indigenous or social values. Moisey and McCool (2001) used their model to suggest the identification and development of sustainability indicators, significantly noting the dissent between those advocating the adoption of a standardized set of indicators versus the use of site-specific indicators.

Thus, it became apparent that there was a need for the development of at least one integrated process or framework, which may be adopted generically, yet could be defined specifically with respect to the use of indicators or measurable variables. With respect to the accumulation of the reviewed material thus far, such a framework should possibly aim to involve:

- the ascertainment of community values;
- the identification of those values which are relevant to the hosts with respect to attracting appropriate clientele to their region;
- the ability to incorporate these values into the tourism and marketing functions; and
- the comparison of these values with those of the tourists, their expectations and perceptions of the people and place being visited and the personally significant outcomes of their visit.

As pointed out by Ham and Weiler (2002), it is only when the customers are satisfied that tourism can be sustainable, for without the customer there is no sustainable tourism. It is suggested, however, the potential process described above provides a method by which both the visitors' and hosts' satisfaction of the tourism experience can be assessed and compared, forming a linkage which facilitates increased understanding between the community and the tourist. For it is only with community support of the tourism activity can tourism be considered under the principles of sustainability, and it is only with increased understanding of the tourist and their activities can a community critically evaluate the outcomes of tourism within this concept.

The Role of Interpretation and Ecotourism in Sustainable Tourism

The role of ecotourism within the sustainable tourism concept and the role of interpretation in ecotourism have been addressed quite convincingly in the literature, thus will only be briefly reviewed here in order to establish the basis for construction of the new framework. According to Wearing and Neil (1999) an essential feature of ecotourism is sustainability, with its fundamental concerns including environmental degradation, impact on local communities and the need for high-quality tourism management. Although ecotourism involves the natural environment, it is differentiated from nature-based tourism by the characteristic that it contributes to conservation. The primary motivation of ecotourists is their focus on increasing knowledge and awareness of nature, and that the ecotourism activities contribute positively to conservation of the destination area or host community. Weaver (2001) suggests the goals inherent in ecotourism are conservation and education regarding the natural and cultural environment. The educational component and management of the activities in most ecotourism operations are usually conducted by the tour guides and facilitated through what is termed 'interpretation'. Weiler and Ham (2001) work on the premise that interpretation is an indispensable element of the ecotour guide's role, critical to achieving the goals of ecotourism.

Moscardo (1998) also suggests that interpretation could play a critical role in achieving sustainability. Moscardo and Woods (1998) elaborate further to suggest that interpretation and tourism are in fact mutually beneficial activities, which when working together support the development of more sustainable tourism. Moscardo (2000, p. 327) identifies three core functions:

- to enhance visitor experiences;
- to improve visitor knowledge or understanding; and
- to assist in the protection or conservation of places or culture.

It is through these three core functions that interpretation can contribute to the sustainability of tourism operations (Walker and Moscardo, 2006) and achieve conservation goals (Wearing and Neil, 1999; Ham and Weiler, 2002). Interpretation has also been seen as an effective management tool because it endeavours to increase visitor awareness and decrease inappropriate behaviour on a voluntary basis, rather than through enforcement and physical barriers, paths, etc. (McArthur and Hall, 1996; Ballantyne and Uzzell, 1999; Wearing and Neil, 1999).

Ham and Weiler (2002) also link the role of interpretation to the economic sustainability of ecotourism because, for example, successful businesses know that wildlife tourists want to receive information in appropriate forms, and that by providing interpretation these businesses offer more than a physical experience. These businesses offer an intellectual and emotional experience, providing a personal and meaningful connection between the people and the place they are visiting, and thus creating satisfied customers. By employing locals as guides, there is an added contribution to local sustainability. With regard to environmental sustainability, they claim that interpretation not only influences what visitors know and how they behave on site, but also has the potential to influence visitors' beliefs about conservation generally. And by influencing what visitors' believe about conservation and the resources being protected, researchers claim it is possible to influence not only how a person feels, but also how they act with regard to conservation (Ham and Weiler, 2002; Moscardo *et al.*, 2004). This is supported by the suggestion that the combination of providing knowledge and having a rewarding experience may facilitate the development of positive conservation attitudes and changes in values (Moscardo, 1998, 1999; Newsome *et al.*, 2002). Newsome *et al.* (2002) also argue that interpretation can make tourists more aware of human impacts on the global environment and this further contributes to greater support for wider conservation efforts.

Thus, the relationships between the concepts of sustainability, sustainable tourism, ecotourism and interpretation have been established, and it can be assumed that most ecotourism operations incorporate an interpretive component. The implications of the use of interpretation for communities have also been demonstrated with respect to its utilization as a tourism management tool, and one that any community exposed to ecotourism operations will be familiar with at some level, either through observation or participation. Thus, it is potentially a community capacity-building instrument that community representatives are most likely to be involved with, particularly with respect to employment or possibly in a liaison, cultural and language interpretation or advisory role with external ecotourism operators. It is pertinent to note, however, that so far the focus regarding interpretation and ecotourism has been exclusively upon the tourist experience and their increased understanding and awareness and personal values and not upon any reciprocal community understanding or increased awareness in the tourism process.

Community Values, Interpretation and Community Capacity Building

Moscardo (2003) provides support for a model that includes the visitor and incorporates interpretive links with the host community. This model effectively embeds the role of interpretation within the community aspect of the sustainability process. While it provides the key elements involved in interpretation, she suggests that all interpretation, whether it applies to the natural, cultural or historical aspects of a place, is based within the culture and politics of the host community. Moscardo (2003) proposed that the actual interpretive experience brings the interpreter and visitor together and may facilitate a number of fundamental outcomes for the sustainable tourism process. These outcomes include three related to visitors, such as their satisfaction level with regard to continued business viability, information receipt with regard to increasing knowledge and understanding and visitor concern with regard to developing or enhancing a conservation ethic. The possible outcomes identified for the community are economic and sociocultural benefits and minimizing visitor impacts. Economic gains and the management of impacts have both been previously mentioned and are appreciable outcomes, but what are the elements of the sociocultural benefits being referred to here?

Indeed, Moscardo (2003) raises concern about ways in which interpreters choose their interpretive content, noting that it has been argued that local interpreters are often members of the dominant or more powerful groups within a society. Thus, the topics chosen for interpretive presentation may reflect this power, rather than providing a more representative presentation of the community values. This situation may not only diminish the potential sociocultural benefits of the interpretive process but also bias the outcomes. She poses that a major challenge for the development of more sustainable tourism in the Asia-Pacific region is to ensure that the interpretation is effective, and that meeting this challenge requires greater attention to be paid to cross-cultural issues.

Moisey and McCool (2001, p. 349) support this observation and suggest that the protection of local values through community participation is necessary for communities to maintain their identity, their 'sense of place', without which the 'pathway to sustainability becomes lost'. This implies the potential community capacity benefits that can evolve from the interpretive process, empowering the community in its future development by reinforcing important values. Now that some elements of the sociocultural benefits have been raised, such as the identification and retention of community 'identity' and 'sense of place', it is interesting to note the reciprocity with respect to the use of the latter conceptual term. Discussion regarding the 'sense of place' concept has been more recently suggested and debated in interpretive literature where it is considered to be a potentially important component of effective interpretation with respect to being conveyed by the guide and appreciated by the visitor (Beck and Cable, 1998; Walker, 2007). It is a concept that intrigues the researcher and interpreter alike with respect to its facilitation and impact upon outcomes of interpretive programmes, with little currently published about either. Here it appears as an important value with respect to being sustained by the host community and linked to the function of interpretation of a place being embedded within the host community's culture. This is an example of the need for tourist–host reciprocal identification and recognition of community values in order to be able to critically evaluate the sociocultural outcomes of the tourism experience for both host and visitor. Whether the reader considers this value to be more environmentally or culturally orientated with associated sustainable implications, it is more basically a community-embedded value which it seems would be beneficial to inherent community capacity building if recognized by both host and visitor.

A Sustainable Tourism Framework and Tools: Linking the Community to the Tourist

In order to initiate investigation and consideration of the key areas in this approach, a new framework was developed for a sustainable tourism process utilizing ecotourism as the catalyst and source for enhancing community capacity building (Fig. 7.2). The framework identifies the elements discussed and links them together in order to facilitate increased community understanding of the tourist and the identification and comparison of community and personal values with respect to desired and actual tourism activity outcomes. This type of approach provides information that can be fed back into Moscardo's community capacity-building model as previously described (Fig. 7.1) and presents the community or associated agencies with a tool (the Value Model of Interpretation-I (VMI-I)) to critically evaluate the interpretive outcomes of the ecotourism operation.

The framework described in Fig. 7.2 presents a central link between the community and the tourist based on the recognition and significance of their social and environmental values. It demonstrates this through a series of linkages and relationships between the framework's components and the VMI-I. The VMI-I (Fig. 7.3) represents a new model of effective interpretation developed from a number of research studies (Walker, 2005, 2006a,b; Walker and Moscardo, 2006). This central component of the framework offers a model of interpretation (VMI-I) that identifies the core attributes and benefits of the ecotourism activities that are fundamental to facilitating value recognition and identification. A ladder of abstraction approach adapted from the means-end analysis technique of Klenosky *et al.* (1998) provides the cognitive linkages between the interpretive attributes and benefits and the personal value-based significance of the experience for the participant (see Fig. 7.3). This level of abstract responses may represent values such as a deeper appreciation for the people, environment or culture and the placement

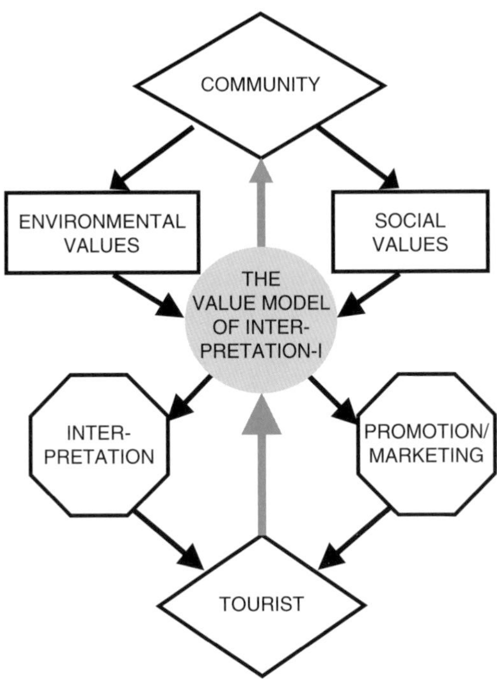

Fig. 7.2. A Sustainable Tourism Framework – linking the community to the tourist.

of this awareness into a global perspective of personal importance to the participant. These initial value-based responses are then linked to a greater personal insight of some significance referred to as 'self-appreciation'. These often include references to environmental concern and responsibility for the place and people visited and a more insightful appreciation of the value of this type of tourism. It is these higher-level value-based responses that are considered most likely to lead to an 'intentional behaviour' of the participant as an outcome of their ecotourism interpretive experience. The evaluation of these outcomes is conducted via an innovative but simple interpretive technique also developed for this research and derived from the ladder of abstraction approach and is referred to as the Personal Insight Approach (see Walker, 2006a for more detail regarding the derivation and application of this approach). This interpretive technique can be used reciprocally to ascertain both the tourists' and hosts' desired or achieved personally significant outcomes of the interpretive tourism experience.

The Sustainable Tourism Framework facilitates the linkage between the community and the tourist via the use of the VMI-I. It can provide information to the community about the tourists involved in the tourism activity, the significant values they are recognizing and placing personal importance upon as a result of the tourism experience, the attributes and benefits of the activity that generate these outcomes and their intentional behaviours based on these personally significant outcomes. This information can be used for the evaluation of the tourism activity via its comparison to the community's desired outcomes, if any had been initially identified. If not, then it provides vital information for the

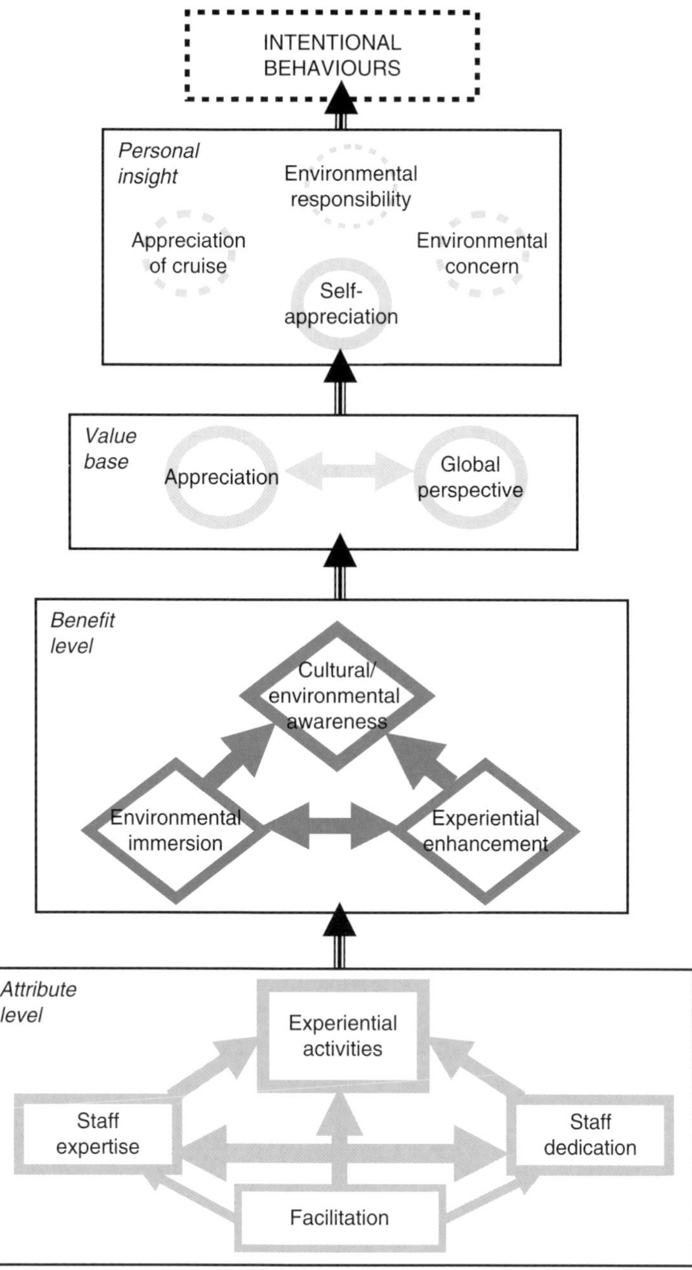

Fig. 7.3. The Value Model of Interpretation-I.

community to be able to consider comparing the recognition of, or alliance with, values the community feels are important outcomes of tourism in their environment. It may stimulate their identification of community-driven environmental and social values which can be fed back into the framework for incorporation into either the interpretive and/or promotional/marketing components. These components have been integrated with respect to their role in facilitating tourist recognition and appreciation of the community's social and environmental values regarding tourism in their environment. If incorporated into the interpretive plan of an ecotourism operation through liaison and or potential participation as a local guide, then the interpretive assessment and evaluation process may be repeated on a progressive basis.

In this way, the framework demonstrates a reciprocal tourist–community relationship. This is facilitated by the loop created through the tourist with respect to the values they identify and recognize being sorted and coded by the analysis procedures associated with the VMI-I for comparison with those identified by the community. The results are fed back to the community, the interpretive tourism outcomes reassessed and new desired outcomes fed back into the model for interpretive incorporation. Thus, the VMI-I presents the opportunity to both deliver and evaluate interpretive activities in order to facilitate tourist recognition and appreciation of values felt to be significant to the community, as well as those significant to the tourist. The concurrent assessment of the preconceived image or perceptions the tourist may have prior to their visit and the sources they attribute these to provides the potential to compare, appraise and comment upon the promotion/marketing component with respect to facilitating tourist recognition of these values, alongside the evaluation of the interpretation received *in situ*.

This framework for sustainable tourism demonstrates a link between the community and the tourist. It provides the opportunity to enhance a community's collective tourism knowledge in such a way as to improve their ability to plan and critically evaluate desired tourist outcomes. It enhances the role of community participation in current externally operated ecotourism operations and relationships, particularly in remote island locations where communities have scant opportunity to learn about tourism from any other source. By incorporating this linkage into the sustainable tourism process it is argued that the effective use of interpretation can contribute to achieving both the environmental and community principles of sustainability and contribute substantially to inherent community capacity building, rather than merely sustaining tourism in their environment.

This is a new framework, new model and interpretive technique, but all of which are grounded in current theoretical knowledge and conducted in current industry application. It is hoped their presentation will stimulate further investigation into how we may complement the potential of sustainable tourism to contribute realistically, intrinsically and significantly to remote communities' sustainability.

References

Ballantyne, R. and Uzzell, D. (1999) International trends in heritage and environmental interpretation: future directions for Australian research and practice. *Journal of Interpretation Research* 4(1), 59–75.

Beck, L. and Cable, T.T. (1998) *Interpretation for the 21st Century*. Sagamore Publishing, Champaign, Illinois.

Bricker, K.S. and Kerstetter, D. (2006) Saravanua ni vanua: exploring sense of place in the rural highlands of Fiji. In: Jennings, G. and Nickerson, N.P. (eds) *Quality Tourism Experiences.* Elsevier, Oxford, pp. 99–111.

Butler, R.W. (1991) Tourism, environment and sustainable development. *Environmental Conservation* 18(3), 201–209.

Department of the Environment and Heritage (2004) *Steps to Sustainable Tourism.* Commonwealth of Australia, Canberra.

Doxey, G.V. (1975) *A Causation Theory of Visitor–Resident Irritants.* Paper presented at the Travel Research Association Conference. TTRA, San Diego, California, no. 6, pp. 195–198.

Ham, S.H. and Weiler, B. (2002) Interpretation as the centrepiece of sustainable wildlife tourism. In: Harris, R., Griffin, T. and Williams, P. (eds) *Sustainable Tourism: A Global Perspective.* Butterworth-Heinemann, Oxford, pp. 35–44.

Jackson, G. and Morpeth, N. (1999) Local Agenda 21 and community participation in tourism policy and planning: future or fallacy. *Current Issues in Tourism* 2(1), 1–38.

Klenosky, D.B., Fraumand, E., Norman, W.C. and Gengler, C.E. (1998) Nature-based tourists use of interpretive services: a means-end investigation. *Journal of Tourism Studies* 9(2), 26–36.

McArthur, S. and Hall, M.H. (1996) Visitor management and interpretation at heritage sites. In: Hall, C.M. and McArthur, S. (eds) *Heritage Management in New Zealand and Australia.* Oxford University Press, Auckland, New Zealand, pp. 18–39.

McCool, S.F. and Moisey, R.N. (2001) Introduction: pathways and pitfalls in the search for sustainable tourism. In: McCool, S.F. and Moisey, R.N. (eds) *Tourism, Recreation and Sustainability: Linking Culture and the Environment.* CAB International, Wallingford, UK, pp. 1–15.

McLaren, D. (1999) The history of indigenous peoples and tourism. *Cultural Survival Quarterly* 23(2), 27–30.

Moisey, R.N. and McCool, S.F. (2001) Sustainable tourism in the 21st century: lessons from the past; challenges to address. In: McCool, S.F. and Moisey, R.N. (eds) *Tourism, Recreation and Sustainability: Linking Culture and the Environment.* CAB International, Wallingford, UK, pp. 1–15.

Moscardo, G. (1998) Interpretation and sustainable tourism: functions, examples and principles. *Journal of Tourism Studies* 9(1), 2–13.

Moscardo, G. (1999) *Making Visitors Mindful: Principles for Creating Sustainable Visitor Experiences Through Effective Communication.* Sagamore Publishing, Champaign, Illinois.

Moscardo, G. (2000) Interpretation. In: Jafari, J. (ed.) *Encyclopedia of Tourism.* Routledge, London, pp. 327–328.

Moscardo, G. (2003) Interpretation: communicating across cultures. In: Griffen, T. and Harris, R. (eds) *Proceedings of the Asia Pacific Tourism Association 9th Annual Conference.* School of Leisure Sport and Tourism, University of Technology, Sydney, Australila, pp. 487–499.

Moscardo, G. and Woods, B. (1998) Managing tourism in the wet tropics world heritage area: interpretation and the experience of visitors on Skyrail. In: Laws, E., Faulkner, B. and Moscardo, G. (eds) *Embracing and Managing Change in Tourism: International Case Studies.* Routledge, London, pp. 285–306.

Moscardo, G., Woods, B. and Saltzer, R. (2004) The role of interpretation in wildlife tourism. In: Higginbottom, K. (ed.) *Wildlife Tourism Impacts, Planning and Management.* Common Ground Publishing, Altona, Australia, pp. 231–252.

Murphy, P. (1985) *Tourism: A Community Approach.* Routledge, New York and London.

Newsome, D., Moore, S.A. and Dowling, R.K. (2002) *Natural Area Tourism: Ecology, Impacts and Management.* Channel View, Clevedon, UK.

Pearce, P.L., Moscardo, G. and Ross, G.F. (1996) *Tourism Community Relationships.* Pergamon, Oxford.

Singh, S., Timothy, D.J. and Dowling, R.K. (eds) (2003) *Tourism in Destination Communities.* CAB International, Wallingford, UK.

Smith, V.L. (2001) Sustainability. In: Smith, V.L. and Brent, M. (eds) *Hosts and Guests Revisited.* Cognizant Communication Corporation, New York, pp. 187–200.

Smith, V.L. and Brent, M. (eds) (2001) *Hosts and Guests Revisited.* Cognizant Communication Corporation, New York.

Stabler, M.J. (1997) *Tourism and Sustainability: From Principles to Practice.* CAB International, Wallingford, UK.

Walker, K. (2005) Expeditions in sustainable tourism: evaluating interpretation on Expedition Cruises. In: Spears, D.L. (ed.) *Winds of Change in Tourism Research: Voyages of Inquiry and Discovery.* Proceedings of the Fourth Annual Asia Pacific Forum for Graduate Student Research in Tourism. 1–3 August, 2005, School of Travel Industry Management, University of Hawaii at Manoa. University of Hawaii, Hawaii, pp. 151–172.

Walker, K. (2006a) A means-end approach to interpretation in sustainable tourism. Cutting edge research in tourism: new directions, challenges and applications. *Proceedings from the University of Surrey School of Management Conference.* University of Surrey, Guildford, UK.

Walker, K. (2006b) Sustainable tourism and the value model of interpretation. New frontiers in global tourism: trends and competitive challenges. *Proceedings from the TTRA 2006 Annual Conference.* G Jennings, Dublin.

Walker, K. (2007) The role of interpretation in sustainable tourism: a qualitative approach to understanding passenger experiences on expedition cruises. PhD thesis, James Cook University, Townsville, Queensland, Australia.

Walker, K. and Moscardo, G. (2006) The impact of interpretation upon passengers of Expedition Cruises. In: Dowling, R.K. (ed.) *Cruise Ship Tourism.* CAB International, Wallingford, UK.

Wearing, S. and Neil, J. (1999) *Ecotourism: Impacts, Potentials and Possibilities.* Butterworth-Heinemann, Oxford.

Weaver, D.B. (2001) Methodologies, research and resources. In: Weaver, D.B. (ed.) *The Encyclopedia of Ecotourism.* CAB International, Wallingford, UK, pp. 595–596.

Weiler, B. and Ham, S.H. (2001) Tour guides and interpretation. In: Weaver, D.B. (ed.) *The Encyclopedia of Ecotourism.* CAB International, Wallingford, UK, pp. 549–563.

World Commission on Environment and Development (WCED) (1987) *Our Common Future.* Oxford University Press, Oxford.

8 Partnerships for Tourism Development

Amanda Stronza

Department of Recreation, Park and Tourism Sciences, Texas A&M University, Texas, USA

Introduction

Many development banks, environmental non-governmental organizations (NGOs) and ecotourism consulting firms are channelling financial and technical resources to local communities with hopes that ecotourism can become a tool for integrated conservation and development. In response, local communities are increasingly seeking to manage tourism operations on their own. As they gain skills and knowledge, a number of communities have joined in partnerships with tour operators and NGOs. These partnerships enable residents with no experience in tourism to participate and benefit from ecotourism. Knowledge of how to forge such partnerships or how to make partnerships truly support local leaders and local community development goals in tourism is nascent. Further, relatively little is known regarding how, or how effectively, local actors are coping with the resources and attention or what people think about their new roles and responsibilities as ecotourism owners and managers.

In this chapter, I describe the experiences and perceptions of local leaders from the three tourism partnerships who participated in a series of workshops aimed at sharing lessons learned. I focus in particular on how they gain new capacities for ecotourism management. Included are details about each of the partnership models, how leaders from each define capacity building, and the challenges and new opportunities they face as ecotourism gains economic and social importance in their regions. I conclude with a summary of factors to consider when lending support to, and working in, partnership with local communities for tourism development.

Global Attention on Local Communities

International environmental organizations, government agencies, multilateral development banks, indigenous federations and the tourism industry have vigorously promoted ecotourism as a potential win–win approach to conservation and development. The US Agency for International Development alone has invested more than US$2 billion in ecotourism (Kiss, 2004). At the World Parks Congress in 2003, representatives from 170 nations called for increased measures to make ecotourism a more effective 'vehicle' for conserving biodiversity and reducing poverty (IUCN, 2003). Much of the optimism has focused especially on community-based forms of ecotourism in which local people play a central role in managing projects, and a major proportion of profits and other benefits remain within the community (Denman, 2001).

In some communities, ecotourism has worked effectively as a strategy to connect biodiversity conservation with sustainable development (Wunder, 1999; Alexander, 2000). In others, it has failed (Belsky, 1999; West and Carrier, 2004). The factors that determine which communities are able to make ecotourism work effectively for goals of conservation and development remain unclear. Some scholars have suggested that ecotourism fails for communities when too little employment or income is channelled to local residents (Bookbinder *et al.*, 1998). Others argue it fails when locals are excluded from the management and decision making behind ecotourism operations (Stem *et al.*, 2003).

If ecotourism has any real potential as a strategy for conservation and sustainable development, we must better understand the reasons why it succeeds or fails within local communities and from the perspective of local residents. In an analysis of 392 case studies in tourism, Moscardo (2005) found that one of the most basic barriers to effective tourism development is a lack of knowledge. Others too have argued that residents of local communities are often lacking appropriate skills and knowledge to manage tourism on their own (Yu *et al.*, 1997; Epler Wood, 2002). This is particularly true for people of rural, indigenous or otherwise traditional communities who have relatively little experience in the global economy or capitalist markets. Even in cases where communities are running their own operations, they may be unprepared to manage ecotourism in ways that can truly serve local needs and priorities. Such barriers must be overcome so that local residents can translate ecotourism into broader benefits for their communities, while also controlling the negative effects of tourism.

For example, when local residents lack leadership or are ill-prepared to manage tourism for themselves, external actors are more likely to dominate, thus perpetuating the marginalization of rural and indigenous communities. In this scenario, tourism is more likely to generate problems rather than benefits. Typical problems associated with externally driven tourism are social conflict, economic disparity and environmental degradation. Alternatively, when local residents are empowered as leaders and decision makers to determine the scope and direction of their own tourism development, net positive outcomes for conservation and development are more likely.

The need for capacity building at the grass roots is a challenge identified by conservationists as well. In the journal *Science*, Rodriguez *et al.* (2007) argued that conservation efforts fail when 'local conservationists have not been trained, or local institutions have not been developed with their own programs and funding'. The authors found that training is usually insufficiently supported, as 'only 4% of the US$3.26 billion invested in Latin American biodiversity conservation between 1990 and 1997 was specifically spent on capacity building' (p. 756). They concluded that more attention and resources should be focused on bolstering abilities of local leaders to manage community-based conservation projects. Some efforts on this front have been made. For example, the Inter-American Development Bank (IDB) and World Bank invested US$9 million to 'strengthen the capacity of indigenous communities' in Central America (World Bank, 2004). Yet, more is needed.

One strategy indigenous leaders throughout the world are using to expand their knowledge, skills and management capacity in ecotourism is to forge partnerships with other actors (Ashley and Jones, 2001; Forstner, 2004). In such partnerships, residents of local communities link their knowledge, land, labour and social capital with the investment capital, business acumen and managerial experience of outside tour operators or NGOs. In a broader sense, the companies and NGOs bring the tourism industry and the globalized economy while people in local communities offer their long-held and intimate knowledge of ecosystems and traditions. In the past, such exchanges represented simply more opportunities for exploitation of local cultural and natural resources. In contrast, more recent collaborations are meant to be true partnerships, meaning that locals participate not just through employment or service, but also as decision makers, managers and owners. Benefits remain in the community, but so does decision-making authority. To make such partnerships possible, strengthened capacity within local communities to assume full control of tourism operations is needed.

The *Trueque Amazonico*

In 2003, leaders of three community-based ecotourism partnerships in the Amazonian regions of Peru, Ecuador and Bolivia joined in a 6-month comparative study called the '*Trueque Amazonico*: Ecotourism Exchanges in the Tropical Andes'. The aim was to bring local voices to the fore in evaluating partnerships for ecotourism. The three ecolodges in the comparison are community-initiated and community-managed, though they all began as partnerships between indigenous peoples, private tourism companies and/or NGOs (see Table 8.1). Community members in each site earn economic benefits from ecotourism, either through shared profits or salaries, but they are also engaged in managing the scope and direction of ecotourism in their own communities. All three partnerships are ultimately aimed at building local capacity for tourism development and strengthening local leadership for effective tourism management at the grass-roots level.

The *Trueque Amazonico* was funded by the Critical Ecosystem Partnership Fund, a consortium of Conservation International (CI), the Global Environmental Facility, the MacArthur Foundation and the Government of Japan. The funding enabled participatory evaluations of ecotourism's effects in each location, and led to case studies about the three kinds of partnerships in the three countries: community–NGO (Chalalán in Bolivia); community–private company (Posada Amazonas in Peru); and federation–private company (Kapawi in Ecuador).

The partnerships in each site have been instrumental in enabling local residents to overcome some of the most salient challenges associated with tourism

Table 8.1. Three community-based partnerships for tourism.

Lodge	Chalalán	Posada Amazonas	Kapawi
Partnership model	Community–NGO	Community–private company	Federation–private company
Country	Bolivia	Peru	Ecuador
Region	Alto Madidi	Tambopata	Pastaza
Protected area	Madidi National Park 1,895,740 ha	Bahuaja-Sonene National Park 1,091,416 ha	Kapawi Reserve 700,131 ha
Community	San José de Uchupiamonas (60–70 families)	Native Community Infierno (120–150 families)	58 Achuar communities (hundreds of families)
Ethnicity	Tacana and Quechua	Ese'eja and riberenho	Achuar
Partner	Conservation International (NGO)	Rainforest Expeditions (private tourism company)	Canodros, S.A. (private tourism company)
Ecosystem	Lowland rainforest	Lowland rainforest	Lowland rainforest
Revenue-sharing model	50% to shareholders (74 families); 50% to community-wide fund	Profits divided 60% to community and 40% to Rainforest Expeditions	Monthly concession fee of US$3,800, plus US$10 per tourist
Tourists/year	1,000	5,400	1,800
Beds	24	60	50

development, as identified by Moscardo in Chapter 1 (this volume). These include environmental degradation, conflict, cultural challenges, disruptions to daily life and disillusionment when tourism development fails to deliver promised benefits. Leaders from each of the partnerships, however, also note that becoming involved in tourism management and acting as full partners in their respective ecolodges has introduced new challenges as well. New challenges include separating social dynamics of the communities from business matters of tourism and determining how best and most equitably to divide and distribute tourism profits.

Methods

The *Trueque Amazonico* was a 'south–south' exchange that involved indigenous leaders of three community-based ecotourism partnerships in Peru, Ecuador and Bolivia in 2003 (Stronza, 2005). The aim was to generate grass-roots consensus on best practices for community-based ecotourism. Several community members from each site were involved in every phase of the analysis and exchange. Together with the author, they proposed the idea of carrying out an exchange to the funder, the Critical Ecosystem Partnership Fund. Once funded, six delegates from each site were selected by their communities to participate in three 5-day workshops held in the lodges. Leading up the workshops, national-level coordinators joined the tri-national team. Each lived in the communities for at least 2 months to conduct ethnographic research and semi-structured household interviews among lodge workers and community members. The inquiries focused on social, economic, cultural and environmental changes introduced by ecotourism.

Building on the results of the ethnographic research, the coordinators worked with the community leaders to develop discussion themes and activities for the workshops. Topics of discussion included impacts of tourism on communal resources, strategies for distributing tourism profits fairly and codes of conduct for interacting with tourists. During the workshops, delegates stayed in each others' lodges as tourists, learned each others' behind-the-scenes operations and exchanged insights on the pros and cons of managing tourism in their communities. Community leaders facilitated plenary discussions and focus groups to build consensus on best practices. At the end of the workshops the tri-national team organized press conferences in La Paz and Quito to share lessons learned with wider audiences. Community leaders made appearances on television and gave interviews to radio and print journalists.

Three Ecotourism Partnerships

The three ecolodges – Posada Amazonas, Kapawi and Chalalán – are community-managed, though all began as partnerships with either a private tourism company or conservation NGO. Descriptions of the three partnerships follow.

Community–NGO

Chalalán is the first ecolodge in Bolivia to be entirely community-owned and community-operated. Yet this achievement in communal tourism management began with a partnership in 1998 between an indigenous community, San José de Uchupiamonas, and two global actors, CI and the IDB. San José is a Quechua-Tacana community of 100 families (approximately 630 people) who live within the borders of Bolivia's Madidi National Park. Madidi's 2,000,000 ha encompass mountain cloud forest, dry tropical forest, humid lowland rainforest and savannah. For its high level of species endemism and abundance, Madidi has been identified as a 'biodiversity hot spot' and thus an important focal point for international organizations seeking to make ecotourism an effective tool for conservation and development (Myers *et al.*, 2000).

The IDB invested US$1.45 million in Chalalán. Most of the money was dedicated to capacity building in the community San José. Capacity building entailed working with residents to construct the lodge with local materials and local labour and skills, providing training for staff in hospitality, management and service through on-site experiential learning and rotating shifts and establishing an organizational and legal structure for the company. The project spanned 5 years from inception in 1998 to transfer of full ownership and management to the community San José in 2002. Local leaders from San José said they partnered with the IDB and CI to help protect their resources while also securing their territory and seeking alternatives to development. The operation attracts roughly 1000 tourists per year and generates US$15,000–20,000 per year for San José. Fifty per cent of all profits go to a community fund, which is used primarily for health and education (Stronza, 2006).

Community–private company

The ecolodge, Posada Amazonas, is the product of a joint venture between the Lima-based private tour company, Rainforest Expeditions, and the Native Community of Infierno. Infierno comprises 10,000 ha of communally owned land in the lowland rainforest region of Madre de Dios, in south-eastern Peru (Stronza, 1999). The community was recognized by the Peruvian government as Ese'eja indigenous territory in 1976, but since that time, the population has increased to about 150 families (approximately 500 people) from various cultural backgrounds, including Ese'eja Indians, mestizos from other parts of the Amazon and Quechua-speaking colonists from the Andes. The members of the community signed a 20-year contract in 1996 with Rainforest Expeditions, agreeing to share in the construction, operation and management of Posada Amazonas. The partners also agreed to split profits – 60% to the community and 40% to the company – and to divide the management 50:50.

A critical tenet of the agreement was that community members should be actively involved in the enterprise, not only as staff, but also as owners, planners and administrators; further, they should join Rainforest Expeditions in making decisions about the future of the company as well as providing services for tourists. The partners also agreed that by 2016, the entire operation would pass to Infierno, and the community would have the choice of either continuing to collaborate with Rainforest Expeditions or taking over as proprietors and managers. To prepare for 2016, capacity building in the community has been a priority for both partners.

The lodge features five main cabins with 60 beds, a lobby, hammock area, a dining room with cathedral ceilings of hand-woven thatch and a 40 m canopy tower. It is located on the Tambopata River, near the Bahuaja-Sonene National Park. Like Madidi, this area is famous among international NGOs for its biodiversity, and thus it has been the locus of efforts to make ecotourism a vehicle for conservation. Key wildlife attractions at Posada Amazonas include a population of giant otters and a macaw clay lick. Business-wise, the lodge has been very successful, attracting 7000–8000 tourists per year and generating annual profits upwards of US$100,000, which are divided equally among households in Infierno.

Federation–private company

The Kapawi Ecolodge in the tropical rainforest of Ecuador is a complex of thatched huts, which shoulder a small lagoon on the north side of the Capahuari River, 100 km from the eastern foothills of the Andes. The habitats surrounding Kapawi are diverse and include terre firme and upland terre firme forests, lowland swamps, oxbow lakes and rivers. The lodge consists of 21 cabins that accommodate a maximum of 70 people, including guests and staff. Not coincidentally, it is about the size of a typical village of the Achuar Indians.

Kapawi is the result of a partnership between the Achuar indigenous federation, FINAE, and Canodros, a private tourism company (Rodriguez, 1999). The

Achuar leased the ecolodge's land to Canodros for 15 years, until 2011, sharing benefits and decision making. To build the lodge, all of the capital came from Canodros, and most of the local materials and labour came from the Achuar. In total, Canodros invested US$2 million to build Kapawi and provide financial support to FINAE during the period of construction. The lodge was built by the Achuar in traditional architectural style, combined with low-impact technology, including waste management and recycling, solar energy, biodegradable soaps and four-stroke engines.

The terms of the 15-year agreement stipulated a monthly rent to the Achuar Federation of US$2000, with an increase of 7% per year, based on banks' interest rates on the dollar that year. In 2002, the amount was renegotiated with FINAE to a fixed rent of US$3400 per month. In addition, a US$10 fee is charged to every visitor for the exclusive benefit of the Achuar community. The partners agreed that Achuar participation would be emphasized in every aspect of lodge. Canodros promised to employ a majority of Achuar people and to purchase supplies for the lodge, including food, wood, palms and fibres, from Achuar communities. More broadly, Canodros agreed to pass know-how to the Achuar co-owners through apprenticeship and training in all aspects of lodge management and operation. The company also committed to improve health and education conditions in Achuar territory while at the same time researching other economic options for the Achuar. In exchange, the Achuar agreed to allow access to their lands and to engage in the establishment and management of the lodge. They also assented to restrict their hunting in areas near the ecotourism lodge. By 2011 or sooner, the lodge will pass entirely to the Achuar.

Kapawi opened for operation in April 1996. By 2002, the number of personnel in Kapawi totalled between 55 and 60, including sales, reservations, logistics assistants based in offices in Quito, Guayaquil and Shell, cooks, administrators, guides, boat drivers, waiters, maintenance workers and housekeepers. The Achuar represent a significant (>60%) portion of the staff. Tourists per year average 1000. By 2011, the lodge will have paid a total of US$612,000 in rent, plus an estimated US$150,000–200,000 in tourist fees (Stronza, 2003). These revenues are divided among the federation, FINAE, and 54 Achuar communities (approximately 5000 people), in a region of 7000 km^2.

Bringing Community Leaders Together

Just 10 years ago, the communities involved in each of these partnerships were lacking in both knowledge and ability to develop or manage tourism on their own. In the case of the community of Infierno in Peru, for example, people were missing even a basic understanding of the concept of tourism. When the joint venture was formed in 1996, just a few leaders were instrumental in making the connection with Rainforest Expeditions. During interviews that year, when residents were asked their opinions about the joint venture for ecotourism, many responded with their own query: 'What do you mean by tourism?' Many quickly acknowledged the increasing numbers of outsiders who were plying the rivers in motorized canoes in front of their homes, but what those outsiders were doing, what they had come to see, how they arrived there, or who had invited them, was beyond easy comprehension. Furthermore, though people in Infierno were curious about tourists, most were oblivious to the possibilities, positive or negative, of what tourism might bring to their community.

When the *Trueque Amazonico* began in 2002, each of the three partnerships was in a different stage of capacity building and each community was assuming increasing responsibilities in tourism management. Community leaders clearly had a lot to learn from each other. Chalalán was held up by many as the model, for they had achieved full autonomy from their NGO partner, CI, in 2000. Yet Kapawi was also perceived as a model because the Achuar communities had been able to shield many of their cultural traditions from the Westernizing influences of tourism. Posada Amazonas was admired by participants in the exchange for its sheer scale, the numbers of visitors it annually drew (more than double the other two combined) and its profitability.

When the delegates from each of the partnerships joined in the workshops to discuss their experiences with ecotourism and capacity building, they discussed the following questions:

- How do we define capacity building?
- What processes are we following to build local capacity?
- What opportunities and difficulties have we faced?

Lessons Learned

How do we define capacity building?

The goal of building local capacity is implicit if not primary in many community-based ecotourism partnerships. For the three partnerships in the *Trueque*, the question of how to build local capacity and eventually transfer ownership entirely to the communities was of special interest. Each lodge had been established with the basic premise that communities and their partners could obtain mutual, material benefits from each other if they joined resources and skills to develop ecotourism. The companies could increase profits by gaining access to communal lands, locally managed wildlife populations, cultural resources and the traditional ecological knowledge of local residents. In exchange, the communities could earn directly from tourism by tapping into the marketing expertise, managerial know-how, financial capital and connections with the Western markets of their partners.

Beyond these instrumental ends, however, a critical aim of the partnerships was to use ecotourism as a means for building environmental stewardship and empowering local residents with the skills and resources to achieve their own development goals. For these social reasons that reached beyond standard business goals of tourism development, the ecolodges were financed with the support of multilateral development agencies and banks, such as the Peru–Canada Bilateral Fund, in the case of Posada Amazonas, and the IDB, in the case of Chalalán. The MacArthur Foundation also provided a grant to the Posada Amazonas partnership so that community members could gain preparation for assuming the most technical and skilled positions in lodge management and operation. Also, for these reasons, the partnerships were established with limited durations (5, 15 and 20 years for Chalalán, Kapawi and Posada Amazonas, respectively) and were meant to evolve from the status of partnerships to entirely community-based tourism (CBT) operations. All of this implies that the success of tourism partnerships is often defined by how well communities are prepared to assume full ownership and management within a given period of time – an outcome that depends on effective capacity building.

Yet, the leaders of each partnership described capacity building in different ways. The partners from Kapawi noted: 'It is a gradual process that allows the partial or total delivery of the necessary elements, including abilities, skills, and knowledge that will lead to proper functioning of the business at the level of the community. It entails passing work from one to the other.' The explanation from Chalalán was more about transferring management from the partnership to the community, which they defined as: 'A process of legally and technically expropriating an ecotourism project from one institution to another.'

In the case of Posada Amazonas, the delegates characterized capacity building as: 'A process which, through time, leads to better management of ecotourism.' They did not concur with the others that a 'successful partnership' is necessarily one that results in complete community control over the enterprise. One of the co-owners of the company partnering with Infierno, Rainforest Expeditions, described instead the concept of long-term collaboration. 'There are two players here', he explained, 'the division of roles between the company and community should be smooth and gradual. It should get to a point at which people in the community have learned, and they know what they do better, and the company too puts more emphasis on what they have learned and can do better.' This allows each to assume roles to which they are best suited. 'Strategic alliance', the delegates from Peru decided, is a better concept than 'transfer'. A strategic alliance does not require a culmination or ending, but rather an ongoing, evolving and mutually beneficial relationship for both. Delegates from all three partnerships agreed that the final outcome of capacity building should not necessarily be total autonomy among communities.

What processes are we following to build local capacity?

The community leaders agreed that training and preparation to assume management of the tourism operations should be gradual. Capacity building for the local community and their involvement in the work and business of tourism also should be specified explicitly in a partnership agreement. They recommended beginning with relatively less-skilled staff positions in the lodge and then continuing with increasingly skilled positions, such as in guiding, finances, marketing or management. This stepwise approach allows direct community participation in all aspects of tourism development, even as people are learning and gaining skills and preparing themselves to assume increasing amounts of responsibility in management.

In the 5 years it took to pass full ownership and management of the Chalalán lodge to the community of San José, the partner, CI, brought in consultants, volunteers, researchers of various disciplines, marketing and design experts, conservationists and community development workers from the USA, Bolivia, Peru and elsewhere to help prepare the community to assume control. For example, a landscape architect from the USA provided pro bono support to work with community members in identifying attractions, scouting sites for trails, cabins and waste systems, coming up with a prospectus for the 24-bed lodge, which included blueprints, marketing plans, cost estimates, a construction schedule and a draft itinerary for potential guests, from backpackers to elite birdwatchers.

In another case, a Peruvian biologist helped 20 trainees from San José to become forest guides. The preparation included 6 months of courses that focused on everything from natural history to English language and first aid. One of the guides said that something he learned was simply to stay with the tourists at all times, making sure they did not get lost or hurt. 'They taught us that tourists can't do the same things that we can do' (Hendrix, 1997). Throughout the training, the prospective guides were encouraged to combine their traditional knowledge of the forest with scientific principles of ecology.

Also important to the process of capacity building in San José was a system of apprenticeships. Community members worked at Chalalán and learned while doing. Their salaries were subsidized by the project (funding from the original IDB loan) for the first 2 years. Also, two community members were granted support to travel to La Paz to gain professional training in accounting, administration and marketing. These leaders now assume management responsibility.

In all, it took just 5 years to transfer full control of the lodge from the partnership with CI to the community of San José. The legal deed for the enterprise was transferred in 2001. One of the leaders remarked during the *Trueque* exchange:

> We felt sure of ourselves even though, in reality, we were never really 'ready'. We are still in an ongoing process of learning and overcoming challenges. We sensed we were ready for the transfer because we already had gained some experience in managing tourism on our own, and then we also participated in a lot of training. As for decision-making, our involvement in that increased a bit more gradually.

The consensus among all of three of the lodges was that capacity building should be defined clearly at the start of any tourism partnership, covering first technical skills and activities and services and gradually moving to more skilled or professional roles, such as guiding, administration and marketing. Delegates also indicated that a time frame for each step of the process should be defined clearly by the partners.

More generally, the delegates agreed that transparency is needed throughout all phases of capacity building. They noted that even well-functioning partnerships can benefit from including an intermediary. For example, to make co-management work at Posada Amazonas, the community created a 'Control Committee' in the first year of the joint venture. The ten-member committee is elected every 2 years by the communal assembly and holds monthly meetings with Rainforest Expeditions' staff to make decisions regarding everything from profit reinvestment to administration to marketing and personnel. The committee is also responsible for overseeing Rainforest Expeditions' operations and management and communicating decisions to the rest of the assembly.

While discussing the idea of intermediaries, the delegates determined that an ideal model for community-based ecotourism is one that includes three-way collaboration between a local community, a private company and an NGO. An intermediary can help address expectations the community may have with regard to how ecotourism is addressing – or not – local development needs. As ecotourism cannot serve as the sole source of community development, an intermediary actor can help establish alternative, or 'satellite', projects that complement ecotourism. In the cases of Posada Amazonas and Chalalán, for example, satellite projects have included fish farming, agroforestry, small livestock production and handicraft production.

What opportunities and difficulties have we faced?

An overriding challenge for community leaders associated with their involvement in tourism management was making the transition from a mostly subsistence-based economy to one that depends increasingly on outside markets. Despite initial expectations – and hopes – that ecotourism could generate profits and improve livelihoods for all, all of the *Trueque* delegates acknowledged that tourism was not, and would not be, able to meet everyone's needs.

There are also conflicts between people within the communities who advocate a shift to tourism, and those who choose to continue working in other activities, such as agriculture or hunting, activities that can be in opposition to ecotourism (i.e. local residents hunting wildlife near or in the same areas as other local residents who are guiding tourists on hikes to see wildlife). As an economic alternative, ecotourism has limited opportunities for employment – 15–20 salaried positions in any of the lodges at a time – and even substantial profits (as in the case of Posada Amazonas, US$100,000 per year) are not sufficient to address the full range of local needs. Agriculture and the collection of forest products are integral to peoples' livelihoods in all three communities and would remain so. A challenge is planning how to make agriculture and forest extraction more sustainable for those who continue to rely on those activities for their livelihoods while also making them compatible with ecotourism. In fact, the demand for agricultural and forest products can be enhanced through ecotourism, thus creating complementary economic activities for community members, such as sales of handicrafts and other value-added items crafted from local materials.

There are also social differences that become more marked as some people become increasingly involved in tourism management and others do not. For example, the Chalalán project has strengthened ties with the market economy and Western world. These ties have led to various forms of cultural change in San José. Chalalán leaders in particular are now quite familiar with a variety of concepts that are decidedly Western, including 'quality control', 'market niche', 'cost–benefit analysis' and 'strategic planning'. In addition, there were fundamental challenges in preparing the leaders of San José to assume lodge management over a period of just a few years. Education levels in San José are relatively low: the mean number of years of education completed by 66 adults interviewed in 2003 was 7.8. The learning curve for anyone taking on a new business is steep. In the case of Chalalán, members of San José had to learn how to manage a business while they were also adjusting to a whole new way of earning a living and interacting with each other – from friends, family and neighbours to business partners, employees and managers.

Another challenge that comes with new engagement in tourism is conflict over the distribution of economic benefits and decision-making authority. Delegates noted that it is critical to define who 'partners' and 'shareholders' are in the company. This entails identifying what members contribute or invest in the operation, such as land, work, materials or some other form of capital. In San José, the profits from Chalalán are distributed 50% to shareholders and 50% to a communal fund. That way, even community members who did not originally invest in the construction of the lodge benefit none the less by virtue of the fact they are residents of San José.

The delegates of the *Trueque* also described conflicts that result from the fact that their roles and interactions with others (within their own communities) are shifting in relation to tourism. As people take on new roles as managers, employees, shareholders and service providers, traditional relations between individuals and families have become increasingly contractual in nature. Essentially, the tourism enterprises have begun to intersect with communal and family concerns. To combat this problem, the residents of Infierno decided to organize separate communal meetings – ones that would deal only with matters of tourism and others that would focus on more traditional concerns.

Yet, community involvement in each of the partnerships enabled local residents to overcome many of the challenges that can arise from conventional tourism. Here, the descriptions will shift to just one of the three cases, Posada Amazonas, to provide more detail. Because the local residents of Infierno have gained skills and knowledge to co-manage ecotourism, they have also gained skills and knowledge – and decision-making experience – to overcome many of the challenges inherent to tourism development. These are identified by Moscardo in Chapter 1 (this volume) as environmental degradation, conflict, cultural challenges, disruptions to daily life and disillusionment. While the people of Infierno have not escaped these challenges, they are arguably better prepared than most indigenous communities to manage them. Here the impacts are categorized as economic, environmental and cultural impacts.

Economic impacts

In 2006, the lodge hosted between 6000 and 7000 tourists, a total that generates significant profits for the company and the 154 families of Infierno. In 2004, profits were US$182,583, and US$109,550 went to the community. In 2005, profits increased to US$208,328, and US$124,996 was used for the community. Profits were distributed evenly to families and each household earned approximately US$550 per year. This represents a 25% increase over the average household income families earn through other activities in agriculture, hunting, fishing and forest extraction (Stronza, 2007). Another portion of profits has been used in a communal fund to improve local infrastructure for health, education and transportation. In addition to profits distributed in the community, a rotating pool of workers fills 18 of 21 full-time employment positions at the lodge, including housekeepers, cooks, boat drivers and guides.

Cultural impacts

These have been managed carefully by the partners since the inception of the project in 1996. The lodge is located within the 10,000 ha native territory of Infierno, but all of the infrastructure and activities for tourism are restricted to an area that lies far upriver from the centre of most communal activities. Tourists visit the school and homes only on special occasion, such as when a donation is being made or some kind of controlled interaction with guests has been organized by the community. Otherwise, the community maintains strong codes of conduct, including no unsolicited visits to private homes or communal meetings and no cultural displays or productions for tourists. In a number of ways, tourism in the community has led to a resurgence of cultural pride. Longitudinal ethnographic research since 1996 shows that people have begun to show renewed pride in indigenous culture. Indicators of this are increased efforts to learn indigenous language, stories and songs from elders, heightened interest in presenting indigenous culture to tourists, coupled with debates over intellectual property rights and the adoption of native identity by some non-native members of the community.

Environmental impacts

Communal involvement in Posada Amazonas has also led to improved communal management of forests, lakes and wildlife in the native territory in Infierno. The lodge is located in a 3000 ha communal reserve that is protected by local families, and all hunting, timber harvesting and farming is prohibited within the reserve. Although the regulations are sometimes broken, the community none the less has shown increased willingness and capacity to manage their natural resources for ecotourism and conservation. This has been revealed, for example, when community members have been caught hunting in the reserve. Communal assemblies were called, and people collectively determined appropriate sanctions, such as withholding the hunter's tourism profits for that year. Another example occurred when a logger from another community came to Infierno to harvest a stand of hardwoods located near the communal lake. Though the logger tried coercion and bribes, the community assembly notified regional authorities and had the timber and harvesting equipment expropriated.

Conclusion

Community-based ecotourism is a potentially effective strategy for connecting the business of tourism with local goals of sustainable development and long-term environmental conservation. Because community-based ecotourism is more likely than other forms of tourism to build new skills and leadership in communities, it arguably has better chances of also building environmental stewardship. Community-based ecotourism can deliver economic benefits as well as effective local leadership, and even empowerment. These changes, in turn, are prerequisites for sustaining strong local institutions and strategies for managing and protecting natural resources.

Getting people involved as decision makers enables local residents to translate tourism benefits into broader community goals while also staving off – or at least learning to cope with – negative impacts. In this way, the tourism partnerships described in this chapter have been enabling local residents to overcome some of the most salient challenges associated with tourism development, including environmental degradation, conflict, cultural challenges and disruptions to daily life.

Practical lessons about capacity building from the Kapawi, Chalalán and Posada Amazonas partnerships are fourfold. One is the importance of transparency, clear communication, trust and even written legal agreements, which clearly define responsibilities, goals and timelines for each partner. Potential private and non-profit partners to communities may be eager to initiate the processes of training, building capacity and teaching community leaders how to run a tourism business of their own. Such preparation, however, should ideally work within a context of respecting local leaders, local processes for making decisions, local institutions and local knowledge. Invariably, any effort to work within local approaches to getting things done will take considerably longer than standard Western business practices. Potential partners to communities must factor in the extra time collaborative decision making will require, as this is a prerequisite for making the community-based operation manageable, 'transferable' and ultimately sustainable.

A second lesson is that the concept of capacity building to the point of 'transfer' from company to community is perhaps too short-sighted. Instead, the idea of strategic alliances may be more tenable. The first implies a termination of collaboration, whereas the second focuses on continual expansion of skills and knowledge coupled with increased social understanding and trust on both sides. In these kinds of long-term alliances, a third partner, such as an NGO, an individual or a community board, can be valuable and necessary mediators.

Although ecotourism is often described as an endeavour that has the potential to meet the needs of all members of a community equally, not all members of most communities invest equally in ecotourism. Equal returns to all in the face of unequal investments can lead to conflict and resentment. To ensure that returns are distributed fairly according to investments, company 'partners' or 'shareholders' should be defined clearly. Among community members, fair distribution may entail defining what a resident of the community must do to become a partner, whether it is contributing land, labour or some other form of capital.

Finally, a lesson from all three partnerships is to expect heterogeneity in communities that appear, at least on the surface, or in the beginning, to think and act in unison. Conflicts are likely to emerge, especially as new opportunities and responsibilities are introduced in the context of a new project. The disputes over who participates, who is a partner, who benefits and who pays are inherent to the process of establishing a community-based business, and managing such discussions and conflicts should also be factored in as start-up and fixed costs.

References

Alexander, S.E. (2000) Resident attitudes towards conservation and black howler monkeys in Belize: the community baboon sanctuary. *Environmental Conservation* 27(4), 341–350.

Ashley, C. and Jones, B. (2001) Joint ventures between communities and tourism investors. *Experience in Southern Africa* 3, 407–424.

Belsky, J.M. (1999) Misrepresenting communities: the politics of community-based rural ecotourism in gales point manatee, Belize. *Rural Sociology* 64(4), 641–666.

Bookbinder, M.P., Dinerstein, E., Rijal, A., Cauley, H. and Rajouria, A. (1998) Ecotourism's support of biodiversity conservation. *Conservation Biology* 12(6), 1399–1404.

Denman, R. (2001) *Guidelines for Community-based Ecotourism Development.* World Wildlife Fund International (WWF), Gland, Switzerland.

Epler Wood, M. (2002) *Ecotourism: Principles, Practices and Policies for Sustainability.* United Nations Publications, Paris.

Forstner, K. (2004) Community ventures and access to markets: the role of intermediaries in marketing rural tourism products. *Development Policy Review* 22(5), 497–514.

Hendrix, S. (1997) Bolivia's Outpost of Hope. *Wildlife International* January/February, 12–15.

International Union for the Conservation of Nature (IUCN) (2003) World parks congress recommendation 5.12 approved: tourism as a vehicle for conservation and support of protected areas. Available at: http://www.iucn.org/themes/wcpa/wpc2003/pdfs/outputs/recommendations/approved/english/html/r12.htm

Kiss, A. (2004) Is community-based ecotourism a good use of biodiversity conservation funds? *Trends in Ecology and Evolution* 19(5), 231–237.

Moscardo, G. (2005) Peripheral tourism development: challenges, issues and success factors. *Tourism Recreation Research* 30, 27–43.

Myers, N.R.A., Mittermeier, C.G., Mittermeier, R., da Fonseca, G.A.B. and Kent, J. (2000) Biodiversity hotspots for conservation priorities. *Nature* 403, 853–858.

Rodriguez, A. (1999) Kapawi: a model of sustainable development in Ecuadorean Amazonia. *Cultural Survival Quarterly* 23, 43–44.

Rodriguez, J.P., Taber, A.B., Daszak, P., Sukumar, R., Valladares-Padua, C., Padua, S., Aguirre, L.F., Medellín, R.A., Acosta, M., Aguirre, A., Bonacic, C., Bordino, P., Bruschini, J., Buchori, D., González, S., Mathew, T., Méndez, M., Mugica, L., Pacheco, L.F., Dobson, A.P., Pearl, M. (2007) Globalization of conservation: a view from the South. *Science 10 August 2007* 317(5839), 755–756.

Stem, C.J., Lassoie, J.P., Lee, D.R., Deshler, D.D., Schelhas, J.W. (2003) Community participation in ecotourism benefits: the link to conservation practices and perspectives. *Society and Natural Resources* 16(1), 387–413.

Stronza, A. (1999) Learning both ways: lessons from a corporate and community ecotourism collaboration. *Cultural Survival Quarterly* 23(2), 36–39.

Stronza, A. (2003) *The Kapawi Indigenous-Corporate Partnership for Ecotourism in Ecuador.* Case Number SI-42, Stanford Graduate School of Business, Stanford, California.

Stronza, A. (2005) *Trueque Amazónico: Lessons in Community-based Ecotourism.* Critical Ecosystem Partnership Fund, Washington, DC.

Stronza, A. (2006) *See the Amazon Through Our Eyes: History of the Chalalan Ecolodge.* Conservation International, Washington, DC.

Stronza, A. (2007) The economic promise of ecotourism for conservation. *Journal of Ecotourism* 6(3), 170–190.

West, P. and Carrier, J. (2004) Ecotourism and authenticity: getting away from it all? *Current Anthropology* 45(4), 483–491.

World Bank (2004) Central American indigenous communities to strengthen ecosystem management with US$9 million grant. Available at: http://go.worldbank.org/THTBWWL5T0

Wunder, S. (1999) *Promoting Forest Conservation Through Ecotourism Income? A Case Study from the Ecuadorian Amazon Region.* CIFOR, Bogor, Indonesia.

Yu, D.W., Hendrickson, T. and Castillo, A. (1997) Ecotourism and conservation in Amazonian Peru: short-term and long-term challenges. *Environmental Conservation* 24, 130–138.

9 Enhancing Participation of Women in Tourism

Haretsebe Manwa

Department of Management, University of Botswana, Gaborone, Botswana

Introduction

The United Nations World Tourism Organization (UNWTO) has designated 'Tourism opening doors for women' as the theme for the 2007 Tourism Day celebrations (UNWTO, 2007; http://unwto.org/newsroom/releases/2007/march/women/htm). The question that will be on everybody's mind is whether indeed tourism is opening doors for women. The Millennium Development Goals have outlined a commitment to combat global poverty and hunger (World Bank, 2004). Most developing countries see tourism as an engine for economic development especially of marginal areas (Cattarinich, 2001). These marginal areas are dominated by women with no other forms of livelihood, hence the argument that tourism is indeed opening doors for women. The first section of this chapter contextualizes the position of women in tourism businesses and reasons accounting for their paucity as senior employees in tourism businesses. The second section explores the informal sector and how it has successfully opened doors for women. The chapter concludes by recommending ways of enhancing the participation of women in the tourism industry.

Women in Formal Employment

It is estimated that the tourism industry employs over 200 million people, of whom 70% are women (Marshall, 2001). Gender stereotypes and traditional gender roles are among the most prominent reasons why women and men tend to pursue different occupations and hence horizontal and vertical segregation of labour markets prevail (Mackie and Hamilton, 1993). Gender role stereotyping of jobs is not tourism-specific; rather it seems that the tourism industry is yet another example where traditional gender role stereotyping comes into play (McKenzie, 2007). A gender pyramid prevails in the tourism sector as in other career sectors whereby women occupy positions with few career prospects because it is assumed that they lack managerial traits normally associated with men (Levy and Lerch, 1991; Manwa, 2002). In addition, organizational cultures are averse to women through human resource policies that are hostile to women, for example, less pay for women, long hours and shift work which characterize the hospitality industry (Purcell, 1997; Manwa, 2003; Skalpe, 2007; Parrett, undated).

The following sections address both challenges and opportunities facing women in the formal sector.

Challenges facing women in the formal sector

The literature outlined above has demonstrated the 'glass ceiling' which exists in formal employment in general and is not unique to tourism. This section will highlight some of the challenges women face in formal sector employment.

Women are generally located in jobs stereotypically associated with their nurturing and care-giving role in society. These are jobs at the lower levels of organizations. As a result, women miss out on the opportunity to set the agenda and formulate the long-term strategic focus of the organization. Other factors which militate against women include a lack of the necessary skills and training to enable them to move to senior managerial jobs. Lower-level jobs are generally casual, temporary or part-time jobs which therefore mean that they have to supplement their livelihoods somehow, since they cannot rely on tourism jobs to provide for their full upkeep (Skalpe, 2007).

In several instances, women face the challenge of being taken as part of the product, with only attractive and young females securing employment in the industry as they are perceived to be able to satisfy the sexual needs of the tourists. Studies have shown that women are expected to dress in an 'attractive' manner, to look beautiful (i.e. slim, young and pretty) and to 'play along' with sexual harassment by customers (Griffiths, 1999).

Positive outcomes in the formal sector

Studies in developing countries have shown that tourism creates employment for the less privileged the majority of whom are women (Cattarinich, 2001). Low-level skill requirements and labour intensity mean that many people with low-level skills can be absorbed into the tourism industry. These are people who would otherwise be unemployed. Unlike developed countries, most developing countries do not have social security to provide for needs of the poor. Without the employment tourism brings women would not have any other means of sustaining their livelihood. Therefore, the money earned through tourism has a multiplier effect on the economy, which in turn promotes development.

Other opportunities offered by tourism are its flexible nature in terms of employment, allowing women flexible hours so they continue carrying out their traditional roles. Alternatively, the situation allows women to enter the tourism workforce based on their traditional roles and their own confidence to fulfil them. The nature of work is not as physically straining to women as agricultural or industrial work which, as Hemmati (2000) noted, is dependent on physical strength.

The Informal Sector

The majority of women especially in the developing world are employed in the informal sector as either owners of tourism services or providers of complimentary services to the tourism industry. Most developing countries tend to have a significant informal sector that is dependent on tourism, including arts, crafts, artefacts, basket making, food venting, bead making, pottery, stone and wood carving, batik and other artefacts and services. The informal sector has had a significant impact in opening doors for women. The next section looks at a few case studies where tourism has had a significant positive impact on women, including reducing reliance on men and pressure to get married at a young age (McKenzie, 2007).

Basket making in the Okavango Delta

The Okavango Delta attracts the majority of tourists into Botswana (Mbaiwa, 2004). Women in the delta earn their livelihood through the production of baskets from reeds and beads, as well as from artefacts made from ostrich eggshells. This trade is of economic value and a source of livelihood in the Okavango Delta. It is also a skill that is acquired mostly by women. In the 1980s it provided self-employment to between 400 and 1500 women (Terry, 1994). The economic benefit of the trade is estimated at around P225,140 (US$1 = P8.00). Money acquired from selling the baskets is used for buying food, school uniforms for children and clothing for the family. The driving force behind the success of basket making has been the support from international non-governmental organizations (NGOs) and Botswana Craft Marketing. These organizations have been instrumental in marketing the baskets and the beads both locally and in overseas markets such as Europe.

The Vulamehlo handicraft project

The Vulamehlo handicraft project in Kwazulu Natal in South Africa is aimed at uplifting the living standards of women in Kwazulu Natal (Kruger and Vester, 2001). Successes of the project are attributable to the flexible working arrangements where women can work from home and therefore be able to carry out other traditional role demands. Similar to the Okavango project, the skills are passed on from generation to generation. Kruger and Vester (2001) have also noted that the project has facilitated acquisition of business skills such as financial management and some financial independence. Other benefits include environmental protection, preservation of culture and skills.

The batik project in Jambi, Sumatra, in Indonesia

The batik project in Indonesia does not differ significantly from the other case studies above in that it capitalizes on women's skills and benefits mainly women. More importantly the project has been able to target the most disadvantaged women to be the beneficiaries of the project (Hitchcock and Kerlogue, 2000). In addition, the project has been able to provide needed technical support for example, training, access to capital and marketing of the products.

NGOs have also been instrumental in influencing changes in gender relations in the community by ensuring that women take the lead in project management and benefits accruing from it (Scheyvens, 2000). The Dutch organization RETOUR took the role of a change agent by convincing the community that they would not finance the project unless women took full control of the project, and that potential tourists would only come if women were in charge. Other success stories include the Sandy Beach Women's cooperative in Belize. This project successfully managed to challenge gender role stereotyping, and niche their product towards local culture and environmental sustainability by focusing on nature tourists.

Key factors that led to successful outcomes

Factors which were instrumental towards the successful outcomes in the case studies discussed above can be classified as public–private sector partnerships, gender role stereotyping, presence of an external change agent, capacity building, training and development of niche markets.

The case studies have demonstrated the importance of public–private sector partnerships. These were in the form of private operators facilitating business linkages with women's organizations through outsourcing of some of their services, marketing and acting as a wholesaler of their products. Women's products were guaranteed markets with high return on investments. Other partnerships were with local authorities and national parks. Local authorities spearheaded availability of land for business operation. National park authorities adopted a philosophy of involving local community in natural resource management within the parks and women were therefore able to utilize raw materials for their products which were mainly located within national parks.

Gender role stereotyping prescribes what women's roles are. The case studies show that activities like weaving are exclusively female activities. These skills are passed from generation to generation using the matrilineal line. NGOs have been instrumental in the development of peripheral areas. They took advantage of their respected position in marginal societies to advocate for women empowerment as a precondition to their continued support to tourism businesses which they had helped set up.

Other enabling factors included capacity building and training of women in business skills and decision making. Women attended courses to learn basic business skills like bookkeeping, marketing, even how to speak English so that they can communicate better with their customers. Lastly, tourism is a service and as a result it is very easy to copy, hence the importance of being innovative. The above projects were based on niche markets.

Challenges facing women in the informal sector

Women are most adversely affected by negative environmental impacts of tourism development. For example, the development of the Highland Water scheme in Lesotho has had serious implications on people living along the Malibamatso River in the Highlands of Lesotho. Less water availability downstream of the scheme means that there is now less agricultural output in some villages. Similarly the flooding of some villages' agricultural fields has caused reduced output. Firewood which used to be accessible along the river banks has also been made inaccessible as a result of the flooding of the dam (Manwa, in press) and women now have to travel long distances in search of firewood and water for cooking.

Zimbabwe has also experienced similar problems as characterized by the Communal Areas Management Programmes for Indigenous Resources (CAMPFIRE) projects whereby fencing of parks to stop troublesome animals encroaching on villages did not take into consideration the special needs of women as providers of food and drinking water for the families (Hemingway, 2004). In some instances cited in the literature, while women were responsible for the weaving and production of souvenirs, men still controlled the wholesaling in the urban areas, giving women a smaller share of the profits (Williams, 2002).

Conclusion

The Millennium Development Goals' commitments are geared to reduce poverty. The MDGs are geared to specifically 'Promote gender equality and empower women'.

Women have been shown to make up the majority of the poor especially in marginalized communities. The use of pro-poor strategies (many of which were highlighted in the case studies earlier) can also enhance opportunities for women, for example, when local employment is sought and large businesses adopt positive discrimination in their recruitment of labour by favouring local women. Capacity building is another pro-poor strategy which seeks to remedy skills gaps among the local population. Large corporations could bridge these gaps by offering training in quality, acceptable standards and consistency in their products and service.

Organizations could go further and borrow from good practices from South Africa where the Sun group of hotels has gone a long way in implementing pro-poor strategies, including outsourcing to small, medium or micro enterprises (SMMEs) souvenir supply to the group, furniture, medication and laundry functions (Rogerson, 2006). Large operators could also come up with mentoring programmes for small operators through internship/attachment to their facilities for a specified period for small operators to gain a hands-on experience. Other intervention strategies could include supporting communal- and rural-based tourism, i.e. tourism outside the major tourist circuits. This type of tourism emphasizes people's culture and heritage and it is generally perceived to be environmentally and culturally sustainable. The key players for the success of this type of tourism would include local women who are the custodians of a nation's culture. At the top of pro-poor agenda is empowerment of the poor in deciding their own destiny. NGOs could play a pivotal role in improving women's status in the developing world and marginalized areas (Ashley, 2006).

In addition to these pro-poor strategies governments could enhance local economic linkages by supporting community- and rural-based tourism, developing a quality standards framework and providing marketing guidelines, providing training and mentoring programmes. The central government could also give incentives to the private sector to work with women and disadvantaged communities and to invest in building infrastructure in these remote areas, thereby ensuring that the local people have access to infrastructure and services. Research is still needed, however, to find suitable opportunities to empower women on a case-by-case basis, and the benefits would go a long way towards meeting the Millennium Development Goals and alleviating global poverty and hunger.

References

Ashley, C. (2006) Pro-Poor Tourism Report No.2. Facilitating pro-poor tourism with the private sector. Lessons learned from pro-poor tourism pilots in Southern Africa. Available at: http://www.propoortourism.org.uk/ppt_report2-0206.pdf

Cattarinich, X. (2001) Pro-poor tourism initiatives in developing countries: analysis of secondary case studies. Available at: http://www.propoortourism.org.uk/initiatives_cs.pdf

Griffiths, B. (1999) Women's sexual objectification in the tourism industry in the United Kingdom. In: Hemmati, M. (ed.) *Gender and Tourism: Women's Employment and Participation.* UNED–UK, London.

Hemmati, M. (2000) Women's employment and participation in tourism. *Sustainable Travel and Tourism*, 17–20.

Hemingway, S. (2004) The impact of tourism on the human rights of women in South East Asia. *International Journal of Human Rights* B(3), 275–304.

Hitchcock, M. and Kerlogue, F. (2000) Tourism, development and Batik in Jambi. *Indonesia and the Malay World* 28(82), 221–241.

Kruger, S. and Vester, R. (2001) An appraisal of the Velamehlo handicraft project. *Development Southern Africa* 18(2), 239–252.

Levy, E. and Lerch, P.B. (1991) Tourism as a factor in development implications for gender and work in Barbados. *Gender and Society* 5(1), 67–85.

Mackie, D.M. and Hamilton, D.L. (1993) *Affect Cognition and Interactive Processes in Group Perception.* Academic Press, San Diego, California.

Manwa, H. (2002) 'Think manager, think male': does it apply to Zimbabwe? *Zambezia* 29(1), 60–75.

Manwa, H. (2003) Wildlife-based tourism, ecology, sustainability: a tug-of-war among competing interests in Zimbabwe. *Journal of Tourism Studies* 14(2), 45–54.

Manwa, H. (2008) Tourism in Lesotho. Paper presented at *Sustainable Tourism in Southern Africa: Local Communities and Natural Resources in Transition* Conference, University of Pretoria, 24–26 January.

Marshall, J. (2001) Women and strangers: issues of marginalization in seasonal tourism. *Tourism Geographies* 3(2), 165–186.

Mbaiwa, J.E. (2004) Prospects of basket production in promoting sustainable rural livelihoods in the Okavango delta, Botswana. *International Journal of Tourism Research* 6, 221–235.

McKenzie, K. (2007) Belizean woman and tourism work: opportunity or impediment. *Annals of Tourism Research* 34(2), 477–496.

Parrett, L. (2005) London Thames Gateway Forum. Women in Tourism Employment. A Guided Tour of the Greenwich Experience.

Purcell, K. (1997) Women's employment in UK tourism. In: Sinclair, M.T. (ed.) *Gender, Work and Tourism*. Routledge, New York and London, pp. 33–59.

Rogerson, C.M. (2006) Pro-poor local economic development in South Africa: the role of pro-poor tourism. *Local Environment* 11(1), 37–60.

Scheyvens, R. (2000) Promoting women's empowerment through involvement in ecotourism: experiences from the third world. *Journal of Sustainable Tourism* 8(3), 232–248.

Skalpe, O. (2007) The CEO gender pay gap in the tourism industry – evidence from Norway. *Tourism Management* 28(3), 845–853.

Terry, M.E. (1994) The Botswana handicraft industry: moving from 20th to 21st century. In: Hemos, J. and Ntetas K. (eds) *Botswana in the 21st Century*. Botswana Society, Gaborone, pp. 571–583.

UNWTO (2007) World Tourism Day 27 September 2007. Available at: http://world-tourism.org

Williams, M. (2002) Economic Literacy Series: General Agreement on Trade in Services, Number 5: Tourism and Liberalization, Gender and the GATS. International Gender and Trade Network – Secretariat, Washington, DC.

World Bank (2004) Millennium development goals: eradicate extreme poverty and hunger. Available at: http://www.developmentgoals.org/poverty.htm

10 Entrepreneurship and the Rural Tourism Industry: a Primer

Nancy Gard McGehee[1] and Carol S. Kline[2]

[1]*Hospitality and Tourism Management, Virginia Tech, USA;* [2]*Hospitality and Tourism Administration, North Carolina Central University, USA*

Introduction

Many rural and underdeveloped regions of the world are turning to tourism as a strategy for increasing community wealth. At the same time, community and business leaders are also focusing their attention on entrepreneurship development as part of a sound economic plan. The overlap of these two areas, tourism development and entrepreneurship development, is a burgeoning but critical field to study, expand and support. This chapter will outline the role of entrepreneurs in tourism, differentiate types of entrepreneurs, summarize the methods for measuring entrepreneurial activity, discuss the climate needed for entrepreneurs to succeed and propose an agenda for future research in the area of entrepreneurship in the tourism industry. While much of the discussion will centre on US-based initiatives and examples, many of the concepts transcend geopolitical boundaries.

Entrepreneurship is currently a very sought-after activity within the context of rural tourism development, often because it is an application of many current community development philosophies. Entrepreneurship harmonizes with the philosophy that problems are best solved by solutions generated from inside the community, and that external consultants are not needed to propose successful strategies for economic redemption (HandMade in America, 2003; Putnam and Feldstein, 2003; Morse, 2004). The Rural Sociological Society refers to this as catalytic development, which is mobilizing local talent and resources to create community-economic development from within (2006). Further, entrepreneurship can encourage regional interplay as well as a regional identity when entrepreneurs build off each other's efforts, initiating complementary enterprises. This economic strategy has manifested recently in what is termed cluster or corridor development efforts (Rural Sociological Society, 2006). In addition, entrepreneurship compliments the 'buy local' philosophy and place-based initiatives that have become popular in recent years across a number of industry sectors, including tourism (C.S. Kline, North Carolina, 2007, unpublished data).

 Building Community Capacity for Tourism Development (ed. G. Moscardo)

Although it comes with its own level of uncertainty, entrepreneurial activity is attractive for rural regions because it does not bear the dependency that exists when an outside corporation that has no ties to the community controls a large proportion of employment. Locally based entrepreneurs have a connection with the community and will reinvest financially and emotionally in the local area (Henderson, 2002). As most rural communities do not have a complete business infrastructure, the adaptive and flexible nature of entrepreneurship is also advantageous.

Defining entrepreneurship

The origin of the word entrepreneur comes from the French term *entreprendre*, which means 'to undertake' (Lordkipanidze *et al.*, 2005, p. 788). In the USA, the Kellogg Foundation defines entrepreneurs as people who create and grow enterprises. This definition is thought to include all types of entrepreneurs, including those working outside the private sector. Schumpeter (1934) was an economist credited with initiating popular attention to entrepreneurs. He presumed that entrepreneurs respond to changes and events in their environment. This response could be considered either adaptive or creative, depending on whether the actor changed something within existing practices or created an entirely new practice (Lindgren and Packendorff, 2003).

It is also important to differentiate entrepreneurs from small business owners. While communities want to encourage both groups, their needs are not always the same. The difference is summarized in the following quote:

> An entrepreneur is also a small business owner, but there is an important difference. The entrepreneur envisions something that did not exist before, creates something new or provides an existing product or service in a new way. . . . Being entrepreneurial is an approach to business that relies on innovation, ambition and growth.
>
> (Rightmyre *et al.*, 2004, p. 7)

Likewise, entrepreneurial *traits* and small business managerial *traits* can be differentiated. While an entrepreneur must have business management skills, regardless of the sector in which he/she works, an entrepreneur's intent goes beyond keeping a business's bottom line in the black. 'The primary task in enterprise *creation* (emphasis added) is to make decisions under uncertainty arising from imperfect information; the primary task in enterprise *management* (emphasis added) is to successfully carry out an established plan' (Koh, 1996, p. 35).

Characteristics and motivations of an entrepreneur

According to Koh (2002), personal characteristics and skills of entrepreneurs can include risk-bearing, decision making, market-filling, creativity and facilitation of production factors. Flora (2006) also found non-conformity, self-efficacy, achievement motivation, preference for innovation and low uncertainty avoidance. Other personality traits may include an excessive need for control, need for applause, defensive operations and a sense of distrust (McKenna, 1996).

Of course, not all entrepreneurs are alike. Some have a greater impact upon the community than others. McKercher (1999) as well as Russell and Faulkner (1999, 2004) argued that specific individuals should be credited for creating major impacts in their communities through the development of tourism. McKercher called them rogues and Russell and Faulkner referred to them as chaos-makers, but in essence they are both terms for the entrepreneurs who yield profound influence on the direction of tourism development. In a series of articles ranging from the late 1990s to 2002, Koh asserts that the presence of tourism entrepreneurs in a community largely determines the pace and success of tourism development overall; he even argued that tourism entrepreneurs are the 'persona causa' (Koh and Hatten, 2002, cited in Koh, 2006, p. 117) of tourism development, yet they are overlooked players in tourism development studies. Similarly, Shaw and Williams (1994, p. 132) credited entrepreneurs within the tourism industry as being the 'captains of tourism'.

Differentiating the tourism entrepreneur: legitimate differences or just splitting hairs?

While tourism entrepreneurship parallels many general entrepreneurship principles, there are some distinctions between the two groups. Koh (2002) offers several ways that tourism entrepreneurship differs:

- The tourism product is harder to test before launch because it is intangible.
- Service management skills are needed in tourism as opposed to tangible goods management skills.
- The product is consumed where it is produced, so a tourism entrepreneur is subject to less control over operating and distribution environments.
- Because some tourist attractions are government-operated (e.g. parks and museums), the free market system is not completely at play in tourism, as it may be in other goods industries.
- Outside of agriculture, tourism entrepreneurs are possibly affected by seasonality more than many other industries.

Koh makes a valid argument in differentiating tourism entrepreneurs from general entrepreneurs, but there is still much to be learned and applied from the existing literature on general entrepreneurs. Perhaps recent lessons learned from the demand side of tourism may assist those who study this area. Specifically, attempts have been made for decades to categorize tourists in discrete, supply-based ways (e.g. ecotourists, agritourists, adventure tourists), when in fact tourists do not view themselves in this way at all. Rather, they are tourists who happen to be engaged in adventure activities, eco-activities or rural activities, and they may engage in something quite different within the course of the same vacation. Similarly, general entrepreneurs may be involved in an enterprise that appeals to their neighbours as well as the tourists who visit their community and therefore may not consider themselves 'tourism entrepreneurs'. It is for this reason that both entrepreneurs (a general, all-encompassing term) and entrepreneurs in tourism (i.e. entrepreneurs who may be all or partially involved in the tourism industry) will be referenced throughout this chapter.

Typologies of Tourism Entrepreneurs

While many types of entrepreneurs have been defined and differentiated, an inclusive typology that accounts for all of the existing literature within the context of tourism is elusive. Much of the general literature on entrepreneurship focuses on the individual, rather than on the business. For example, the Kauffman Center for Entrepreneurial Leadership defines and describes a *high-growth entrepreneur* as one who generates benefits socially and economically beyond the direct benefits to him or her. In other words, a high-growth entrepreneur has expanded a business so that it employs others and has a visible economic and social benefit in its community (Kauffman Foundation, 2005). Conversely, Dabson for RUPRI (2006) defines three types of entrepreneurs based on their motivations: lifestyle, survival and serial entrepreneurs. *Lifestyle entrepreneurs* are those who choose self-employment to satisfy personal goals; *survival entrepreneurs* are those who are pushed into entrepreneurship after an unexpected and unwanted loss of employment; *serial entrepreneurs* are those who will create and launch several businesses over a lifetime. While these are each viable types, they are neither an all-inclusive nor a mutually exclusive typology. In another motivation-based example, Hamilton and Harper (1994) describe *latent entrepreneurs* as those who are called to action when they surmise the pay-off of being self-employed is greater than other alternatives (Hamilton and Harper, 1994). Thompson (2002) has a slightly different and somewhat more innovative approach. He characterized two types of entrepreneurs: *private sector* and *social entrepreneurs*. While social entrepreneurs can be found in businesses, social enterprises and the volunteer sector, they use their entrepreneurial talents for caring and helping rather than making money. The social entrepreneur often plays a major role in communities, generating innovations in the public or non-profit sectors. Thompson (2002) outlines 20 categories of causes taken on by social entrepreneurs, including several with direct relevance to the rural tourism industry:

- community festivals;
- historic building preservation;
- fund-raising;
- skills training;
- job creation in deprived areas;
- programmes for youth.

Thompson differentiates social entrepreneurs from their private sector counterparts in that they have a strong commitment to help others. However, they are similar in that they identify a need and related opportunity, bring imagination and vision to the solution, motivate others to the cause and build essential networks, secure the necessary resources, overcome obstacles and handle the inherent risks and include measures for controlling and sustaining the venture (2002). According to Thompson (2002, p. 416), 'they [social entrepreneurs] listen to the voice of the community. Many initiatives are successful because they relate to community needs.' Social entrepreneurship supports a community's amenities and quality of life, which in turn contributes significantly to tourism development as it creates a suitable setting for a tourism destination as well as tourism business start-ups. Specific to an *environmental* proclivity, green entrepreneurs or ecopreneurs (Volery, 2002) are other terms for socially minded visionaries who balance a business model with ecological ideals.

The preceding literature identifying entrepreneur types no doubt played an important role in the development of Koh and Hatten's typology of tourism entrepreneurship (2002). Nine types of tourism entrepreneurs were outlined: inventive, innovative, imitative, social, lifestyle, marginal, closet, nascent and serial. See Table 10.1 for a description of each type. This is a very important step in the study and development of a solid research agenda for entrepreneurship within the tourism industry. However, as with general entrepreneurship classifications, Koh and Hatten's (2002) typology is neither mutually exclusive nor all-inclusive. For example, a tourism entrepreneur may be both a lifestyle entrepreneur and a social entrepreneur. Additionally, we are again seeing a typology based primarily on motivation, although it is important to note that Koh and Hatten did identify three types (inventive, innovative and imitative) as being based on product type. Motivation-based typologies may be a valuable way to differentiate entrepreneurs for some research, but not all. For example, if a community is searching for the optimal entrepreneurial mix as it pertains to the tourism industry, they may be less interested in motivation and more concerned with enterprise type.

Measuring the Supply of Tourism Entrepreneurs

The challenging task of tracking entrepreneurial activity has gained significant momentum in the last decade across all types of enterprises. Typical measures include number of new businesses created, number of self-employed individuals, number of jobs created, change in regional economic growth, number of new loans and income of the self-employed. In addition to business births, business deaths have also been monitored to provide a realistic picture of the net gain or loss of a community's economic condition (Henderson, 2006). Entrepreneur enterprises are typically categorized as nascent (less than 3 months), new (3–42 months) or established (42 months or older).

A number of organizations in the last several years have undertaken the measurement of entrepreneurial activity. The most well-known and currently the most comprehensive report on entrepreneurship, the Global Entrepreneurship Monitor (GEM), is managed by Babson College and London Business School and funded by the Ewing Marion Kauffman Foundation (www.gemconsortium.org). The GEM was started in 1999, at that time estimating the entrepreneurial activity in ten countries (Minniti *et al.*, 2005a). To date, the GEM includes 35 countries and aims to answer three questions:

- Does the level of entrepreneurial activity vary between countries and, if so, by how much?
- Are differences in entrepreneurial activity associated with national economic growth?
- What national characteristics are related to differences in entrepreneurial activity? (Minniti and Bygrave, 2003).

Table 10.1. Koh and Hatten's (2002) typology of tourism entrepreneurs.

I. Product-based typology	Definition	Example
Inventive tourism entrepreneur	One whose commercialized product is truly new to the tourism industry	American Express travellers cheques
Innovative tourism entrepreneur	One whose commercialized product is not new but is an adaptation of an existing product or the discovery of a previously untapped market	Orbitz.com
Imitative tourism entrepreneur	One whose product is not significantly different from existing products	A franchise hotel or restaurant that is not new to the marketplace but may be new to the community
II. Behaviour- or motivation-based typology	**Definition**	**Example**
Social tourism entrepreneur	One who starts a non-profit touristic enterprise	A regional tourism industry association
Lifestyle tourism entrepreneur	One who starts an enterprise in order to support a desired lifestyle; generally, these types of tourism entrepreneurs have no desire to 'grow' the business beyond a certain size	B&B owner and avid kayaker who specializes in guided kayak adventures
Marginal tourism entrepreneur	One who starts and operates a tourism enterprise within the informal and peripheral sector of the tourism industry	Unlicensed roadside farmer's market
Closet tourism entrepreneur	One who operates a tourism enterprise while maintaining a full-time job as an employee elsewhere	A high school teacher who offers guide services during the summer
Nascent tourism entrepreneur	One who is in the process of developing a tourism enterprise	An individual developing a business plan or in the process of attracting capital investment
Serial tourism entrepreneur	One who has founded a succession of tourism enterprises, either due to failure of the previous enterprise or the evolution of one enterprise into another form	Tourism enterprise A becomes a corporation, whereupon the serial entrepreneur sells the business and starts tourism enterprise B

The GEM explores both opportunity-based and necessity-based new and nascent activity as it relates to demographic factors such as age, gender, education, household income, ethnic background, access to physical capital, financial capital, education and training and four 'attitudinal factors' (is there an opportunity seen, perception of one's own skills, fear of failure and personal familiarity with an entrepreneur). In 2005, the GEM began tracking established businesses, those in existence for 42 months or more, noting that the conditions that are ripe for starting a business may differ from those to sustain and grow a business. Also, in 2005, the GEM began clustering countries according to their income level (high or medium) and gross domestic product (GDP) growth level (high or low). Interestingly, a pattern exists that medium-income countries have higher business start-up rates than high-income countries, while the established business rates are just slightly higher in high-income countries. Also of note, entrepreneurial activity in all G7 countries over the last 4 years tended to be concentrated in the business-to-business industry sector (23–25%) and consumer-services industry sector (42–51%). In addition to national accounts, GEM analysts examined niche populations such as in the High-Expectation Entrepreneurship Report (Autio, 2005), Report on Women and Entrepreneurship (Minniti *et al.*, 2005a) and Social Entrepreneurship Monitor UK 2006 (Harding, 2006).

There are also a number of tracking mechanisms for general entrepreneurship in the USA, including the Kauffman Index and the measures from the Center for the Study of Rural America (CSRA). Using a matched sample of data from the US Census Bureau, the Kauffman Index baselines the number of adults, ages 20–64, who do not own a business as their main job. From there, the Index tracks the rate of business births per month by these individuals yielding the per cent of non-business owners who start a business each month. The Kauffman Index notes the gender, race, nativity, age, education, geographic region and industry sector. Between 1996 and 2004, the average Index was 0.36%, representing 550,000 new businesses started in the USA every month (Kauffman Foundation, 2005).

The CSRA is an arm of the Federal Reserve Bank of Kansas City which monitors many types of economic trends in rural America, including entrepreneurial activity (www.kansascityfed.org/RegionalAffairs/Regionalmain.htm). The CSRA measures entrepreneurship using two indices: entrepreneur depth and entrepreneur breadth (Low, 2004). Entrepreneur breadth is a function of self-employment to overall employment. Entrepreneur depth is measured in two ways: by entrepreneur income and a 'value-added' ratio of entrepreneur income to receipts. Each of these measures is offered for each of the 3000+ counties in the USA as a localized look at entrepreneurial activity that is helpful for community leaders to track over time.

While the above indicators are extremely useful in understanding the big picture of general entrepreneurial activity, they are limited to traditional outputs, are mega in scope, and largely relate to private sector ventures. These limitations have been cited in entrepreneurship literature as well as being the recent focus of discussion at the conference entitled 'Exploring Rural Entrepreneurship: Imperatives and Opportunities for Research', held in Washington, DC, in October 2006. In a presentation regarding entrepreneurs in creative industries (often a valuable component of the rural tourism industry), Rosenfeld (2006) noted that creative jobs are often under-represented in census-type counts because they are not reported, or are misreported or embedded in other industries. When he undertook an inventory of artists and performers in the Toe River Valley of North Carolina, a range of results occurred, concluding that between zero and 388 artists were employed in the region, depending on the organizational source used (2006). At the same conference, Pages (2006) noted the unrealistic way that entrepreneurial activity was measured in regards to time, stating that short-term job creation is simply not the purpose of entrepreneurial development programmes. He aptly compared the annual measurement of entrepreneurial activity to measuring a person's ability to pay a loan on monthly basis (2006). Closing comments at the conference included a call for new measurements of entrepreneurial activity, entrepreneurial climate (e-climate) and entrepreneurial process that fit the diversity and reality of the rural context (Markley, 2006).

Local, niche and social entrepreneurial activities are absent in the majority of reports on general entrepreneurial activity. These are all issues that are problematic for entrepreneurs in the rural tourism industry, where a venture might be a seasonal job, or the bulk of entrepreneurial activity may be manifest in the public and non-profit sectors. As a result, large portions of entrepreneurial activity within rural tourism are left uncounted.

Supporting Tourism Entrepreneurs

Rural disadvantage: can it be overcome?

Dr Deborah Markley, co-director of the Center for Rural Entrepreneurship in the USA (2007; http://www.ruraleship.org/index_html?page = content/about_the_center.htm), notes that rural entrepreneurs may be at a disadvantage for a number of reasons. For example, opportunities for financial capital may be limited, local politics may interfere with entrepreneurial freedom, there may be a lack of entrepreneurial role models or a support network, or the overall culture may be too conservative to foster change (Genera, 2005). Other potential shortcomings of rural areas include access to density of suppliers and customers, labour markets and transportation systems (Acs and Malecki, 2003).

While these socio-economic hindrances can be daunting, Flora and Flora (1993) argue that there is evidence of success among rural communities who demonstrate a strong Entrepreneurial Social Infrastructure (ESI). ESI includes three elements: symbolic diversity, resource mobilization and quality of networks. Symbolic diversity involves not only the acceptance of conflict, but also its full acceptance as a vital part of 'constructive controversy' (1993, p. 48) that is necessary for healthy communities and an environment ripe for entrepreneurial growth. Anyone who has worked with rural communities that are interested in tourism entrepreneurship development can relate to the existence of controversy – and to the observation that most successful communities recognize and even embrace it. Resource mobilization, the second component of ESI, originates in the social movement literature and implies that community success can only come through the pooling of local resources, the sharing of risk and a general collective investment in the community. Again, entrepreneurship in the rural tourism industry is often founded on the pooling of resources in innovative ways, including barter, cooperatives or collectives. Flora and Flora (1993) label the third component of ESI as quality networks: 'Quality networks include establishing linkages with others in similar circumstances and developing vertical networks to provide diverse sources, both within and outside the community, of experience and knowledge' (p. 43). Often successful tourism Destination Management Organizations (DMOs) located in rural communities may act as conduits for quality networks for all types of tourism enterprises, including those with an entrepreneurial bent.

In addition to the development of ESI, Flora (1997) and Flora (2004) have also created a model that streamlines the varied models of community development into seven forms of capital. Along with the more traditional elements of financial capital, human capital and built capital, they include four other less common types: political capital, social capital, natural capital and cultural capital. Flora and Flora argue that each community possesses a unique mix of the various forms of capital. In order for communities to thrive, they must first determine their overall goals, and then work to match the various capitals with those goals. While the model was designed for overall community development, it most certainly can be used when an overall community goal includes entrepreneurial tourism development. For example, if a community has a primary goal of fostering a climate for healthy entrepreneurship that is based on local heritage, then their cultural capital must be strong, but perhaps strong financial capital is not as necessary. Together, the various types and levels within each form of capital create an overall economic environment, or climate.

Entrepreneurial climate

Just as plants need specific soil in which to thrive, entrepreneurs need a certain environment to nurture their growth. The characteristics of this environment are as important to identify as the characteristics and supply of the entrepreneurs themselves. A number of factors comprise the environment or 'climate' needed for entrepreneurs to succeed and these influential factors occur at many levels: macro (international and national), meso (regional) and micro (local, firm, family, individual) (Bryant, 1989). Examples of factors existing in the macro e-climate are demographic trends, in-migration and out-migration, economic surges and downturns, unemployment rates, interest rates, national political priorities, market/trade policies, technologies acquired and cultural norms. National and cultural factors are key building blocks for entrepreneurial development in that they play an enormous role in access to market, infrastructure, training, motivation and productivity. Meso e-climate examples might include seasonal conditions, transportation networks and historical industries. Elements of micro e-climate are currently receiving the most attention in economic development circles. Therefore, a more detailed discussion of this category follows.

A key aspect of the micro e-climate is flexibility. Entrepreneurs are linked to instability and flux in that this is their preferred operating environment (Faulkner and Russell, 1997; Genera, 2005). Innovative activity can only emerge when the environment is malleable or vulnerable to change as opposed to a rigid, corporate or highly regulated community environment.

At the CSRA (located in the USA) conference entitled 'Growing and Financing Rural Entrepreneurs', Sampson stated that 'policy's role is to help regions create an entrepreneurial ecosystem' (Drabenstott *et al.*, 2003, p. 77). Sampson elaborated that this ecosystem should consist of education and training, recognition programmes, networks in many directions, access to capital, infrastructure and institutional support (Drabenstott *et al.*, 2003). In a series of articles released in mid-2006, CSRA provided snapshots of conditions that may play a role in building an entrepreneurial ecosystem by measuring and mapping *regional asset indicators*, which are abstract qualities thought to contribute to a nurturing environment for innovation. These indicators are found at varying degrees in communities and could help explain why some communities are entrepreneurial hot spots. Examples of regional asset indicators developed to date are Human Amenities, Creative Workers, Infrastructure, Innovation and Wealth Indicators. Counties with more Human Amenities have access to health care, scenic appeal, restaurants and a variety of recreation and entertainment opportunities. The Creative Workers Index measures professions that require a high degree of creativity, but excludes those creative jobs that must be present in any community, such as teachers and health care professionals. The Infrastructure Index measures highway operation expenditures, commercial aircraft traffic and high-speed Internet access. For the Innovation Index, CSRA counts the number of patents and Wealth Indicators are computed using elements of residential real estate, agricultural real estate and financial investments (Low *et al.*, 2005; Center for the Study of Rural America, Federal Reserve of Kansas City, 2006). While the measures themselves are dependent on secondary data collected, the compilation of these data to form scales of abstract environmental qualities is quite an innovative undertaking. Further, the data are mapped on a county-by-county basis, allowing for comparison at a local level. The regional asset indicators are a good start in explaining trends in entrepreneurial activity and will be useful to communities to track longitudinally. CSRA has used their indicators of regional assets to examine their effects on entrepreneurial breadth and depth.

The micro e-climate is of particular interest to business and community leaders, because it can be more easily manipulated than regional or national conditions. Micro e-climate is comprised of many elements that can be divided into broad categories. After each category listed below, a few example elements or descriptors are provided:

- Physical infrastructure – roads, affordable and available real estate, water and sewer services, Internet access.
- Financial infrastructure – flexible and inclusive of lending programmes, community project funds, financial literacy assistance.
- Business support services – legal, tax and accounting services, marketing and printing services.
- Networking – opportunities to network with other entrepreneurs and seasoned business owners, various segments of the community, venture capitalists, employees and markets.
- Human resources – the quantity and quality of labour.
- Education and training – formal classes on entrepreneurship and business management offered in secondary institutions and colleges, informal workshops to address industry-specific issues, internships and mentoring programmes.

- Organizational capacity – the number and effectiveness of non-governmental organizations working in the community to enhance quality of life.
- Governance/leadership – the level that government is responsive to new/ small business, free-flowing information, regional thinking, tax structures that are favourable to new or expanding businesses, leadership that equally supports urban and rural populations.
- Marketing – local business mindset to pursue markets both local and beyond and to take advantage of trends and new marketing strategies.
- Quality of life – attractiveness of area, stewardship of natural resources, affordable housing, affordable health care, low crime, recreational and cultural opportunities, family-friendly activities.
- Community and cultural norms – progressive environment open to change and supportive of creative professions, 'buy local' mentality, sense of community identity, cooperative and celebratory community spirit.
- General context – the size of the community population, the diversity of the population, proximity to urban areas.

Community and cultural norms represent one of the most abstract of e-climate categories. A community culture that supports entrepreneurship could mean many things. In addition to the items above, a brief survey of e-climate literature revealed these key descriptors of a supportive community culture:

- Community media that represents all interests.
- Programmes that publicly celebrate entrepreneurs and small businesses.
- Community understanding and appreciation of entrepreneurship, its cycles, potential for failure and need for anonymity.
- Acceptance of controversy as normal.
- Leadership that is broadly shared in community.
- Economic development efforts are widely supported by community and institutions.
- Development efforts are depersonalized and community focus is on process.
- Willingness to tax oneself for maintenance of community infrastructure.
- Fair treatment within community/inclusiveness of various ethnicities.
- Assimilation of new residents.
- Environment that supports young adults in business.
- General community belief in reinvesting in community.
- Community residents with generally positive, can-do, problem-solving attitudes.

(Flora and Flora, 1988, 1993, 1997; Lerner and Haber, 2000; Koh, 2002; Community Policy Analysis Center, 2003; Corporation for Enterprise Development & W. K. Kellogg Foundation, 2003; Bolton and Thompson, 2004; Pages and Markley, 2004; Chatman and Johnson, 2005, unpublished data; Minniti *et al.*, 2005a; Rural Sociological Society and the National Coalition for Rural Entrepreneurship, 2006.)

Clearly, the 12 e-climate categories are not mutually exclusive but can overlap, contradict and influence one another. But unlike other industries, in tourism, a savvy destination marketing organization must be a part of the environment in order to maximize the assets of the area and draw in visitors, essentially bringing a tourism entrepreneur's customers to them. This element of e-climate might fall under 'organizational capacity' or 'business support services'. Also needed for entrepreneurs in tourism are supportive resident attitudes towards tourism itself. And finally, there are e-climate elements that are critical to tourism, that otherwise may be only marginally important to dissimilar industries. Quality of life, community culture and general contextual elements are the foundation of the tourism destination. Likewise, the organizational capacity of the destination would influence the quality of life and culture. These elements, manifested in the very *feel* of the place, the uniqueness, the public art scene, the visible variety of pubs and coffee shops, the landscaping or planning of the streets, offer an impression of the destination to visitors long before they experience the entrepreneur's tourism product.

Of particular interest is the fact that visitors come to the product source to purchase their tourism wares, thus entering into the e-climate where the entrepreneur operates. For example, the idea that visitors penetrate and experience the same environment that supports the entrepreneur is part of HandMade in America's success in drawing visitors to the studios and galleries in rural western North Carolina (www.handmadeinamerica.org). This truly sets tourism apart in its dependency on the e-climate, not only as a supporting mechanism for the operations of the tourism entrepreneur, but also as part of the 'storefront' of the operation. While other industries may distribute their goods away from the community, or offer a service that is deliverable over space, tourism entrepreneurs depend on their village, town, city or region to provide the backdrop for their business. For this reason, the tourism industry is even more vulnerable than others to e-climate.

Measuring e-climate

To improve e-climate, stakeholders must first assess the current state of the community before implementing policy or programmatic improvements. The evaluation of e-climate is in its infancy, likely due to its expansiveness and difficult-to-measure components. While some of the tangible factors of e-climate such as number of training programmes or quality of roads can be corroborated with secondary data, the intangible factors such as sense of community identity cannot.

In 2006, Kline created a scale to measure the e-climate of several counties in North Carolina, a state located in the south-eastern USA. The intent was to explore a correlation between counties that had a supportive climate for entrepreneurs and the status of the tourism industry in that county. The scale used was adapted from two instruments forged in the USA. The first came from the Rural Entrepreneurship Initiative created by the Community Policy Analysis Center (CPAC) out of the University of Missouri (2003). After field testing the instrument, the CPAC team now offers it as an appendix in the manual 'Growing Entrepreneurship from the Ground Up: A Community-based Approach to Growing Your Own Business' (Rightmyre *et al.*, 2004) as well as an online questionnaire at http://www.mrdp.net/RuralEntrepreneurshipInitiative/tabid/66/Default.aspx. The second source was the Energizing Entrepreneurs Programme (E2) developed by the Center for Rural Entrepreneurship (Rural Policy Research Initiative, undated).

E2 is also a resource for communities that would like to expand entrepreneurial activity by creating the right climate and assembling the necessary resources for existing and future entrepreneurs (http://www.energizingentrepreneurs.org/). Kline discovered the e-climate factors that contributed most to the success of tourism in the study counties were the natural resources, business services, physical infrastructure, current economic situation of the county and proximity to urban areas (C.S. Kline, North Carolina, 2007, unpublished data).

The Council for Entrepreneurial Development has posted the results of their Entrepreneurial Satisfaction Survey (2007) on the web, which includes an importance-performance scale of 28 key factors needed by entrepreneurs to thrive (www.cednc.org/resources/reports_and_surveys/entrepreneurial_satisfaction_survey/). Certainly, these instruments are culturally biased and the results apply only to the particular region of study. In the coming decade, there will be an increase in the assessment of e-climate factors, tools will be refined and become more sophisticated and new applications will be discovered relating to e-climate's impact on tourism development.

Improving e-climate

There are many resources for communities who wish to improve their e-climate and much of it is extremely relevant to entrepreneurship within the tourism industry. Stakeholders wishing to advance the entrepreneurial status of their community only have to spend a few minutes searching the Web to find that the number of service providers and programmes aimed at assisting entrepreneurs is staggering. A few key examples follow. On the global level, the Organization for Economic Cooperation and Development (2007; www.oecd.org) has documented an exhaustive list, organized by country, of conferences, programmes and publications that are designed to assist both entrepreneurs and service providers. The OECD's Centre for Entrepreneurship, SMEs and Local Development organizes its resources into three main programmes: (i) Local Economic and Employment Development Programme; (ii) Small and Medium-sized Enterprises (SME) and Entrepreneurship; and (iii) Tourism. The United Nations World Tourism Organization (2007; http://www.world-tourism.org/) also addresses entrepreneurship, although their programmes and resources can be found primarily embedded in the section on Regional Activities.

An example of a multinational initiative would be the train-the-trainers curriculum in *The Entrepreneur in Rural Tourism* developed by the Rural Tourism International Training Network (2007; http://www.ruraltourisminternational.org/). This network works with the European Federation for Farm and Countryside Tourism as well as the European Centre for Eco Agro Tourism. On national and regional levels, the governmental department of Economic Development and Tourism located in the Western Cape of South Africa has developed the web site 'How we can support your tourism business' and offers an annual award to the Emerging Tourism Entrepreneur of the Year (2007; www.capegateway.gov.za/eng/your_gov/97842). The Singapore Tourism Board also offers awards to the Tourism Entrepreneur of the Year and the New Tourism Entrepreneur of the Year (Singapore Tourism Board Tourism Entrepreneur Awards, 2007; http://www.tourismawards.com/video.htm), as do many national tourism boards. An analysis of the US Department of Agriculture Current Research Information System database found that most of the entrepreneurial research and outreach programming is conducted through the four Regional Rural Development Centers (2007; http://srdc.msstate.edu/about/rdmap.htm); the national agency Rural Policy Research Initiative (2007; www.rupri.org); university colleges of business, management and economics; land-grant universities' research and extension programmes; and non-profit, community-based organizations (Zuiches, 2006). As an example of a state- or provincial-level programme is the *Resources to Assist Tourism Entrepreneurship in your Community* online offered by the state of Wisconsin, USA (Community Toolbox: Resources to Assist Tourism Entrepreneurship in your Community, 2007; http://www.uwex.edu/ces/cced/economies/tourism/index.cfm).

In addition to the resources listed above, there are rich resources available for those interested in entrepreneurship within the academic literature. Suggestions for improving e-climate from this group include providing networking opportunities, offering recognition of entrepreneurs, growing a 'pipeline of entrepreneurs' by including youth and young adults, encouraging service providers to collaborate, offering training programmes based on local needs, providing a range of financing options, electing officials who 'think regionally' and improving physical infrastructure when possible (Lyons, 2003; Pages and Markley, 2004; Rightmyre *et al.*, 2004; Low *et al.*, 2005; Dabson for RUPRI, 2006).

Specific to entrepreneurship in tourism, Koh has promoted a two-pronged approach that includes: (i) increasing the supply of entrepreneurs through training; and (ii) cultivating an environment to support them. He has proposed that these two factors, which he refers to as the supply of entrepreneurial people (SEP) and the quality of entrepreneurial climate (QEC), would significantly affect how tourism develops within a community, i.e. the type, scale, form, enterprise birth rates and impact in which tourism develops. He offers examples of practical programmes that might be initiated to support both SEP and QEC:

- creating a public awareness programme on the benefits of tourism industry which includes training on the opportunities within tourism;
- offering tourism entrepreneur/business/hospitality skills training at academic institutions;
- establishing advisory/technical assistance programmes at existing businesses much like the SME Collaborative Research (SCORE) programme;
- searching for regional financial investment system that supports small businesses by offering loans to micro-enterprises;
- lobbying local government to consider policies, tax incentives and government programmes that support tourism-related small business;
- celebrating/honouring tourism entrepreneurs in the local media;
- establishing mentoring/shadowing with successful tourism entrepreneurs.

Koh's work, as well as the work of those cited above, has provided a great deal of information for communities looking to develop and improve their potential for entrepreneurial opportunities with the tourism industry. Certain community climates are more supportive of entrepreneurial activity and thereby reap the rewards of entrepreneurial thinking and action. Policy makers and service providers are increasingly recognizing entrepreneurship as the economic driver that will keep nations strong in a global marketplace. Entrepreneurship in tourism indeed has a 'place at the table' in the future global economy.

Propositions for a Research Agenda in Tourism Entrepreneurship

This chapter draws together valuable research and information useful for entrepreneurs involved in the rural tourism industry from several different areas of literature, including community development, rural development, general entrepreneurship and tourism entrepreneurship. The chapter began with the presentation of a definition of entrepreneurship, a review of the characteristics and motivations of entrepreneurs and a discussion of whether differentiating the tourism entrepreneur from the general entrepreneur was useful and/or necessary. This last component of the introduction presents an important starting point for the next phase of research in entrepreneurship:

> **RQ1:** What are the differences and similarities between general entrepreneurial activity and more specific tourism-related entrepreneurial enterprise? Are there sufficient differences between general entrepreneurship and entrepreneurship within the tourism industry to warrant its own separate line of research?

Obviously, for some researchers (Koh, 1996, 2006; Koh and Hatten, 2002; Brunner-Sperdin and Peters, 2004), the answer is yes, but additional research is necessary before this question can be definitively answered. Perhaps, upon closer inspection, a more appropriate question would involve the examination of entrepreneurship overall and the varying degrees in which any variety of enterprises may be involved in tourism. For example, an artist may have a large online following, but a portion of sales may come from devotees travelling near the artist's studios who wish to meet the artist and make purchases directly. Likewise, a local winery or brewpub whose product is exported away from their home community may also attract a following of visitors. Sometimes even the original location or corporate office of an entrepreneur becomes a tourist attraction in its own right, such as the garage where software icon Bill Gates first began his work. Thus, a second research directive is suggested:

> **RQ2:** How can various forms of entrepreneurial activities, including those in the realm of social entrepreneurship, be familiarized within the tourism industry as a valuable niche market worth considering, and subsequently encouraged and supported?

The next section of the chapter dealt with identifying the various types of entrepreneurs. While the bulk of existing research in entrepreneurial typologies is found in the general entrepreneurship literature, some important work has been conducted in the context of tourism. However, typologies have focused primarily on behaviour or motivation of the entrepreneur, while very little work was found to focus on the product or the enterprise's position as part of an ideal entrepreneurial mix within a community. From this finding the next research question was developed:

> **RQ3:** How can communities determine their optimal mix of entrepreneurial activity, and how can they determine what proportion of that mix should include tourism enterprises?

One commonality that exists between the tourism industry and entrepreneurial enterprises of all kinds is the difficulty in capturing a complete and exhaustive picture of the existing supply. Both have considerable components that exist in the margins of the economic reporting measures. Both consist of enterprises that may only partially fall within the parameters of strict definitions of entrepreneurship or tourism. Finally, both are attractive to groups traditionally excluded from, or under-represented in, corporate industry. These matters were discussed in the section on issues involved in measuring the supply of tourism entrepreneurs. As a result, the following research question begs to be explored:

> **RQ4:** How can new measurements of entrepreneurial activity be developed and implemented that allow for its uniqueness, and be particularly inclusive of those forms of enterprise that are involved in the tourism industry?

The final, and perhaps most important, section in the chapter centred around the difficulties faced by often economically strapped rural communities in their efforts to support entrepreneurs and the potential solutions for those communities. Utilization of ESI, assessment of the various capitals within a community and maximizing the e-climate of a community are all useful tools for communities to utilize to assess and improve their potential for entrepreneurial success of all types. However, anyone who has spent time in the field knows that while the keys to a community's success may be relatively easy to assess and present, in the final analysis, those rural communities that are successful often possess an intangible ability to engage in cooperation and resource mobilization while embracing conflict. It cannot be taught, nor can it be 'consulted' from the outside, it must come from within. However, researchers can locate case studies and best practices, as well as analyse cases of how *not* to do it, and can promote and disseminate that information. This is where the process of entrepreneurship development, both at the individual level and within a community, comes into play. Therefore, the authors ask a final, three-part research question:

> **RQ5:** At both the individual and community levels, what is the entrepreneurial process? How are information search, information assimilation and decision making approached by the tourism entrepreneur within his/her operating environment? What is the optimal combination of environmental elements needed for an entrepreneur in tourism to succeed?

The entrepreneurial process would seem to be a thread linking the individual characteristics of an entrepreneur, the internal and external motivations of an entrepreneur, the climate and community that the entrepreneur operates within, and the outputs of the entrepreneur.

The tourism industry with its breadth of niches and variety of experiences is a fertile ground for entrepreneurs to invest their energy. As the world's largest industry, it shows no signs of slowing in growth, particularly in rural communities. Additionally, entrepreneurs will continue to emerge as key stakeholders around the globe, especially in economically developing nations and rural regions. It is vital for policy makers, educators and service providers to recognize that 'the task ahead is to make our efforts more community-driven, regionally oriented, entrepreneur-focused, and continuously learning' (Corporation for Enterprise Development & W. K. Kellogg Foundation, 2003, p. 59).

References

Acs, Z.J. and Malecki, E.J. (2003) Entrepreneurship in rural America: the big picture. Main Streets of Tomorrow: Growing and Financing Entrepreneurs conference proceedings. Available at: www.kansascityfed.org/PUBLICAT/MainStreets03/RC03_Acs_Malecki.pdf

Autio, E. (2005) Global Entrepreneurship Monitor: High Expectation Entrepreneurship 2005 Summary Report, Babson College and the London School of Business. Available at: www.gemconsortium.org

Bolton, B. and Thompson, J. (2004) *Entrepreneurs – Talent, Temperament, Technique*, 2nd edn. Elsevier Butterworth-Heinemann, Oxford.

Brunner-Sperdin, A. and Peters, M. (2004) Importance and measurement of entrepreneurial quality and processes in tourism. *Journal of Quality Assurance in Hospitality & Tourism* 5(1), 73–90.

Bryant, C. (1989) Entrepreneurs in the rural environment. *Journal of Rural Studies* 5(4), 337–348.

Center for the Study of Rural America (CSRA), Federal Reserve of Kansas City (2006) Regional asset indicators. Available at: www.kansascityfed.org/ruralcenter

Center for Rural Entrepreneurship (undated) Community toolbox. Available at: www.energizingentrepreneurs.org/

Community Policy Analysis Center (CPAC) (2003) Rural Entrepreneurship Initiative Report. Available at: www.mrdp.net/portals/0/REI%20Guidebook_web.pdf

Corporation for Enterprise Development (CFED) & W. K. Kellogg Foundation (2003) Mapping rural entrepreneurship. Available at: http://www.energizingentrepreneurs.org/content/cr_5/2_000049.pdf

Dabson, B. for RUPRI (2006) Why Entrepreneurship? A Vision and Policy Pointers for Maine. Powerpoint presentation at Enterprise Development Works Policy Forum, Maine. Available at: www.rupri.org/Forms/dabson060106.pdf

Drabenstott, M., Novack, N. and Abraham, B. (2003) Main Streets of Tomorrow: Growing and Financing Rural Entrepreneurs – A conference summary. Center for the Study of Rural America, Federal Reserve of Kansas City. Available at: www.kansascityfed.org/PUBLICAT/MainStreets03/RC03_Summary.pdf.

Faulkner, B. and Russell, R. (1997) Chaos and complexity in tourism: in search of a new perspective. *Pacific Tourism Review* 1(1), 93–102.

Flora, C. (2006) Are entrepreneurs born or made? *Rural Development News* 28/4. Available at: http://www.ag.iastate.edu/centers/rdev/newsletter/Vol28No4–2006/born-or-made.htm

Flora, C. and Flora, J. (1993) Entrepreneurial social infrastructure: a necessary ingredient. *Annals of the Academy of Social and Political Science* 529, 48–58.

Flora, C.B. (1997) Building social capital: the importance of entrepreneurial social infrastructure. *Rural Development News*, 21, 2.

Flora, C.B. (2004) Community dynamics and social capital. In: Rickerl, D. and Francis, C. (eds) *Agroecosystems Analysis*. American Society of Agronomy, Madison, Wisconsin, pp. 93–108.

Flora, C.B. and Flora, J.L. (1988) Characteristics of entrepreneurial communities in a time of crisis. *Rural Development News* 12, 2.

Genera, C. (2005) Nature vs. nurture. *Region Focus. The Federal Reserve Bank of Richmond,* Fall 9(4), 17–20.

Hamilton, R.T. and Harper, D.A. (1994) The entrepreneur in theory and practice. *The Journal of Economic Studies* 21(6), 3–18.

HandMade in America (2003) *Craft Heritage Trails of Western North Carolina.* HandMade in America, Asheville, North Carolina.

Harding, R. (2006) Global Entrepreneurship Monitor: Social Entrepreneurship Monitor: United Kingdom 2006. Babson College and London School of Business. Available at: www.gemconsortium.org

Henderson, J. (2002) Building the rural economy with high-growth entrepreneurs. Economic review. Federal Reserve of Kansas City. Available at: http://www.kansascityfed.org/3q02hend.pdf

Henderson, J. (2006) Understanding rural entrepreneurs at the county level: data challenges. Exploring Rural Entrepreneurship: Imperatives and Opportunities for Research. Conference held at USDA-ERS, Washington, DC. Available at: http://www.energizingentrepreneurs.org/content/cr.php?id = 4&sel = 10

Kauffman Foundation (2005) Understanding Entrepreneurship: A Research and Policy Report. Kaufmann Center for Entrepreneurial Leadership. Available at: http://www.energizingentrepreneurs.org/content/cr_5/2_000050.pdf

Koh, K. (1996) The tourism entrepreneurial process: a conceptualization and implications for research and development. *The Tourist Review* (4), 24–40.

Koh, K. (2002) Explaining a community touristscape: an entrepreneurism model. *International Journal of Hospitality and Tourism Administration* 3(2), 21–48.

Koh, K. (2006) Tourism entrepreneurship: people, place, and process. *Tourism Analysis* 11(2), 115–131.

Koh, K. and Hatten, T. (2002) The tourism entrepreneur: an overlooked player in tourism development studies. *International Journal of Hospitality and Tourism Administration* 3(1), 21–48.

Lerner, M. and Haber, S. (2000) Performance factors of small tourism ventures: the interface of tourism, entrepreneurship, and the environment. *Journal of Business Venturing* 16, 77–100.

Lindgren, M. and Packendorff, L. (2003) A project-based view of entrepreneurship, towards action-orientation, seriality and collectivity. In: Steyaert, C. and Hjorth, D. (eds) *New Movements in Entrepreneurship*. Edward Elgar, Cheltenham, UK, pp. 86–102.

Lordkipanidze, M., Brezet, H. and Backman, M. (2005) The entrepreneurism factor in sustainable tourism development. *Journal for Cleaner Production* 13(8), 787–798.

Low, S. (2004) Regional assets indicators: entrepreneurship breadth and depth. Center for the Study of Rural America, Federal Reserve of Kansas City. Available at: http://www.kansascityfed.org/RuralCenter/ruralstudies/studiesmain.htm

Low, S., Henderson, J. and Weiler, S. (2005) Gauging a region's entrepreneurial potential. Center for the Study of Rural America, Federal Reserve of Kansas City. Available at: http://www.kansascityfed.org/RuralCenter/ruralstudies/studiesmain.htm

Lyons, T. (2003) Policies for creating an entrepreneurial region. Main Streets of Tomorrow: Growing and Financing Entrepreneurs conference proceedings. Center for the Study of Rural Ameria, Federal Reserve of Kansas City. Available at: www.kansascityfed.org/PUBLICAT/MainStreets03/RC03_Acs_Malecki.pdf.

Markley, D. (2006) Closing remarks. Paper presented at the RUPRI-ERS Conference Exploring Rural Entrepreneurship: Imperatives and Opportunities for Research Conference, 26–27 October, 2006, Washington, DC.

McKenna, S.D. (1996) The darker side of the entrepreneur. *Leadership and Organizational Development Journal* (17)6, 41–45.

McKercher, B. (1999) A chaos approach to tourism. *Tourism Management* 20, 425–434.

Minniti, M. and Bygrave, W. (2003) Global Entrepreneurship Monitor: National Entrepreneurship Assessment – United States of America: 2003 Executive Report. Available at: www.gemconsortium.org

Minniti, M., Bygrave, W. and Autio, E. (2005a) Global Entrepreneurship Monitor: 2005 Executive Report. Babson College and George Mason University. Available at: www.gemconsortium.org

Minniti, M., Allen, I.E. and Langowitz, N. (2005b) Global Entrepreneurship Monitor: 2005 Report on Women & Entrepreneurship. The Center for Women's Leadership at Babson College and London School of Business. Available at: www.gemconsortium.org

Morse, S. (2004) *Smart Communities.* Wiley, Jossey-Bass, San Francisco, California.

Pages, E. (2006) Entrepreneurship policy innovation and performance measurement in the States. Paper presented at the RUPRI-ERS Conference Exploring Rural Entrepreneurship: Imperatives and Opportunities for Research Conference, 26–27 October, 2006, Washington, DC.

Pages, E. and Markley, D. (2004) Understanding the environment for entrepreneurship in rural North Carolina. A report to NC Rural Economic Development Center. Available at: www.ncruralcenter.org/entrepreneurship/markleypagesreport.pdf

Putnam, R.D. and Feldstein, L.M. (2003) *Better Together: Restoring the American Community.* Simon & Schuster, New York.

Rightmyre, V.M., Johnson, T.G. and Chatman, D. for Community Policy Analysis Center (2004) Growing entrepreneurship from the ground up: a community-based approach to growing your own business. Available at: www.mrdp.net/portals/0/REI%200Guidebook_web.pdf

Rosenfeld, S. (2006) Creativity and entrepreneurship presentation at the Exploring Rural Entrepreneurship Paper presented at the RUPRI-ERS Conference Exploring Rural Entrepreneurship: Imperatives and Opportunities for Research Conference, 26–27 October, 2006, Washington, DC. Available at: http://www.energizingentrepreneurs.org/content/cr.php?id=4&sel=10

Rural Sociological Society and the National Coalition for Rural Entrepreneurship (2006) Catalytic Community Development. Issue Brief: Challenges for Rural America in the Twenty-first Century, No. 6. Available at: http://www.ruralsociology.org/briefs/brief6.pdf

Rural Policy Research Initiative (RUPRI) Center for Rural Entrepreneurship (undated) Energizing Entrepreneurs: Readiness. Available at: www.energizingentrepreneurs.org/content/chapter3.pdf

Rural Policy Research Initiative (RUPRI) Center for Rural Entrepreneurship (undated) Energizing Entrepreneurs: Assessment. Available at: www.energizingentrepreneurs.org/content/chapter4.pdf

Russell, R. and Faulkner, B. (1999) Movers and shakers: chaos makers in tourism development. *Tourism Management* 20, 411–423.

Russell, R. and Faulkner, B. (2004) Entrepreneurship, chaos and the tourism area life cycle. *Annals of Tourism Research* 31(3), 556–579.

Schumpeter, J.A. (1934) *The Theory of Economic Development.* Harvard University Press, Cambridge, Massachusetts.

Shaw, G. and Williams, A.M. (1994) *Critical Issues in Tourism: A Geographical Perspective.* Blackwell Publishers, Oxford.

Thompson, J.L. (2002) The world of the social entrepreneur. *International Journal of Public Sector Management* 15(5), 412–431.

Volery, T. (2002) An entrepreneur commercialises conservation: the case of Earth. *Sanctuaries, GMI* 38, 109–116.

Zuiches, J. (2006) Analysis of the inventory of current CRIS projects on Rural Economic and Entrepreneurship Development. Powerpoint presentation for the Experiment Station Committee on Organization and Policy Social Science Subcommittee Meeting in Washington, DC. Available at: www.nationalcoalition.wsu.edu/documents/CRIS-final.pdf

11 Perspectives on Leadership Coaching for Regional Tourism Managers and Entrepreneurs

Anna Blackman

School of Business, James Cook University, Townsville, Australia

Introduction

'Peripheral areas experiencing an economic downturn in traditional industries such as agriculture often consider tourism to be a viable alternative. Unfortunately these areas do not always enter into the business of tourism with a very clear understanding of the associated difficulties and challenges' (Blackman *et al.*, 2004). Blackman *et al.* (2004) analysed 11 case studies describing tourism development in peripheral regions from different parts around the world. A number of factors were found to contribute to successful tourism development in peripheral regions, including the use of private–public sector partnerships, the development of specialist attractions, strong government control and funding support, sound market research and community involvement lead by a local 'champion' (Blackman *et al.*, 2004). This chapter will critically analyse the use of business coaching as a leadership development tool for tourism operators in regional destinations.

Leadership Development Tools

A number of different practices have developed to support leadership development, including mentoring, job assignment, action learning, formal class room style programmes and more recently business coaching. Mentoring is a practice that can be used in leadership development in the form of a formal relationship where on-the-job experience is used. Mentoring has traditionally been seen as older, more senior people who informally take on a guiding role for the younger, newer employees (Brown, 1990). Mentoring is said to be a one-on-one process helping individuals to learn and develop new skills and it takes a long-term perspective on the development of that person's career (Tabbron *et al.*, 1997). While Van Velsor and Leslie (1995) warn of the potential for over-dependence by the mentee, Day (2001) argues that the benefits from the mentoring practice far outweigh any risks of over-dependence. Networking is one of these benefits and a highly recommended practice in the field of leadership development. One of the important initiatives of leadership development is to develop leaders who are able to go beyond the knowing of *what* and *how* and into the *who* in terms of resources and support for the individual and the organization (Day, 2001).

Job assignment (Giber and Friedman, 2006) has also been recognized as a practice for developing leadership. Job assignments help individuals to learn through specific roles, responsibilities and tasks assigned to them at work (Day, 2001). The experience gained on the job helps the individual to learn, acquire leadership skills, undergo change, work better within their roles and manage responsibilities and tasks encountered within their jobs (McCauley and Brutus, 1998; Day, 2001). While job assignment may be highly regarded by some in the development of leadership, Day (2001) argues that this approach can 'lack the kind of intentionality in terms of implementation and follow-up to be confident in understanding the amount and type of development that has occurred' (Day, 2001).

Action learning is similar to job assignment in that learning is done on the job, the difference being that the process of learning is reflected upon, and supported by, other colleagues (Day, 2001). The practice of action learning assumes that individuals learn more effectively when they work on real-time business problems (Revans, 1980). Alimo-Metcalfe and Lawler (2001) found that 'a strong action learning approach, using direct personal and business issues as the focus of activity, encouraging and expecting participants to implement changes in their work environments, and having the strong support of senior management and the support of line managers' was effective for leadership development (Boaden, 2006).

Each of these leadership development tools has been developed within the context of a structured organization and so can be difficult to apply and manage in the less-structured situation of a developing tourism destination. Two options which seem more suited to destinations are classroom programmes and business coaching.

Classroom programmes (workshops) are used widely for leadership development (Day, 2001). These workshop or classroom environments allow for participants to interact and develop social capital through the use of networking. They also help with the increasing difficulty of participants being able to find time in their busy work schedules to participate in the other leadership development options (Boaden, 2006). Workshop or classroom programmes can, however, suffer from transfer of training problems and the cost involved (Day, 2001).

Another form of practice to help develop leadership is the use of business coaching (Giber and Friedman, 2006). This practice helps to focus the individual on particular goals through the use of one-on-one sessions which help with learning and behavioural change (Peterson, 1996; Hall *et al.*, 1999; Day, 2001). The link between the use of goal setting and higher performance has been established in the literature (Locke and Latham, 1990; Garman *et al.*, 2000). The approach is more of a long-term practice and is supposed to be more comprehensive in terms of assessment, challenge and support (Day, 2001).

Collins and Holton III (2004) conducted a meta-analysis of the literature on leadership development programmes and their effectiveness. They found that this field was limited in reporting on what is or what is not effective, especially when it came to organization outcomes. Many of the leadership development programmes varied in their effectiveness with some rating highly effective while others rated poorly. The research was not able to identify which types of programme were effective and which were not, suggesting the need for more evaluation of the various methods.

Business coaching can often include a number of different leadership development tools and can either focus on one specific tool or combine a number of different tools to help maximize effectiveness. For example, the use of workshops to relay generic coaching skills and follow up one-on-one coaching sessions has been suggested as an effective combination (Damon, 2007).

Leadership and Coaching in the Tourism Sector

To date there is no empirical literature on business coaching in the tourism sector (Moscardo, 2005). Research into the role that leadership plays in developing tourism in regional areas has, however, been conducted in a wide range of countries, including Australia (Kenyon and Black, 2001), Norway (Holmefjord, 2000), Portugal (Edwards and Fernandes, 1999), the Slovak Republic (Clarke *et al.*, 2001), the USA (Lewis, 2001), Croatia (Petric, 2003) and Romania (Muica and Turnock, 2000). Leadership was identified as a key factor in developing tourism in regional areas and one of the key features associated with effective tourism leaders was the access that they had to business networks (Long and Nuckolls, 1994; Teare, 1998; Wilson *et al.*, 2001). This finding is similar to the work conducted by House and Aditya (1997) who argue that networking is a beneficial way to develop leadership skills.

Moscardo (2005) lists a summary of key leadership features and one of the specific themes for leadership in the tourism sector is to have extensive local networks. She puts forward three reasons for this. First, that it is unlikely that one person would be able to provide all of the skills and support necessary, a view supported by Sorensen and Epps (1996). Second, it would be difficult for one person to have enough time to support the number of activities needed for rural regional development (Blackman *et al.*, 2004). Third, an individual would have to deal with a large number of stresses alone and having a network could help lessen the burden placed on the individual leader (Teare, 1998; Wilson *et al.*, 2001; Hartley, 2002; McKenzie, 2002; Wituk *et al.*, 2003; Kirk and Shutte, 2004).

In summary, the literature on leadership development from the tourism sector is sparse. There is a need for more in-depth knowledge on the role that business coaching might play in leadership development for developing destinations. This chapter will describe a case study of a programme combining two different leadership development tools, workshops and one-on-one business coaching sessions for tourism operators in a regional destination.

The Context

The case study was set in a regional destination in north-eastern Australia. Traditionally the region has been considered as peripheral in terms of tourism because it lies between two major established international destinations. Recent statistics indicate that although total visitor numbers are still low compared to other destinations the rate of increase is significant with annual growth in international visitation of 24% and 18% in domestic visitation (Tourism Queensland, 2006). This is an example of a rapidly emerging regional destination.

Methodology

The first stage of the research project consisted of a 1-day workshop held with eight local tourism managers and business owners. Stage two consisted of a series of one-on-one coaching sessions with three volunteer participants from this group, starting 1 month after the initial workshop. This allowed the participants enough time to implement the strategies that were discussed at the workshop. At this stage participants were able to go over the goals that they set in the workshop and to decide on what the next step should be. Evaluations were conducted at the conclusion of the workshop and with all participants at the end of the one-on-one sessions.

Sample

The sample was made up of eight participants: three were graduate students in tourism management, one was a project officer, two were small tourism business owners, one was a festival director and one was a museum curator. Respondents were asked if they had 'any previous experience attending work related workshops' and if they had 'any previous experience with business coaching before'. Seven respondents had experienced work-related workshops, while only two respondents stated that they had previous experience with business coaching.

The Workshop

The workshop lasted for approximately 6 hours and the day was broken into four different sessions. The first session included the introduction of the workshop coordinator and a little background information. Respondents were also asked to introduce themselves to the rest of the group. The workshop coordinator then went through what goal setting was and how it could benefit them: the group then defined their individual values and vision. The second session consisted of setting goals, objectives, identifying critical success factors and developing strategies. The third session helped participants to develop an action plan, and the fourth and final session included a guest speaker presenting information on current tourism trends. This final session also allowed for a group discussion with the guest speaker about any particular regional challenges or opportunities. Participants were then informed that the coordinator would be conducting follow-up one-on-one coaching sessions with those who were interested. Box 11.1 provides an overview of the evaluation forms used.

Box 11.1. Evaluation Forms.

Workshop evaluation

1. Overall how satisfied were you with the workshop? (scale 1–10, very dissatisfied–very satisfied)

2. Please rate the following on how helpful they were (scale very helpful–very unhelpful)
- a. Helped me identify my goals
- b. Related my personal goals to organization goals
- c. Used priorities and timelines
- d. Encouraged me to take appropriate action
- e. Provided an opportunity to network

3. How useful was each of the following sessions to you (scale very–not at all)
- a. Values and vision session
- b. Goal setting session
- c. Critical success factor session
- d. Developing an action plan session
- e. Guest speaker session

4. What were the three best things about the workshop?

5. What three things could be changed/improved about the workshop?

6. Have you had any previous experience attending work-related workshops?

7. Have you ever had any previous experience with business coaching before?

8. Any further comments about the workshop?

Final evaluation

1. Thinking back to the coaching workshop, have you been able to implement or use anything you learnt from the workshop? If yes please list?

2. If not, why not?

3. What do you remember most from the workshop?

4. If you had the opportunity to do something more on your leadership skills, which of the following would you choose? (you may choose more than one thing)
- a. Attend another coaching workshop
- b. Have one-on-one coaching sessions
- c. Keep working on the goals and strategies set at workshop on your own
- d. Do more networking
- e. Other

5. If you were to go to another workshop, what areas would you like to see included?

6. Any further comments about the workshop experience?

One-on-one coaching sessions

(same as final evaluation with extra questions about the one-on-one sessions)

1. Overall how satisfied were you with the one-on-one coaching sessions? (scale 1–10 very dissatisfied–very satisfied)

2. What were the three best things about the one-on-one coaching sessions?

3. What three things could be improved about the one-on-one coaching sessions?

4. How important do you feel it is that you have a good relationship with your coach? (scale very important–not at all important)

5. How supportive was your organization in regard to you attending one-on-one sessions? (scale very supportive–not at all supportive)

6. Any further comments about the one-on-one coaching sessions?

Results from the Workshop Evaluation

All statements related to the helpfulness of the workshop were rated highly overall, generally receiving a mean rating between one and two meaning that most participants found the workshop either helpful or very helpful in these areas (see Table 11.1). Respondents were also asked to rate each session during the workshop on how useful the session was to them on a scale from one being 'very helpful' and five being 'not at all helpful'. Again mean scores for all the components were low suggesting positive evaluations. In summary, in order of helpfulness, the sessions were Guest Speaker ($x = 1.13$), Values and Visions ($x = 1.50$), Critical Success Factors ($x = 1.50$), Goal Setting ($x = 1.63$), Developing an Action Plan ($x = 1.63$) and Developing Strategies ($x = 1.63$).

Respondents were then asked a set of open-ended questions. First, 'What were the three best things about the workshop?' The responses were content analysed and key categories emerged. Responses were grouped into three main categories: goals, strategies and the workshop itself. The category 'goals' included any response that had to do specifically with either developing goals or the goal setting session or with defining values. Under the term 'goals' respondents seemed particularly concerned with 'setting values' and 'identifying goals'. Values need to be determined before one can set goals; respondents needed to understand and define what they valued so that they could go on to set goals for themselves that were in line with their values. Examples of comments from participants included 'approach to defining values', 'clarify my goals' and 'how important it is to set goals'. The importance of setting goals and values is consistent with the broader organizational literature (Diedrich, 2001; Koestner *et al.*, 2002; Newell, 2002; Presby Kodish, 2002).

Under the theme of 'strategy', participants commented on being able to identify and learn specific tasks that were completed during the workshop which could then be taken away with them to be used again later. Examples of participant responses included 'the workshop forced me to look at how I do or do not complete tasks', 'action plan session' and 'critical success factor session'. The idea of wanting to

Table 11.1. Workshop helpfulness.

Comment	Mean	Response	Frequency
Helped me identify my goals	1.375	Very helpful	5
		Helpful	3
Related my personal goals to organizational goals	1.625	Very helpful	4
		Helpful	3
		Neither	1
Used priorities and timelines	1.375	Very helpful	5
		Helpful	3
Encouraged me to take appropriate action	1.250	Very helpful	6
		Helpful	2
Provided an opportunity to network	1.750	Very helpful	2
		Helpful	6

learn new skills is supported by Presby Kodish (2002). Many participants felt that actually being shown how to develop an action plan was one of the best things about the workshop. Responses like 'now know what to do/developing an action plan' were the most common overall.

During the workshop participants were asked to reflect on goals set for themselves in the past and analyse the reasons why some of these goals may not have been achieved. This technique of analysing past goals is recommended by several authors in the coaching literature (Kiel *et al.*, 1996; Brotman *et al.*, 1998; Newell, 2002). Through this step participants were able to identify particular barriers and could realize how to overcome them by developing certain strategies.

The final category that the responses were grouped under was 'workshop'. Under this theme responses were grouped according to specific things about the workshop, i.e. these things could only have been executed in the workshop. As stated previously workshops are useful in providing participants with the opportunity to network and receive information on a number of topics (Day, 2001).

The majority of participants felt that the best thing about the workshop was the 'guest speaker'. The guest speaker was able to provide specific knowledge, trends and information on particular issues for the tourism sector. While participants thought that the general coaching skills gained were beneficial, the use of a guest speaker to provide specific sector knowledge was highly supported. Also noted by participants as being one of the best things about the workshop was the information from the coordinator, the goal setting process followed, the workbook provided and the atmosphere of the group workshop.

The second open-ended question asked respondents 'What three things could be changed/improved about the workshop?' Again because respondents could answer in a number of different ways, a multiple response analysis was carried out. Responses were again grouped into larger categories, this time being strategies and the workshop itself.

Under the 'strategy' category, refining the timeline and having to complete the action plan were considered aspects that could be improved. They were also listed as some of the best parts about the workshop. This may be an individual perspective where some people are happy to work within the workshop environment to complete certain tasks and others prefer to do it in their own time.

The category of 'workshop' included the most responses. Results included having more networking time. This was reported in responses from participants, for example, 'a bit more discussion time'. The use of networking is supported by Day (2001) as an effective tool for leadership development and seems to be something that participants felt would make the coaching experience more effective. The need for the coach to provide coachees the opportunity to network is something that is not included in a typical organizational approach as business coaching is often one-on-one (Hall *et al.*, 1999; Orenstein, 2000; McCauley and Hezlett, 2001; Bacon and Spear, 2003). Other responses under the category 'workshop' included topics to do with the logistics of the day such as providing more time for certain sessions or tasks.

The final question asked was if the respondents would like to add any further comments about the workshop. This basically gave the respondents the opportunity to write down anything they felt had not been covered in the evaluation sheet. Most opted to write some words of thanks to the researcher. However, four respondents stated that the workshop had allowed them the time to think about their personal and professional aims and how important these were to them.

Results from the One-on-one Coaching Sessions

The first five questions of the final evaluation form were asked to both one-on-one coaching participants and those who had only attended the workshop. The first question on the final evaluation form asked respondents to think back to the workshop to see if they had been able to implement anything that they had learnt at the workshop. This question was important as a common limitation to workshops is that they are a single training session which does not produce any transfer of training once the workshop is completed (Collins and Holton III, 2004).

Nearly all respondents listed something about looking at their future and where they would like to be or what directions they should be taking. Participant responses included 'I have learned that among other things I was a mess. I had no goals set and no defined tasks. I have since coaching set and achieved short-term goals. I am constantly working to a goal', 'It has definitely helped me realize goals that I would like to work towards' and 'Able to work on goals. Given me more motivation to make small changes to enable me to meet goals. Become more reflective about direction of career.' They were able to do this by listing goals and then using the processes outlined in the workshop to make sure that goals could be actioned and attained. Some had already achieved specific goals set for themselves during the workshop.

The comments from the first question suggest that participants were able to take away with them what they learned during the workshop and implement it into their daily lives so that their goals could be achieved. The strategies used during the workshop of making the participants actually go through goal setting and writing an action plan meant that the participants had done all the hard work of deciding where they wanted to go and what they needed to do. They then had to follow the steps that they had set out for themselves.

The second question asked respondents: 'If they hadn't been able to implement anything why not?' Only one respondent had stated that they found it hard to implement certain things due to time constraints but had also commented that they had been able to implement linking their goals to their values. All other respondents left this question blank. The overwhelming response to the first question with nearly all respondents stating that they had been able to implement something indicates that the skills learnt during the workshop were able to be transferred into the participants work and personal lives after the coaching workshop.

The third question asked respondents: 'What do you remember most about the workshop?' Again the majority of the respondents felt that reflecting and looking at future directions were the main things that they remember from the workshop. Going through the goal setting process and helping them to prioritize their goals and put them into manageable steps was also mentioned as memorable. A few respondents noted the values activity as the most memorable thing from the workshop as did a few about the guest speaker. Responses included 'It reinforced what we already knew, but motivated me to put it into practice', 'value selection, converting to goals, format for developing objectives, guest speaker', 'I really enjoyed the first activity on values and the guest speaker's presentation' and 'The workshop encouraged me to focus on what goals I wanted to achieve and steps to take to achieve the goals I had set'. It is interesting to note that at the workshop the guest speaker was rated very highly in terms of usefulness, which would suggest that coaches need industry experience, but when it came to what respondents remembered most about the workshops they mostly listed the goal setting process.

The fourth question was a close-ended question: 'If you had the opportunity to do something more on your leadership skills, which of the following would you choose?' Responses included 'attend another coaching workshop', 'have one-on-one coaching sessions', 'keep working on the goals and strategies set at workshop on your own', 'do more networking' and 'other'. The first response of 'attend another coaching workshop' was chosen by three participants. The next option was to 'have one-on-one coaching sessions' with four choosing this option. 'Keep working on the goals and strategies set at workshop on your own' was the next response with five participants choosing this option. 'Do more networking' was next with three respondents choosing this option.

Overall, participants felt that being able to work on strategies and goals set at the workshop are important but also listed attending another coaching workshop and having one-on-one coaching sessions as important. More than half of the respondents noted these three options as something that they would like to do.

The next question asked participants: 'If you were to attend another workshop what areas would you like to see included?' A theme that emerged was that of attaining specific skills, three areas were specifically highlighted by respondents. These areas included 'people management and communication skills', 'time management skills' and 'networking'.

Five extra questions were asked to those respondents who participated in the one-on-one coaching sessions. These were questions specifically about the one-on-one coaching sessions they had participated in. Three volunteers from the workshops participated in the one-on-one sessions. The first of the five extra questions was a scale question that asked the participants: 'Overall how satisfied were you with the one-on-one coaching sessions?' with one being very dissatisfied and ten being very satisfied. Two participants rated the one-on-one coaching sessions a ten, the other participant rated it an eight.

The next question asked participants: 'What were the three best things about the one-on-one coaching sessions?' Participants felt that the individual focus on them was good and that having to meet up with a coach at a specified time meant that they had to make sure something had been achieved or worked towards before they met, ultimately helping them to achieve their goals. Some respondents also liked that they were able to get more personalized advice from the coach. The responses reaffirm that having an ongoing process where participants are returning to goals set and continuously working on their goals as being a more effective strategy for achievement (Koestner *et al.*, 2002; Presby Kodish, 2002).

Having a coach who was outside the normal working context where participants felt they were in a safe environment and could discuss any topic was also a benefit of the one-on-one coaching sessions (Witherspoon and White, 1996; Goodstone and Diamante, 1998).

Overall, participants who attended the workshop and those who participated in the one-on-one coaching sessions saw benefits for themselves. Those who did participate in the one-on-one sessions felt that they had a more personalized and individual service and reported that the relationship between the coach and coachee was important. The sessions were rated very highly and participants commented that not much was in need of change for future one-on-one sessions.

Implications for Coaching in Tourism

The tourism sector is one that is diverse in terms of the types of employment and few local leaders will be based in a highly structured organization. Many leadership development programmes are designed with a structured organization in mind. The results from this case study have shown that the use of coaching workshops and one-on-one sessions may be an effective alternative for tourism in regional destinations. As previously stated regional tourism operators do not always understand the difficult challenges that may arise (Blackman *et al.*, 2004). The use of coaching workshops where local tourism managers and business owners were able to learn skills and were provided the opportunity to network and use of one-on-one follow-up coaching sessions was found to be an effective way for these potential tourism leaders to deal with some of the challenges faced by their sector.

If coaching is to be effectively used to help develop local tourism leaders it is important to understand what an effective coaching process needs. The workshop provided a key platform as the start of the coaching process to encourage participants to focus on their values and goals and to encourage a positive attitude towards change. In this first phase tourism-specific information was valuable in helping participants to formulate detailed goals and translate these into action plans. It also provided the participants an opportunity to network with others from the local tourism sector. The one-on-one sessions then allowed for maintenance of change and further development. In this maintenance phase the coach's general skills and support become more important than their technical expertise or sector experience. The respondents who reported on this second phase also expressed a desire to engage in a wide range of development activities including more workshops. This suggests that an effective tourism leadership development approach could be a cycle between group and individual work such as that set out in Fig. 11.1 (Damon, 2007).

In the review phase coachees with internal motivation and those who have more experience seek to further their self-development goals, again striving to achieve or perform at a higher level (Presby Kodish, 2002). While the coachees with more of an external motivation and/or less experience need to be motivated for further development with a stronger internal focus. The final step is to have the coachee implement the new behaviour in order to achieve a goal. After the

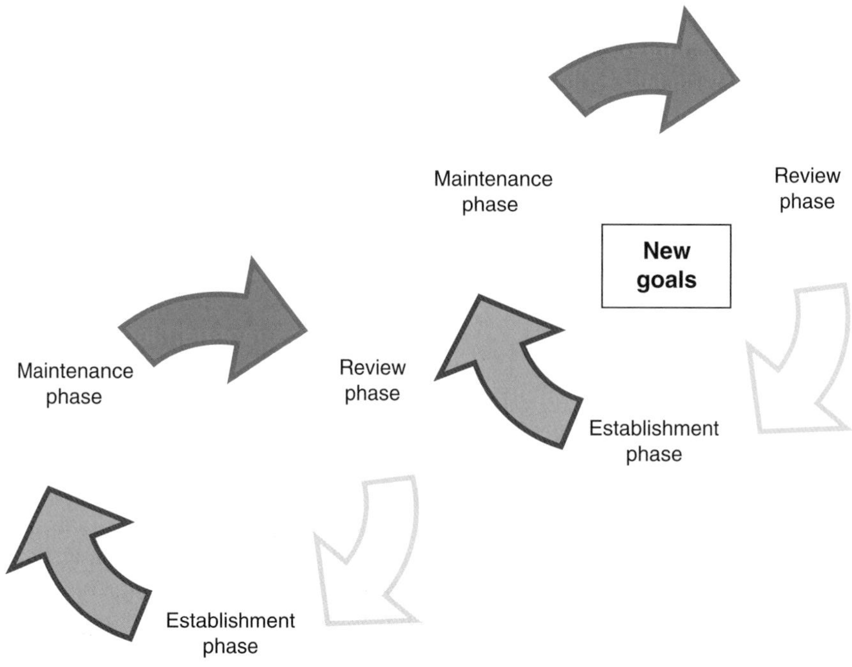

Fig. 11.1. Spiral of coaching.

review stage the coachee can start again at the establishment phase with new goals or priorities but functioning at a higher level. A response from one of the participants sums up the spiral of coaching process quite nicely:

> I have learned that, among other things I was in a mess. I had no goals set and no defined tasks. I have since coaching set and achieved short term goals. I am constantly working to a goal. I believe the workshop was run well with good content. I would not be inclined to change it a great deal and I would benefit from sitting through the same again. I think we would all pick up more a second time around. One-on-one made me look at what I had done and at what I had not. We or at least I tend to get lazy and think I will do it soon. Coaching helps eliminate that. You [the coach] were very professional, well presented and knowledgeable. I am pleased to have had this time and will value it.

References

Tourism Queensland (2006) Townsville Region – Regional Update. Research Department Tourism Queensland, Brisbane, Australia.

Alimo-Metcalfe, B. and Lawler, J. (2001) Leadership development in UK companies at the beginning of the twenty-first century – lessons for the NHS? *Journal of Management in Medicine* 15, 387–404.

Bacon, T. and Spear, K. (2003) *Adaptive Coaching: The Art and Practice of a Client-centered Approach to Performance Improvement.* Davies-Black, Palo Alto, California.

Blackman, A., Foster, F., Hyvonen, T., Jewell, B., Kuilboer, A. and Moscardo, G. (2004) Factors contributing to successful tourism development in peripheral regions. *Journal of Tourism Studies* 15, 59–70.

Boaden, R. (2006) Leadership development: does it make a difference? *Leadership & Organization Developement Journal* 27, 5–27.

Brotman, L., Liberi, W. and Wasylyshyn, K. (1998) Executive coaching: the need for standards of competence. *Consulting Psychology Journal: Practice and Research* 50, 40–46.

Brown, T. (1990) Match up with a mentor. *Industry Week* 239.

Clarke, J., Denman, R., Hickman, G. and Slovak, J. (2001) Rural tourism in Roznava Okres: a Slovak case study. *Tourism Management* 22, 193–202.

Collins, D. and Holton III, E. (2004) The effectiveness of managerial leadership development programs: a meta-analysis of studies from 1982 to 2001. *Human Resource Development Quarterly* 15, 217–248.

Damon, N. (2007) Follow the successful leader. *Training & Coaching Today*, 10–11.

Day, D. (2001) Leadership development: a review in context. *Leadership Quarterly* 11, 581–613.

Diedrich, R. (2001) Lesson learned in – and guidelines for – coaching executive teams. *Consulting Psychology Journal: Practice and Research* 53, 238–239.

Edwards, J. and Fernandes, C. (1999) Emigrants and espigueiros – tourism activities in a peripheral area of Portugal. *International Journal of Tourism Studies* 1, 329–340.

Garman, A., Whiston, D. and Zlatoper, K. (2000) Media perceptions of executive coaching and the formal preparation of coaches. *Consulting Psychology Journal: Practice and Research* 52, 201–205.

Giber, D. and Friedman, D. (2006) Leaders of the future. *Leadership Excellence* 23, 12–13.

Goodstone, M. and Diamante, T. (1998) Organizational use of therapeutic change: strengthening mutlisource feedback systems through interdisciplinary coaching. *Consulting Psychology Journal: Practice and Research* 50, 152–163.

Hall, D., Otazo, K. and Hollenback, G. (1999) Behind closed doors. *Organizational Dynamics* 27, 39–53.

Hartley, J. (2002) Leading communities: capabilities and cultures. *Leadership & Organization Developement Journal* 24, 273–284.

Holmefjord, K. (2000) Synergies in linking products, industries and place? Is co-operation between tourism and food industries a local coping strategy in Lofoten and Hardanger. *Whether, How and Why Regional Policies are Working in Concert with Coping Strategies Locally Workshop*, Joensuu, Finland.

House, R. and Aditya, R. (1997) The social scientific study of leadership: quo vadis? *Journal of Management* 23, 409–465.

Kenyon, P. and Black, A. (2001) Small town renewal: overview and case studies. Rural Industries Research and Development Corporation, Canberra.

Kiel, F., Rimmer, E., Williams, K. and Doyle, M. (1996) Coaching at the top. *Consulting Psychology Journal: Practice and Research* 48, 67–77.

Kirk, P. and Shutte, A. (2004) Community leadership development. *Community Development Journal* 39, 234–251.

Koestner, R., Lekes, N., Powers, T. and Chicoine, E. (2002) Attaining personal goals: self-concordance plus implementation equals success. *Journal of Personality and Social Psychology* 83, 231–244.

Lewis, J. (2001) Self-developed rural tourism: a method of sustainable tourism development. In: McCool, S. and Moisey, R. (eds) *Tourism, Recreation and Sustainability: Linking Culture and the Environment.* CAB International, Wallingford, UK.

Locke, E. and Latham, G. (1990) *A Theory of Goal Setting and Task Performance.* Prentice-Hall, Englewood Cliffs, New Jersey.

Long, P. and Nuckolls, J. (1994) Organising resources for rural tourism development: the importance of leadership, planning and technical assistance. *Tourism Recreation Research* 19, 19–34.

McCauley, C. and Brutus, S. (1998) Management development through job experiences: an annotated bibliography. Center for Creative Leadership, Greensboro, North Carolina.

McCauley, C. and Hezlett, S. (2001) Individual development in the workplace. In: Anderson, N., Ones, D., Sinangil, H. and Viswesvaran, C. (eds) *Handbook of Industrial, Work, and Organizational Psychology*. Sage, London.

McKenzie, F. (2002) Leadership development: flogging a dead horse or the kiss of life for regional Western Australia? *Sustaining Regions* 1, 24–31.

Moscardo, G. (2005) Peripheral tourism development: challenges, issues and success factors. *Tourism Recreation Research* 30, 27–43.

Muica, N. and Turnock, D. (2000) Maramures: expanding human resources on the Romanian periphery. *GeoJournal* 50, 181–198.

Newell, D. (2002) The smarter they are the harder they fail. *Career Development International* 7, 288–291.

Orenstein, R. (2000) Executive coaching: an intergrative model. *Dissertation Abstracts International* 61/04, 2257.

Peterson, D. (1996) Executive coaching at work: the art of one-on-one change. *Consulting Psychology Journal: Practice and Research* 48, 78–86.

Petric, L. (2003) Constraints and possibilities of the rural tourism development with special stress on the case of Crotia. *European Regional Science Association 2003 Congress.* Finland.

Presby Kodish, S. (2002) Rational emotive behavior coaching. *Journal of Rational-Emotive & Cognitive-Behavior Therapy* 20, 235–246.

Revans, R. (1980) *Action learning.* Blond & Briggs, London.

Sorensen, T. and Epps, R. (1996) Leadership and local development: dimensions of leadership in four Central Queensland towns. *Journal of Rural Studies* 12, 113–125.

Tabbron, A., Macaulay, S. and Cook, S. (1997) Making mentoring work. *Training for Quality* 5, 6–9.

Teare, R. (1998) Enabling organizational learning. In: Teare, R., Bowen, J. and Hing, N. (eds) *New Directions in Hospitality and Tourism: A Worldwide Review.* Cassell, London.

Van Velsor, E. and Leslie, J. (1995) Why executives derail: perspectives across time and cultures. *Academy of Management Executive* 9, 62–72.

Wilson, S., Fesenmaier, D., Fesenmaier, J. and Van Es, J. (2001) Factors for success in rural tourism development. *Journal of Travel Research* 40, 132–138.

Witherspoon, R. and White, R. (1996) Executive coaching: a continuum of roles. *Consulting Psychology Journal: Practice and Research* 48, 124–133.

Wituk, S., Warren, M., Heiny, P., Clark, M., Power, C. and Meissen, G. (2003) Developing communities of leaders: outcomes of a statewide initiative. *Journal of Leadership and Organizational Studies* 9, 76–86.

12 Capacity Building Through Cooperation

Richard Monypenny

School of Business, James Cook University, Townsville, Australia

Introduction

In the introduction to this book it was suggested that the key question driving all the contributions in this book was – how can we improve the process of tourism development and enhance its benefits for destinations in developing, rural and/or peripheral regions? Our answer to this question is to improve community capacity building before the process of tourism planning even begins. This answer is supported by the literature and research evidence from health (see, e.g. Onyx *et al.*, 2005; Hannah, 2006; George *et al.*, 2007), education (see, e.g. Ishisaka *et al.*, 2004; Chino and DeBruyn, 2006; Greenfields and Home, 2006) and agriculture (see, e.g. Dollahite *et al.*, 2005; Lennie *et al.*, 2005) which highlights the importance of the key elements of community capacity building occurring before specific development options or programmes are chosen or pursued. This answer is also supported by the literature and research evidence from networking (see, e.g. O'Neill and Whatmore, 2000; Tinsley and Lynch, 2001; Huybers and Bennett, 2003; Novelli *et al.*, 2006).

Community capacity building is a continuous activity. The sophistication of the task increases from the early stages in which there are few, if any, local organizations available with which to leverage off, to well-developed stages with many capable local organizations. Once there are local organizations, local networking can be encouraged by leveraging off the organizations that are already in place. The more local organizations that exist, the easier it is to leverage off them.

This book seeks:

- to improve our understanding of what happens when communities turn to, or are subjected to, tourism as a development strategy;
- to use our understanding to change the process of tourism planning and development in ways that will lead to improved outcomes for destination residents;

- to address some of the knowledge gaps and to further develop some aspects of building community capacity to help better manage and to better benefit from tourism development; and
- to focus on what does and/or should happen in a community before any tourism development is initiated.

The above four outcomes are often expressed in terms of achieving sustainable regional development. Achieving sustainable development in small regional economies is increasingly being looked at by practitioners, professionals and researchers, to see how it might contribute to the tourism sector.

The local region is the geographical unit of measure that is relevant for the development of any one or several of the economic sectors that operate in that region. In general, it a region that is developed rather than just one sector that operates in the region. In a given region that is interested in developing the tourism sector, if the other sectors that provide goods and services to the tourism sector are underdeveloped, the tourism sector will be limited in its development. Thus, this chapter focuses on those aspects of regional development that apply to the whole region.

This chapter will identify some of the key themes from the regional development literature that are of value in understanding how to build community capacity for tourism development. This literature is relevant in understanding how to build community capacity for tourism development because building community capacity for tourism development is only in part directly related to the tourism sector and in part related to the wider development of the relevant region. The main challenge for community capacity building to improve the process of tourism development is in maintaining an appropriate balance between an improved understanding of local capacity building from both the perspective of the tourism sector and from the perspective of the wider regional development.

Much of the tourism literature has focused on the perspective of the tourism sector (see, e.g. Halme and Fadeeva, 2000; Moulin and Boniface, 2001; Jackson, 2005; Jones, 2005; Vernon *et al.*, 2005; Yuksel *et al.*, 2005; Jackson and Murphy, 2006; Stokes, 2006). Much of the regional development literature has focused on the wider regional development perspective. The challenge is for the tourism sector to learn to apply to tourism what has been learnt from the wider regional development literature because despite the significant tourism literature, the history and the exploration of regional development in tourism is still relatively new.

The area of regional development has a long history both with practitioners, professionals, researchers and in the refereed literature; and a number of different aspects of regional development have been well tested in various industries both in developed and developing countries. Regional development is especially relevant in relatively open economies, like Australia, and especially in a world of globalizing international trade in both goods and services. Despite this history the exploration of regional development in tourism is still relatively new.

This chapter will first identify some of the key themes from the regional development literature that will be of value in understanding how to build community capacity for tourism development. It will then provide a set of hints derived from practical experience, for local communities for building capacity.

The key themes from the regional development literature to be discussed are:

- systems thinking;
- industrial clustering;
- a baseline for/of progress;
- increasing project facilitation skills;
- combining social and private capital;
- sustaining competitive advantage;
- good governance, not good government; and
- collaboration.

This chapter will close with some suggestions for possible next steps to see how the regional development literature might contribute to the tourism sector.

Key Themes from the Regional Development Literature

One of the most important findings from the regional development literature is that each community needs to start with what they already have and then to progress gradually towards achieving their objectives (Dollahite *et al.*, 2005; Salinger *et al.*, 2005; Greenfields and Home, 2006).

Increased cooperation between locals is one way to help residents focus on what they already have as they start on the road, often the long road, towards sustainable regional development (Zaferatos, 2004; Brown *et al.*, 2005). Other key take-home messages from the broader regional development area, following Coombs (2001), are:

- Sustainable development in small regional economies is like a combination lock – certain factors need to be in place before it happens.
- Regions should do what comes naturally to the region.
- There are opportunities in all regions, they have not all been picked up through arbitrage.
- Regional development is about more than just economic development. Sustainable regional development in financial, environmental and social terms is what is needed.
- Regional development critically depends on the regions themselves leading the process of developing strategies and plans for realizing their region's potential.
- There is nothing unique about the general drivers of sustainable regional development. Small regional economies (like all economies) basically grow or decline according both to the demand for, and the supply of, the natural and human resources to which they have access and according to the investments that businesses are prepared to make (in the region).
- The institutions, policies and social and cultural values of the community, the way in which firms and individuals organize to work together and how

firms and individuals relate with the external environment – these factors are the fundamental drivers that form the structure or framework within which incentives are created for bad or good local economic behaviour.

Increased cooperation between local residents and stakeholders is one of the processes that regional development practitioners can take to help communities to focus on regional development. The following sections describe some of the drivers of regional development that can be used to identify the starting point for increased cooperation between locals. In practice, it matters little which topic you use to start; it matters much more that you actually start to increase cooperation between locals.

Systems thinking

Systems thinking, action research and experiential learning are some of the main tools that practitioners can use to help them improve their understanding and management of complex systems (Checkland and Scholes, 1990; Flood, 1990; Senge, 1990; Maani and Cavana, 2000). Monypenny (2001, 2003) argues that systems thinking skills are critical in helping practitioners to prioritize which variables are more, and which variables are less, important in terms of the specific challenge that they currently face, for them to achieve their medium-term objectives. These skills are important because in the real world everything is usually related to everything. Systems thinking skills help practitioners prioritize which of these relationships should be considered in looking for a solution to the specific challenge that they currently face, and which relationships should be taken as being low enough down the priority list to be ignored for the moment.

There are two good sources of systems thinking skills that you can use for local capacity building. First, there is an extensive, refereed literature that can help practitioners to improve their systems thinking skills. Second, good systems thinking skills are also widely available in the local community, even though they are not likely to be referred to as such. All that matters is that the person has good skills to prioritize which variables are more, and which variables are less, important in terms of the specific challenge that they currently face. We suggest that you allocate some resources in capacity-building programmes to the enhancement of systems thinking skills.

The other two tools – action research and experiential learning – help practitioners learn from regularly using their systems thinking skills. There is an extensive, refereed literature that can help practitioners to improve their action research and experiential learning skills (e.g. Ohl, 2006; Stokols, 2006).

Industrial clustering

Industrial clustering and cluster theory are often used by practitioners to help them provide an economic policy that is widely accepted for increasing production efficiency. A good understanding of industrial clustering can be seen as a precursor to increasing regional development, especially in industries linked to international trade. Increased cooperation between locals can be seen as one of the early stages in the development process that might lead in the medium term to the establishment of a formal cooperation agreement or to an industrial cluster. The potential benefits of the implementation of industrial clustering and cluster theory are extensive and well documented in the literature (Lines and Monypenny, 2006). Further industrial clustering readings include Carrie (1999), Maskell (2001), Porter (2003), Porter and Stern (2001) and Roberts and Enright (2004).

A baseline for/of progress

One of the first steps in increasing the effectiveness of regional development is to establish just what is already available locally and/or just what has worked well locally and what still needs your attention so that you can continue to improve your whole of community outcomes (Arlett and Monypenny, 2006). Setting out to establish a baseline for progress is really not the appropriate aim. What you really need to develop is a baseline for each of those few variables that you require to support informed decision making on the next few significant issues and/or questions upon which you want to be able to make an informed decision. Developing these baseline variables is only the first step in an ongoing iterative process of action, evaluation, renewed action and renewed informed decision making.

The available refereed literature can be a significant help so that you maximize your returns in what you actually do. We suggest that you allocate some resources to exploring this literature. The next significant step that you need to make related to actually developing baselines is in fact to identify those few variables that will be used or should be used in any programme to increase cooperation between locals.

Increasing project facilitation skills

Improved project facilitation skills can be seen as an important precursor to increasing cooperation between locals. Increased cooperation between locals is seen as one of the early stages in the development process that might lead in the medium term (5–8 years) to the establishment of a formal cooperation agreement (Monypenny, 2006).

Improved facilitation skills can be more easily achieved by mentoring or coaching in actual real-world tasks, that is, learning by doing in actual projects (Monypenny, 2006). Mentoring usually happens within a given organizational, institutional or community context. Mentoring is more likely to be successful when the context provides a very positive environment within which to mentor and to facilitate the early stages in the development process towards the establishment of a closer cooperation agreement or an industrial cluster. From an organizational, institutional or community point of view, mentoring is a relatively low-risk venture. But more importantly from the local organizational, institutional or community point of view, mentoring can be used as an opportunity to explore the potential contribution that locals could make in using the improved skills achieved through local mentoring. One of the expected outcomes from mentoring locals is that they will have not only improved their project facilitation skills, but they will have also taken local ownership of their project facilitation skills and can see these improved skills as a precursor to them making a contribution to increasing cooperation between locals.

Combination of social and private capital

A combination of private and social capital is often required in the case of large public infrastructure regional development projects that are usually the backbone of regional communities (see, e.g. Coombs, 2001; Porter, 2003; State Department of Development and Innovation, 2005a,b). These projects are usually more complex than private capital projects because they typically have a number of main stakeholders (Scheuber and Monypenny, 2006).

The current widespread practice of supplying public capital to introduce 'sustainable' models of service delivery into regional centres where 'normal market forces' have failed, with the view that this funding will be withdrawn once the service is 'up and running' needs to be rethought (Adema and Ladaique, 2005). Often the predominant reason that market forces have failed in the first place is because the size of the target population is too small to support the sort of sustainable business case required for the potential service providers to enter that particular market segment in the first place. For some of the relevant wider policy issues, see Australian Medical Workforce Advisory Committee (2005), Queensland Government, Queensland Health (2002, 2005) and Queensland Health Systems Review (2005).

Some of the issues for these projects, following Scheuber and Monypenny (2006), are:

- There is usually an ongoing mismatch between stakeholder expectations and reality.
- This mismatch between expectations and reality is an important factor that needs to be understood when you are considering the local economic, social, environmental and political underpinnings that are usually associated with local regional development.
- This mismatch between expectations and reality is clearly evident when it comes to education, transport and the many other public infrastructures that form the backbone of regional development in most regional communities.
- This mismatch between expectations and reality is usually underpinned by one or more of the following trade-offs in local decision making:
  - between the amount of private capital and social capital to be used;
  - between short-term and long-term objectives to be achieved;
  - between the magnitude and impact of private costs and private benefits;
  - between the magnitude and impact of public costs and public benefits; and
  - the most usual trade-off, between the magnitude of short-term private cost and the magnitude of long-term public benefit.

Good local, ongoing, working relationships between these main stakeholders will usually help bring this sort of project to fruition. Developing a local working partnership and complementarities between the private capital contribution and the social capital contribution is easier when there is an effective mechanism for first expressing and then arriving at appropriate local policy decisions and policy implementations.

Sustaining competitive advantage

There is no mistaking the fact that we live in a rapidly changing competitive environment where individuals, organizations and the region are all vying for a share in often scarce resources. No one is going to stop the world and let us get off, so we need to review the way we work to develop the communities we live in and to be prepared to adapt to the ever-changing environment so that these communities remain vibrant and responsive to our needs (Castorina and Monypenny, 2006).

All regions have some basic factors that influence the growth of their region. But some regions perform better than others. So what drives growth to achieve sustainable competitive advantage and economic growth? One way that we find useful in looking at the drivers of competitiveness in a regional system is that they usually have the common thread of being local: local knowledge, local relationships, local connectivity, local productivity and local social cohesion (Porter, 1998; Arbonies and Moso, 2002). These factors are those found in regions that are innovative and entrepreneurial in their efforts to sustain their competitive advantage. These regions understand that they are in control of their fate and they know the importance of building strategic alliances, networks and partnerships that will allow them to develop the new products (goods and services) unique to the global market that will afford them a competitive advantage that will then sustain their growth and development.

Good governance not good government

The fundamental factors of regional development are the driving forces of establishing incentives that reward good economic behaviour. This is brought to bear through strong democratic relationships between government, private firms and the community. Regional development has in the past, often been characterized by a central approach led by the government. However, it is now governance not government that will promote sustainable economic development of regions.

When there is confusion between the meaning of government and governance there is likely to be important practical consequences. Government can be seen as a set of institutions. On the other hand, governance is about how governments and other social organizations interact, how they relate to citizens and how decisions get taken in an increasingly complex world (Plumptre and Graham, 1999). Good governance is usually done by coordinating the efforts to achieve a blending of natural, material, human and financial resources for increasing the socio-economic welfare of the population (Coombs, 2001).

In the real world of several levels of government, it is sometimes convenient to suggest that regions control their own economic growth and development. To some degree that is true but we would be remiss if we thought that they did it entirely on their own. Government does play an important role in sustaining regional economic growth by providing low-cost public services, infrastructure, an efficient tax system and providing social goods that the private sector does not supply or undersupplies. Globalization of the world economy and increased competition means that the role of government has changed. Government and its institutions are now charged with influencing the capacity and willingness of firms and households to meet the challenges of changing economic conditions. Changing attitudes and culture are difficult but paramount in the pursuit of sustaining regional economic growth in an increasingly competitive global economy.

Collaboration

Collaboration is a broad term like many others used to explain people working together such as partnership, cooperation or network. All are used indiscriminately and quite often interchanged. In the basic sense collaboration can be described as a vehicle that organizations are trying to use to reinvent their business and maintain their competitive advantage (Bititci *et al.*, 2004). The same literature suggests that most definitions of collaboration are based on the following assumptions. Collaboration is:

- taken to imply a very positive form of working in association with others for some form of mutual benefit (Bititci *et al.*, 2004);
- a distinct mode of organizing that implies a positive, purposeful relationship between organizations that retain autonomy, integrity and distinct identity, and thus, the potential to withdraw from the relationship (Bititci *et al.*, 2004);
- a number of companies linked to create and support a product (good or service) for its service life, including final disposal (Bititci *et al.*, 2004);
- a focus on joint planning, coordination and process integration between supplier, customers and other partners in a supply chain; and also involves strategic joint decision making about partnership and network design (Bititci *et al.*, 2004); and
- a process in which organizations exchange information, alter activities, share resources and enhance each other's capacity for mutual benefit and a common purpose by sharing risks, responsibilities and rewards (Bititci *et al.*, 2004).

Many different types of business structures are formulated around collaboration to gain access to new or complementary competencies, technologies and opportunities (Beacham *et al.*, 2005) but the culture of collaboration should remain the same: mutual trust, respect, sharing of information and open communication. The important issue regarding collaboration to sustain competitive advantage is in understanding when and with whom it is best to collaborate and when and with whom it is best to compete? Competition is an interactive process where individual, and thereby organizational, perceptions and experience affect organizational action, and thus affect interactions between competitors (Bengtsson and Kock, 1999).

Practical Hints to Help Local Capacity Building

Each individual community needs to take small practical steps to make progress. Each individual community will always find it difficult to make small practical steps because each new step is a new experience for the individual local community. These difficulties will always be there both for those communities that are geographically disperse and for communities that are geographically close. This will even be the case when a given local community has outside help because the outside help will have experience but the local community will not.

Two of the implications from each community making small practical steps are that most of these steps are relatively unique to the specific community and that they often only become obvious with the benefit of hindsight. The practical outcome from these two implications is that there are very few references to support the practical hints identified in this section. It would be very nice for us to be able to indicate appropriate references but that is unrealistic.

One of the current difficulties for all communities is that the environment in which local firms now operate is much more turbulent than it was in the recent past. One of the benefits from this increased turbulence is that there is also likely to be an increase in opportunities to arise from serendipity. However, if an organization is not organizationally equipped to be able to take advantage of such opportunities they will be of little use in increasing local well-being.

However, there are significant advantages in dwelling on the differences and similarities between communities in terms of individual communities identifying the next practical step that they will take. This is because identifying the next practical step that the community will take in capacity building is in part about copying what others do well but it is also about differentiating what the community does from what others do.

This section outlines the following practical hints for local community capacity building:

- understand the dynamics of individuals in a small group;
- look after group maintenance;
- maintain your (internal) communications network;
- manage your outside communications network;
- leverage off what is already available locally;
- learning by doing; and
- reflection.

This section will close with some suggestions for possible next steps in using some of these hints to help your local capacity building.

Understand small group dynamics

The behaviour of small groups has been well understood for some time. Awareness of this understanding can help people manage their groups. The management of a small group can range from the one hand where there is a clear authority figure to the other hand where there is total collective responsibility. The basic level of understanding is the stages that groups go through such as forming, storming, etc. (Jessup, 1992; Taraschi, 1998). More advanced levels of understanding help the group (or the group leader) to minimize the difficulties that arise in managing small groups and to maximize the strengths and the high levels of productivity that can be delivered by small groups (Crowe and Hill, 2006; Hurley and Allen, 2007). One extension to this more advanced understanding is the group being able to actually incorporate action research into their own development and the design of their own learning (e.g. Ohl, 2006; Stokols, 2006).

Look after group maintenance

It is relatively easy to start a small group to work towards a given objective. It is also relatively easy to understand and to use an understanding of group dynamics to help manage a small group; however, the maintenance of the group is often ignored or overlooked. Group maintenance activities can be formal, for example a training session facilitated by an external facilitator. Group maintenance activities can be informal and can be incorporated in normal group activities by the group leader. It is often good practice for a member of the group, other than the group leader, to be given the task of ongoing group maintenance. A well-functioning small group can survive without formal group maintenance activities in the short run, but in the medium term the lack of ongoing group maintenance is likely to create behaviour in some group members that is similar to that displayed in the storming stage of small group dynamics.

Maintain your (internal) communications network

Most small groups require a communications network. The form of the communications network that is most suited to a given small group could be as varied as there are small groups. On the one hand, it could be very centralized in the hands of one individual. On the other hand, it could be very diverse with individual members' communicating with different individuals for different purposes. It matters little how each small group arranges their communications network, but it does matter very much that the communications network does work well. The communications network needs to work well because if it does not it is likely to create behaviour in some group members that is similar to that displayed in the storming stage of small group dynamics.

Manage your outside communications network

It is relatively easy for a small group to develop and maintain a communications network between all members of the small group. One extension to the internal communications network is to initiate, develop and maintain communications with individuals and networks that are external to the core activities of the small group. External communication is usually very demanding in time for one or more members of the small group. This time demand is in large part because of the information overload that is very likely to exist both externally to the group and to the core activities of the group. There is very likely to be a large amount of external information that is only slightly relevant to the core activities to the small group but that could very easily dilute the group's ability to process external information and easily dilute the group's energy to focus on their core activities.

However, there are usually significant potential benefits from maintaining an outside communications network, in terms of accesses to new ideas and experiences. One way to manage the usual information overload is by using an information gatekeeper. Information gatekeepers are widely used in managing external communications because they are usually a single person or at most a small group of people so that they can all be aware of all the information. Usually the information gatekeeper is charged with filtering out the information that is useful and then passing it on to relevant individuals for their action (see, e.g. Blake, 2002; Ettlie and Elsenbach, 2007).

Leverage from what is already available locally

Community capacity building will at least need access to local resources. Some local resources will be easier to access and some will be difficult to access. One way for locals interested in community capacity building to gain access to local resources is to leverage off existing local groups or local organizations. Two of the resources that both local groups and local organizations have that others may not have are, first, a base from which to operate and from which to expand, and, second, individuals who have experience from having worked in a group or an organization. The cost of using resources that are available locally will often be very little: for example, using an existing meeting room that is not in use to hold a meeting.

Learning by doing

Learning for community capacity building at the local level will usually be largely by doing, rather than by learning before you have to actually do the community task. There are two important features that support learning by doing: first, having a process to capture and evaluate good, small, new ideas; and second, having a process to regularly reflect on how to do better next time.

One extension to learning by doing is for the group leader to explicitly structure 'doing tasks' so that, first, learning does actually happen, rather than the person just doing the required task but without them having any cognition of the required learning that they are expected to achieve, and, second, that the structure of the tasks is such that the learning achieved is enhanced. A longer-term extension to learning by doing is to plan for the formal learning usually required for the next generation.

Reflection

Reflection is a very productive tool to help the group progress its medium-term objectives. Reflection is a significant part in improving community capacity building because reflection skills usually permeate and underpin most of the other drivers of community capacity building. Reflection is important because it helps groups, and individuals within a group, to explore ways by which they can do a given task better next time than it was done the previous time. Reflection is an important tool to help increase local learning.

Connecting to Local Tourism Development

The previous section outlined some practical hints for local community capacity building. These practical hints are relevant in understanding how to build community capacity for tourism development because building community capacity for tourism development is mainly related to making local progress, one local step at a time. Yes, it is true that sometimes large outside interests can and do come into the local community, but the benefits from these outside ventures often largely go to the outside interests.

The main challenge for community capacity building to improve the process of local tourism development is in maintaining the size of local steps taken to make progress such that they keep pace with the required community capacity building. On the one hand, the projects need to be small enough to be able to be implemented with available community capacity but, on the other hand, to be big enough to be able to provide for ongoing community capacity building. The wide range of difference in the level of local community capacity available will largely determine the appropriate size of a given project. The challenge is for the tourism sector to learn from the limited available literature how to apply the appropriate size of project to each individual community at their current stage of community capacity building.

What Next?

At the start of this book it was suggested that the key question driving all the contributions in this book was: how can we improve the process of tourism development and enhance its benefits for destinations in developing, rural and/or peripheral regions?

Our answer to this question is to improve community capacity building before the process of tourism planning even begins. Our answer is supported by the literature and research evidence from health, education and agriculture which highlights the importance of the key elements of community capacity building occurring before specific development options or programmes are chosen or pursued.

Each community needs to start with what they already have and then to progress gradually towards achieving their objectives. Increased cooperation between locals is one way to help locals focus on what they already have as they start on the road, often the long road, towards sustainable regional development.

Increased cooperation between locals is one of the processes that regional development practitioners can take to help locals to focus on regional development. Below are some of the drivers of regional development that can be used to identify the starting point for increased cooperation between locals. In practice, it matters little which topic you use to start, but it matters much more that you actually start to increase cooperation between locals.

This last section of the chapter provides some suggestions for possible next steps to see how cooperation between locals might contribute to the tourism industry in similar ways that cooperation between locals has contributed to other industries. These are:

- Within your local region look at the links that already exist between stakeholders for examples of the characteristics of firms and stakeholders that are functioning well.
- Do a preliminary review of the literature on the characteristics of regional clusters and of the involvement required by individuals, organizations and the region to transform the local challenges of a rapidly changing competitive environment into a sustainable, competitive advantage that creates value and cultivates a vibrant, healthy regional economy.
- Be optimistic about the future for the stakeholders in your local region.
- An engaged community – sustained regional development is easier, when the whole community is engaged. The private sector needs to see that it is to their advantage to work collaboratively to achieve a competitive advantage, to look locally for support and to ask for the right things from the government so that together you can all promote growth. That is, not to simply receive subsidies from different levels of government that ultimately only artificially shifts the level of market competition.
- Effective collaborations – from the literature, it is apparent that more research and analysis is needed on how the adopters of collaboration arrangements effectively put in place both systems to capture the value added of these arrangements and systems to actually measure the level of success achieved.
- Existing collaborations between locals – it is helpful for you to understand what your region actually does naturally: what assets and community values exist that form the basis with which to exploit, and to improve, your competitive advantage. Extending the networks, partnerships and collaborations that already exist into a regional cluster will surely strengthen the region's economy and contribute to your growing into a vibrant, healthy region.
- Formation and development – undertake research into the formation and development of regional clusters, to assist local stakeholders to advance the concepts into reality, particularly in the local tourism industry.
- Improve your understanding of the dynamics of how individuals behave in a small group, especially the interaction between these dynamics and the processes used in project management.

- Improve your understanding of the processes of group maintenance, especially the interaction between these processes and the needs of individuals in the group to receive support by the group for what is going on in their life outside their activities in the group.
- Discuss with the whole group those aspects of your internal communication system that are working well and identify those aspects that need improvement; especially pay attention to the interaction between the required improvements and the opportunity to undertake some community capacity building.
- Evaluate the group's recent experience in managing the groups outside communications network; especially pay attention to the experience in emerging areas of information needs that are expected to have to grow to support the group's medium-term objectives.
- Improve the group's understanding of the group's access to resources that can be used to leverage off locally, especially those resources that are expected to be needed to support the group's medium-term objectives.
- Improve the evaluation of the group's 'doing tasks' used to enhance the group's learning by doing, especially of those 'doing tasks' that are expected to be needed to support the group's medium-term objectives.
- Improve the group's reflection skills, especially those reflection skills specifically used in project management. This is because these reflection skills can easily become all pervasive and can thus easily drive the group in achieving their medium-term objectives.

We wish you every success in using the drivers of regional development as the starting point for increased cooperation between locals.

References

Adema, W. and Ladaique, M. (2005) Net social expenditure, 2005 (edn). More comprehensive measures of social support. OECD Social, Employment and Migration Working Papers. Available at: http://www.oecd.org/document/4/0,2340,en_2649_33729_2380420_1_1_1_1,00.html

Arbonies, A. and Moso, M. (2002) Basue country: the knowledge cluster. *Journal of Knowledge Management* 6(4), 347–355.

Arlett, K. and Monypenny, R. (2006) A baseline for progress. In: Charters, K. and Prasser, S. (eds) *Proceedings Sustainable Economic Growth for Regional Australia National Conference SEGRA 2006,* Launceston, 28–30 August 2006. Available at: http://eprints.jcu.edu.au/1421/

Australian Medical Workforce Advisory Committee (2005) *The General Practice Workforce in Australia: Supply and requirements to 2013,* AMWAC Report 2005.2, Sydney, Australia.

Beacham, B., Kalucy, L., McIntyre, E. and Veale, B. (2005) *Focus on . . . Primary Health Care Research and Information Service.* Department of General Practice, Flinders Press, Adelaide, Australia.

Bengtsson, M. and Kock, S. (1999) Cooperation and competition in relationship between competitors in business networks. *Journal of Business and Industrial Marketing* 14(3), 178–193.

Bititci, U., Martinez, V., Albores, P. and Parung, J. (2004) Creating and managing value in collaborative networks. *International Journal of Physical Distribution and Logistics Management* 34(3/4), 251–268.

Blake, K.S. (2002) Colorado fourteeners and the nature of place identity. *The Geographical Review* 92(2), 155–180.

Brown, N.L., Luna, V., Ramirez, M.H., Vail, K.A. and Clark, W.A. (2005) Developing an effective intervention for IDU women: a harm reduction. *AIDS Education and Prevention* 17(4), 317–333.

Carrie, A. (1999) Integrated cluster: the future basis of competition. *International Journal of Agile Management Systems* 1(1), 45–50.

Castorina, D. and Monypenny, R. (2006) Comparative advantage. In: Charters, K. and Prasser, S. (eds) *Proceedings Sustainable Economic Growth for Regional Australia National Conference SEGRA 2006,* Launceston, 28–30 August 2006. Available at: http://eprints.jcu.edu.au/1422/

Checkland, P. and Scholes, J. (1990) *Soft Systems Methodology in Action.* Wiley, Chichester, UK.

Chino, M. and DeBruyn, L. (2006) Building true capacity: indigenous models for indigenous communities. *American Journal of Public Health* 96(4), 596–599.

Coombs, G. (ed.) (2001) *Essays on Regional Economic Development.* South Australian Centre for Economic Studies, Rundle Mall, South Australia, Australia.

Crowe, M. and Hill, C. (2006) Setting the stage for good group dynamics in semester-long projects in sciences. *Journal of College Science Teaching* 35(4), 32–35.

Dollahite, J.S., Nelson, J.A., Frongillo, E.A. and Griffin, M.R. (2005) Building community capacity through enhanced collaboration in the farmers market nutrition program. *Agriculture and Human Values* 22, 339–354.

Ettlie, J.E. and Elsenbach, J.M. (2007) The changing role of R&D gatekeepers: from primarily a first-line supervisor. *Research-Technology Management* 50(5), 59–67.

Flood, R.L. (1990) *Liberating Systems Theory.* Plenum, New York.

George, L.S., Fulop, M. and Wickham, L. (2007) Building capacity of environmental health services at the local and national levels with the 10-essential-services framework. *Journal of Environmental Health* 70(1), 17–20.

Greenfields, M. and Home, R. (2006) Assessing gypsies and travellers needs: partnership working and 'The Cambridge Project'. *Romani Studies* 16(2), 105–131.

Halme, M. and Fadeeva, Z. (2000) Small and medium-sized tourism enterprises in sustainable development networks. *Greener Management International* 30, 97–118.

Hannah, G. (2006) Maintaining product-process balance in community antipoverty initiatives. *Social Work* 51(1), 9–17.

Hurley, E.A. and Allen, B.A. (2007) Asking the how questions: quantifying group processes behaviours. *The Journal of General Psychology* 134(1), 5–21.

Huybers, T. and Bennett, J. (2003) Inter-firm cooperation at nature-based tourism destinations. *Journal of Socio-Economics* 32, 571–587.

Ishisaka, H.A., Farwell, N., Sohng, S.S.L. and Uehara, E.S. (2004) Partnership for integrated community-based learning: a social work community-campus collaboration. *Journal of Social Work Education* 40(2), 321–336.

Jackson, J. (2005) Developing regional tourism in China: the potential for activating business clusters in a socialist market economy. *Tourism Management* 27, 695–706.

Jackson, J. and Murphy, P. (2006) Clusters in regional tourism: an Australian case. *Annals of Tourism Research* 33(4), 1018–1035.

Jessup, H.R. (1992) The road to results for teams. *Training and Development* 46(9), 65–68.

Jones, C. (2005) Major events, networks and regional development. *Regional Studies* 39(2), 185–195.

Lennie, J., Hearn, G., Simpson, L. and Kimber, M. (2005) Building community capacities in evaluating rural IT projects: success strategies from the LEARNERS project. *International Journal of Education and Development Using Communication Technology* 1(1), 13–31.

Lines, T. and Monypenny, R. (2006) Industrial clustering. In: Charters, K. and Prasser, S. (eds) *Proceedings Sustainable Economic Growth for Regional Australia National Conference SEGRA 2006,* Launceston, 28–30 August 2006. Available at: http://eprints.jcu.edu.au/1392/

Maani, K.E. and Cavana, R.Y. (2000) *Systems Thinking and Modelling: Understanding Change and Complexity.* Prentice-Hall, Auckland, New Zealand.

Maskell, P. (2001) Towards a knowledge-based theory of the geographical cluster. *Industrial and Corporate Change* 10(4), 921–943.

Monypenny, R. (2001) Teaching project management: a systems challenge. In: Hutchinson, W. and Warren, M. (eds) *Proceedings Systems in Management 7th Annual ANZSYS Conference 2001*, Edith Cowan University, Perth, Western Australia, Australia, pp. 31–39.

Monypenny, R. (2003) Regional scale development issues, session B1. *Proceedings of the Modelling and Simulation Society of Australia and New Zealand MODSIM 2003 Conference*, Townsville, July 2003.

Monypenny, R. (2006) Increasing project facilitation skills at the TDGP. In: Charters, K. and Prasser, S. (eds) *Proceedings Sustainable Economic Growth for Regional Australia National Conference SEGRA 2006,* Launceston, 28–30 August 2006.

Moulin, C. and Boniface, P. (2001) Routeing heritage tourism: making heritage and cultural tourism networks for socio-economic development. *International Journal of Heritage Studies* 7(3), 237–248.

Novelli, M., Schmitz, B. and Spencer, T. (2006) Networks, clusters and innovation in tourism: a UK experience. *Tourism Management* 27, 1141–1152.

O'Neill, P. and Whatmore, S. (2000) The business of place: networks of property, partnership and produce. *Geoforum* 31, 121–136.

Ohl, T. (2006) The nature of groups: implications for learning design. *Journal of Interactive Learning Research* 17(1), 71–89.

Onyx, J., Wood, C., Bullan, P. and Osburn, L. (2005) Social capital: a rural youth perspective. *Youth Studies Australia* 42(4), 21–27.

Plumptre, T. and Graham, J. (1999) Governance and good government: international and aboriginal perspective, Institute on Governance. Available at: http://www.iog.ca/publications/govgoodgov.pdf

Porter, M.E. (1998) Cluster and the new economics of competition. *Harvard Business Review* 76(6), 77–90.

Porter, M.E. (2003) The economic performance of regions. *Regional Studies* 37(6,7), 549–578.

Porter, M.E. and Stern, S. (2001) Innovation: location matters. *MIT Sloan Management Review* 42(4), 28–36.

Queensland Government, Queensland Health (2002) Smart State: Health 2020 Directions Statement. Available at: http://www.health.q.d.gov.au/Health2020/2020_directions.pdf

Queensland Government, Queensland Health (2005) Queensland strategy for chronic disease 2005–2015: summary. Available at: http://www.health.qld.gov.au/publications/corporate/chronic_disease/chronstrat_summary.pdf

Queensland Health Systems Review (2005) Final report. Available at: www.health.qld.gov.au/health_sys_review/final/app1.5.pdf

Roberts, B.H. and Enright, M.J. (2004) Industry clusters in Australia: recent trends and prospects. *European Planning Studies* 12(1), 99–121.

Salinger, M.J., Sivakumar, M.V.K. and Motha, R. (2005) Reducing vulnerability of agriculture and forestry to climate variability and change. *Climate Change* 70, 341–362.

Scheuber, J. and Monypenny, R. (2006) The combination of private and social capital in the primary care sector. In: Charters, K. and Prasser, S. (eds) *Proceedings Sustainable Economic Growth for Regional Australia National Conference SEGRA 2006*, Launceston, 28–30 August 2006.

Senge, P.M. (1990) *The Fifth Discipline: The Art and Practice of the Learning Organization.* Doubleday, New York.

State Department of Development and Innovation (2005a) *Queensland Research and Development Priorities.* Available at: www.sdi.qld.gov.au

State Department of Development and Innovation (2005b) *Queensland Research and Development Priorities: Policy and Implementation Plan.* Available at: www.sdi.qld.gov.au

Stokes, R. (2006) Network-based strategy for events tourism. *European Journal of Marketing* 40(5/6), 682–697.

Stokols, D. (2006) Towards a science of transdisciplinary action research. *American Journal of Community Psychology* 38, 63–77.

Taraschi, R. (1998) Cutting the ties that bind (forming self-facilitative work teams). *Training and Development* 52(11), 12–14.

Tinsley, R. and Lynch, P. (2001) Small tourism business networks and destination management. *Hospitality Management* 20, 367–378.

Vernon, J., Essex, S., Pinder, D. and Curry, K. (2005) Collaborative policy making: local sustainable projects. *Annals of Tourism Research* 32(2), 325–345.

Yuksel, F., Bramwell, B. and Yuksel, A. (2005) Centralized and decentralized tourism governance in Turkey. *Annals of Tourism Research* 32(4), 859–886.

Zaferatos, N.C. (2004) Tribal nations, local governments and regional pluralism in Washington State. *Journal of the American Planning Association* 70(1), 81–96.

Building Community Capacity for Tourism Development: Conclusions

GIANNA MOSCARDO

School of Business, James Cook University, Australia

In 1990 Jafari presented a conceptual framework to describe the evolution of tourism research, policy and planning that consisted of four platforms referred to as advocacy, cautionary, adaptancy and knowledge-based. The advocacy platform was the first to appear and was based on the assumption that tourism was a positive tool for development and brought many economic benefits (Jafari, 1990). As tourism emerged and grew in many destinations, a range of negative impacts began to be recognized and this resulted in a more critical and cautionary approach to tourism research and policy (Jafari, 1990). This more critical analysis within the cautionary platform gave rise to the search for alternative forms of tourism that could provide the benefits sought by the advocates for tourism without the negative costs identified by those with a more cautionary approach. This formed the core of the adaptancy platform and within this platform a number of different forms of tourism including ecotourism and community-based tourism were proposed (Jafari, 1990). While there is a historical progression within these three platforms, each still remains very much alive in different areas of tourism research and policy (Macbeth, 2005).

Chapter 1 presents literature from all three of these platforms beginning with a review of government and aid agency investment and belief in tourism as a tool for regional development (advocacy platform), noting the existence of negative as well as positive impacts (cautionary platform) and describing ecotourism and community-based tourism as alternative forms of tourism that have been proposed to overcome the negative impacts that have been identified with tourism development (adaptancy platform).

But Jafari (1990) argued that none of these three approaches was sufficient to fully understand tourism and that tourism researchers, policy makers, planners and managers should adopt the fourth or knowledge-based platform. This fourth knowledge-based platform recognizes that tourism is a complex social, cultural and economic phenomenon and that a better understanding of this complexity and how it operates as a system provides a better basis for making decisions than simplistic views of tourism (Jafari, 1990; Macbeth, 2005). Macbeth (2005) has further extended this framework arguing that the fourth platform should be developed or extended in a number of ways. In particular, he argues for a sustainable paradigm platform which would incorporate sustainable development concepts and principles as a key element for both understanding and managing tourism development.

It is within this fifth sustainable paradigms platform that the present book seeks to analyse and improve processes of tourism development. More specifically, it is assumed that tourism should be considered as one of a range of development options and that destination communities should be centrally involved in its development and management. In Chapter 1 these assumptions supported the development of a new framework for tourism planning that explicitly incorporates a number of additional steps not normally included in formal tourism planning models. The first of these is that of assisting communities to better understand tourism before they participate in tourism planning decisions. The second is to compare tourism to other development options with a particular emphasis on broad sustainable development indicators. In most traditional tourism planning models tourism is considered in isolation from other activities. These two steps then allow communities to make informed choices about whether or not they want tourism. If they then choose tourism (or if tourism development is already under way), then the new model includes the step of enhancing community capacity to control and benefit from any tourism development. But this issue of enhancing community capacity to benefit from tourism has been given little attention in the tourism literature and it is this gap that the chapters in this book seek to address.

In concluding an edited book it is important to assess the extent to which the contributors have achieved the overall aims set out for the book. This concluding chapter will attempt to do this by identifying the key themes that emerge from the chapters, by summarizing the key outcomes of the research, reviews and case studies presented, and by suggesting issues for further analysis and consideration.

Key Themes in Understanding Community Capacity for Tourism Development

Although the chapters were organized into three main sections reflecting gaps in knowledge identified in Chapter 1 (relating to understanding tourism impacts, improving community understanding of tourism and community participation in tourism), five important and recurring themes can be identified that cut across all the sections and chapters. These are:

- Community capacity for tourism development is about community capacity for development in general.
- There is a need to better understand the processes that result in tourism impacts.
- While community-based tourism and ecotourism have not on the whole been as effective or sustainable as promised, they still hold the greatest potential for many regions.

- The importance of tourism development knowledge generation and management.
- The critical role of social capital in community capacity and sustainable development.

The first theme, which suggests that building community capacity for tourism development is actually about building community capacity in general, may not seem at first glance to be a particularly informative statement. For those who work within the broader area of regional development there are fundamental dimensions of community capacity that apply to all areas of development (Chapter 12) and so the statement may seem too obvious to mention. But within the tourism literature, it is important to highlight this point because tourism is often considered, analysed and evaluated in isolation from other activities.

In Chapter 1 it was noted that this tendency contributes to planning models that focus on how to make tourism successful in terms of visitor numbers or yield, without detailed consideration of whether or not communities will benefit from tourism. The advocacy platform is often strong in government policy and many of those involved in tourism development planning assume that tourism will benefit the destination community without contemplating in detail exactly how this will happen.

Chapter 2 continues with this argument, noting that many of the existing economic models for estimating tourism's economic multipliers do not work well at the regional level and economic benefits are often overestimated. This chapter further notes that these economic benefits are likely to be greater if local businesses are able to supply the goods and services required by tourist operations. Traditional tourism planning models focus on the development of tourism businesses, but a broader perspective tells us that tourism benefits are likely to be greater if other businesses are also strong and supported. Similar arguments and evidence to support these arguments are provided in Chapters 8, 10 and 12. Chapter 12, in particular, points out the need to have existing social capital, strong local organizations, positive attitudes among local residents towards cooperative ventures and existing intellectual capital for any development project to be effective.

The second theme that recurs across most of the chapters is that of a better understanding of tourism impacts. A better understanding of tourism impacts is a multifaceted challenge. As noted in Chapter 1, the existing research into tourism impacts can be seen as falling into two main categories. There are those studies that seek to identify and describe the impacts of tourism development and those that focus on resident perceptions of impacts seeking to explain those perceptions by analysing characteristics of the residents. What is missing is more extensive research into the characteristics of the tourism development and how these interact with characteristics of the destination community as a whole (rather than of individual residents) to create different outcomes from types of tourism development. This theme is specifically addressed in Chapters 2 and 3, where both authors seek to provide a more detailed examination of the processes that contribute to various tourism outcomes. But the need to better understand these underlying processes is also noted in Chapters 4, 5, 7 and 9.

The third key theme identified across a number of contributions is that of the value of alternative forms of tourism such as ecotourism or community-based tourism. In Chapter 1 it was suggested that there was little evidence that either of these forms of tourism were any better than any other forms of tourism in terms of their contribution to sustainable development of the destination region. This claim is supported by evidence reviewed and presented in Chapters 4, 5, 7 and 9. But this conclusion needs to be considered in light of two qualifications. First, in the case of community-based tourism the reality in practice has not often matched the ideals in principles (see Chapters 1 and 5). Thus, it could be argued that true community-based tourism has not often been implemented. A similar case could be made for ecotourism, although it could also be argued that ecotourism's roots in ecological sustainability limit its capacity to address all of the dimensions of sustainable development (see critiques of ecotourism reviewed in Chapter 1). Second, in many communities these are the only forms of tourism that are likely to be viable in terms of market demand and/or the physical resources available to the destination community. What is necessary to improve these forms of tourism is a greater awareness of the need to enhance community capacity for their development.

The importance of tourism knowledge generation and management is the fourth theme that was identified and is critical to all of the other themes. At the most basic level it was argued in Chapter 1 that knowledge of a development sector, its requirements for success and its potential impacts is critical to community capacity to control and benefit from any proposed development option. Given the importance of this basic requirement, a whole section of this book (Part II: Chapters 5, 6 and 7) is focused on processes and options for improving community knowledge of tourism development.

But in addition to this direct consideration of the role of knowledge in community capacity, the theme of knowledge generation and management emerges in other chapters in a variety of issues and contexts. For example, Chapters 4 and 7 focus on how the knowledge of a destination community's values and desired outcomes from tourism can be used to enhance the presentation of destinations to tourists and contribute to a greater sense of concern for the destination. In these chapters it is argued that giving destination communities greater control over knowledge about a community, as it is used by tour guides and tour operators to create tourist experiences, is central to better outcomes for the destination community. A second issue is discussed in Chapters 6 and 8, where evaluations of different methods of assisting communities to develop their knowledge of tourism and of partnerships for tourism development highlight the importance of the sharing of knowledge and experience of tourism developments. The importance of networks within and across destination communities for generating and managing tourism knowledge is also discussed in Chapters 10, 11 and 12.

The importance of networks was also raised in the final key theme, which was concerned with the critical role of social capital in community capacity and sustainable development. There are those that would argue that social capital is at the core of community capacity (Pooley *et al.*, 2005). Like any broad social science concept used in a number of areas, there has been much discussion of how to define and measure social capital (see Pawar, 2006 for a review). Despite these debates three interrelated elements or dimensions recur throughout the different approaches – relationships, networks and competencies (Pooley *et al.*, 2005). Relationships include the number and quality of interactions between individuals and within and between social groups in a community (Pooley *et al.*, 2005; Maru *et al.*, 2007). These relationships build linkages between individuals and groups and create the networks that are the second dimension of social capital (Pooley *et al.*, 2005; Waldstrom and Svendsen, 2007). According to Pooley *et al.* (2005), these relationships and networks are based upon and create trust, goodwill and reciprocity. Finally there are competencies and for social capital these include the individual's ability to interact successfully with their environment (Pooley *et al.*, 2005) and to engage in cooperative behaviour (Maru *et al.*, 2005). It is argued that all these things contribute to a community's ability to manage conflict, to generate cooperative ventures to support new business activities and to manage development options (Rutten and Boekema, 2007).

Chapter 1 notes that many of the negative sociocultural impacts of tourism reported in various case studies of regional tourism development were related to changes to some aspect of social capital. This is an issue also discussed in Chapter 8, where it was noted that the global, commercial, market-based nature of tourism is often very different in the type of interactions and relationships it requires and/or generates than those related to more traditional activities. This presented a challenge for the communities in these cases and in some instances they struggled to find ways to connect their traditional social structures to the new ways of interacting required by the tourism business. Networks and cooperative attitudes are also noted in Chapters 2, 3 and 9 as basic requirements for a community to be able to benefit from tourism in both the economic and sociocultural domains.

New Approaches to Tourism Planning and Development

Chapter 1 argued that traditional approaches to tourism planning have taken insufficient account of the need to ensure that destination communities have the capacity to make informed decisions about tourism and to benefit more directly from tourism opportunities. A new tourism development model was proposed and compared to traditional approaches. Figure 1 provides a summary of this new model.

Of particular importance to the present discussion are the elements in the highlighted boxes in this model. The proposed extension to tourism planning includes four major additional steps:

- enhancing community awareness and understanding of tourism;
- comparing tourism against a range of other development options rather than considering it in isolation;
- explicitly making a choice to develop, or further develop, tourism; and
- building community capacity to benefit from and manage proposed tourism options identified in the strategic planning for tourism.

The first step in this list is often considered to be part of community capacity building but is of sufficient importance that it can be considered on its own. Thus, the present book focused on two subsections of community capacity building in relation to tourism – enhancing awareness and knowledge, and other aspects of capacity enhancement. Table 1 summarizes the suggestions for practice provided in the chapters relevant to the first of these subsections – enhancing community awareness and knowledge of tourism.

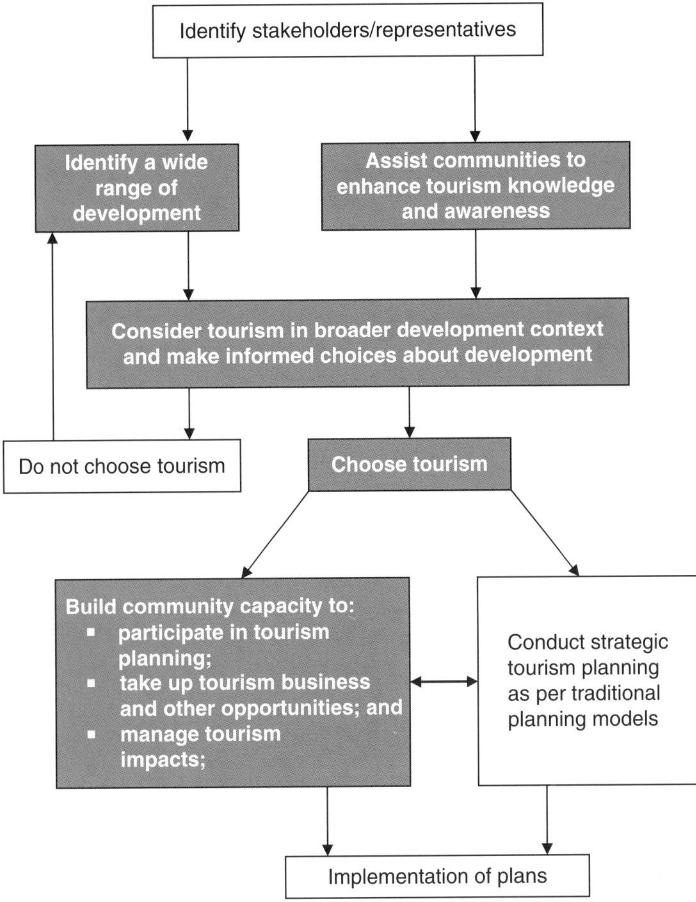

Fig. 1. Incorporating community capacity into tourism planning.

Table 1. Summary of contributors' suggestions for practice to enhance community awareness of tourism.

Chapter	Suggestions for practice
4	A framework and model are proposed in which communities are encouraged to identify the values and images that they would like tourists to have. This is supported by ideas on how to incorporate these into tourist experiences and into sustainability measures
7	The framework and model proposed in Chapter 4 are used to assist destination communities to evaluate different types of tourist activity
6	Three specific techniques, a drawing exercise, role plays and field trips, are evaluated and guidelines for their effective use are provided

Table 2. Summary of contributors' suggestions for practice to elements of community capacity.

Capacity-building element	Chapters offering suggestions for practice
Partnerships	Chapter 8 evaluates three different types of partnerships and provides a set of guidelines for improved practice
Networks and clusters	Chapter 12 offers a number of practical suggestions for developing and maintaining networks Chapter 9 provides examples of the effective use of networks and clusters to enhance the participation of women in tourism
Leaders	Chapter 11 evaluates several options for leadership development and provides specific guidelines for the use of business coaching and goal setting workshops
Entrepreneurs	Chapter 10 provides detailed practical steps for enhancing entrepreneurial climate in a region

Enhancing community knowledge of a development area is one aspect of community capacity building. Other core elements noted in both Chapters 1 and 12 include partnerships, the identification and support of leaders and entrepreneurs, the existence of networks and clusters of organizations and the coordination of tourism stakeholders. Table 2 summarizes the conclusions and practical suggestions provided in the chapters in this book relevant to these other elements of community capacity building. Finally, a number of chapters incorporate guidelines and examples for measuring critical aspects of community capacity for tourism development, including measuring community goals and views (Chapters 4, 5 and 7), assessing tourism impacts (Chapters 2 and 3) and measuring critical elements of entrepreneurial climate (Chapter 10).

Towards a Fifth Platform for Tourism Management

At the beginning of this concluding chapter, Jafari's (1990) concept of tourism research platforms was used to describe the evolution of literature on the value of tourism as a development strategy. Macbeth's (2005) extension of this framework to a fifth sustainable paradigms platform was also highlighted as the best match to the goals of the book. Essentially this book has argued that tourism must be considered within a larger sustainable development framework and assessed more directly in terms of its ability to contribute to community capacity in general. It has been suggested in several chapters in this book that measures of sustainability related to tourism should be expanded to include the extent to which tourism contributes to various elements of community capacity such as social capital, development awareness and skills for development management. In the broader literature on corporate social responsibility it has been noted that businesses need to demonstrate the extent to which they contribute to and enhance the social, intellectual and creative capital of their key stakeholders (Cochrane, 2007). Such discussions have yet to be initiated in tourism, although Macbeth's (2005) idea of a fifth tourism platform based around a consideration of ethics provides a starting point. In conclusion, a consideration of aspects of community capacity and the link between tourism development and community capacity highlights the need to take a broader and more critical perspective on tourism in general and to place consideration of tourism more clearly within a broader sustainable development framework.

References

Cochrane, P.L. (2007) The evolution of corporate social responsibility. *Business Horizons* 50(6), 449–454.

Jafari, J. (1990) The basis of tourism education. *Journal of Tourism Studies* 1, 33–41.

Macbeth, J. (2005) Towards an ethics platform for tourism. *Annals of Tourism Research* 32(4), 962–984.

Maru, Y.T., McAllister, R.R.J. and Smith, M.S. (2007) Modelling community interactions and social capital dynamics: the case of regional and rural communities of Australia. *Agricultural Systems* 92(1–3), 179–200.

Pawar, M. (2006) 'Social' 'capital'? *Social Science Journal* 43(2), 211–226.

Pooley, J.A., Cohen, L. and Pike, L.T. (2005) Can sense of community inform social capital? *Social Science Journal* 42(1), 71–79.

Rutten, R. and Boekema, F. (2007) Regional social capital: embeddedness, innovation networks and regional economic development. *Technological Forecasting and Social Change* 74(9), 1834–1846. Available at: http://www.sciencedirect.com, August 2007.

Waldstrom, C. and Svendsen, G.L.H. (2007) On the capitalization and cultivation of social capital: towards a neo-capital general science? *Journal of Socio-Economics* (in press). Available at: http://www.sciencedirect.com, December 2007.

Index